"The mere fair-weather hunter, who trusts entirely to the exertion of others, and does nothing more than ride or walk about under favorable circumstances, and shoot at what somebody else shows him, is a hunter in name only. Whoever would really deserve the title must be able at a pinch to shift for himself, to grapple with the difficulties and hardships of wilderness life unaided, and not only to hunt, but at times to travel for days, whether on foot or on horseback, alone."

Theodore Roosevelt – 1901

Idaho Elk Seasons
1951

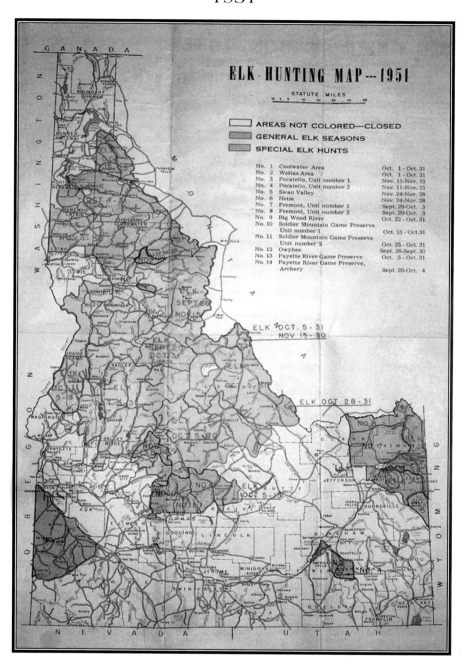

Idaho Big Game Management Units And Elk Zones - 2006

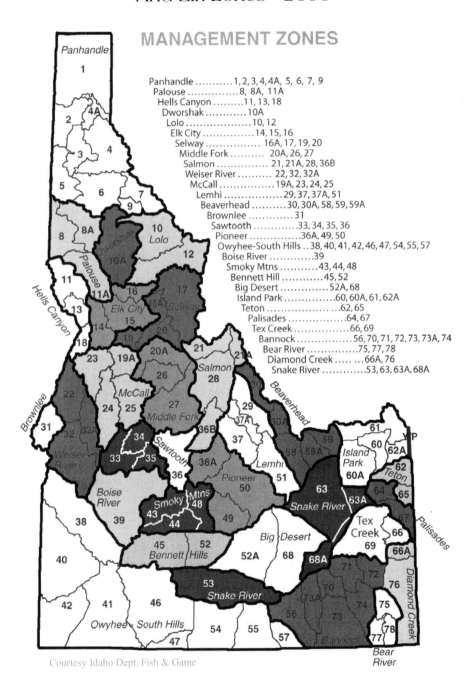

Courtesy Idaho Dept. Fish & Game

Books by this author

Idaho's Greatest Mule Deer
Idaho's Greatest Elk

Coming soon:

Idaho's Greatest Whitetails
Idaho's Greatest Mule Deer, 2nd Edition

To Kylee.
You are the true essence of happiness,
patience, and grace.

And to all hunters who put the future of hunting
above their own personal self-interests.

WANTED

    We are beginning work on the second edition of Idaho's Greatest Mule Deer. We would like to expand sections on big trophy bucks that don't make "the book" and classic old time hunting pictures and stories.

    We will also be adding new record book entries and attempting to discover more information on book entries listed as "hunter unknown". Please send field photos, shoulder mount photos, score sheets, stories, historical journals, and/or other information to the address below for consideration to be included in upcoming editions.

Idaho's Greatest Big Game
P.O. Box 2
Council, Idaho 83612
idahohunting@hotmail.com
www.idahobiggame.com
(208) 253-0002

WANTED

We are also seeking stories, pictures, and other accompanying information on all other Idaho big game animals including elk, whitetails, bighorn sheep, mountain goat, shiras moose, antelope, cougar, and bear for upcoming books in the series. Please send in your photos and stories.

Also, we are trying to chronicle Idaho's hunting heritage by adding old-time hunting photos to our series. Do you have some good ones? Ones such as the one below, or a picture from the '60s of you and your friends? Send them in! Old-time hunting photos are priceless, showing glimpses into days gone by. Please send your best old-time hunting pictures (they can be returned.)

Lastly, funny hunting stories, amazing tales, and harrowing encounters on Idaho hunts to:

Idaho's Greatest Big Game
P.O. Box 2
Council, Idaho 83612
idahohunting@hotmail.com
www.idahobiggame.com
(208) 253-0002

Idaho's Greatest Big Game Series

    This fantastic drawing, titled "Idaho Royalty", was commissioned by Idaho's Greatest Big Game and drawn by nationally renowned artist Dallen Lambson of Pocatello. Dallen is the son of Hayden Lambson, one of the West's finest artists. As you can see, Dallen has come into his own as a top-quality professional.

    This fine 16x20 work pays tribute to four of Idaho's greatest elk, allowing them to be together in their finest form. Featured are Idaho's top three non-typicals and the state record typical. It is limited to 25 signed and numbered artist proofs ($80 each) and 225 signed and numbered prints ($50 each). This is the first piece of a limited series that will accompany future releases of books chronicling Idaho's hunting heritage. We will reserve rights for customers wishing to collect identical numbers throughout the series, which will feature Idaho's greatest mule deer, elk, and whitetail. Call (208) 253-0002 or email idahohunting@hotmail.com to order.

Acknowledgements

A book of this scale cannot be accomplished on one person's efforts. Without the willingness of the hunters and their families to share their stories and photos, we would not have this piece of history. For everyone that gave time, resources, memories, photos, and stories, I am truly grateful.

Thank you to the Boone and Crockett Club for permission to use their copyrighted scoring system and records. Trophy listings in this book were compiled with the permission and assistance of the Boone and Crockett Club. To learn more about the Club and its activities, log onto www.booneandcrockettclub.com. Thanks as well to the Pope and Young Club, The Longhunter Society, and Idaho Department of Fish & Game for permission to list their records.

Special thanks to Dale Toweill for his insights into the past and future of the Clearwater drainage, as well as general insights on elk in Idaho. Also to Dale and Jack Ward Thomas, and others involved in "North American Elk – Ecology and Management". Facts and information obtained from that book were instrumental in the success of a couple of this book's chapters.

Another special thanks to Dana Hollinger, Cabela's, Bass Pro Shops, Don Schaufler, Aly Bruner, Michael Damery, Randy Clark, and others for access to their beautiful collections and photos.

Many other individuals also provided photos, leads, information, or footwork: Thank you to Roger Selner of Trophy Show Productions. Kevin Calaway, Sam McNeill, Julie Houk, George Bettas, Jack Reneau, Jim Peek, Mark Dowse, Mike Rainey, Brad Compton, Ralph Pehrson, Dan McClure, Pete Zager, Brian Farley, Rod Bradley, Jim Hanna, Fred Scott, Tony Jessen, Stan Riddle, Russell & Karen Hatfield, Kylee Hatfield, and numerous others.

Last but not least, a very special thank you to all of the hunters mentioned in this book who were gracious enough to share their personal pictures and stories. The hunters that were able to participate in Idaho's Golden Era of hunting are the foundation and inspiration for this book and will always have my respect and adoration. Over the course of writing this book I had the opportunity to meet many great people and storytellers. It's a pleasure to be able to share their stories.

Author's Note

To put together a book of this magnitude, the author has relied on hundreds of supposedly reliable sources of information. To help ensure its accuracy, all information was scrutinized, all leads followed, and all efforts made wherever possible to find the truth and the complete story. While every piece of information listed in these pages cannot be completely guaranteed, we believe its accuracy is as good as humanly possible.

If you are aware of any inaccuracies presented herein, have any additional information on listed trophies, have any information on trophy-class animals to be included in future editions, or know of old hunting stories and photos, please contact:

Idaho's Greatest Big Game
c/o Ryan Hatfield
Box 2
Council, Idaho 83612
idahohunting@hotmail.com

Cover painting: *"Over the Top"* by Leon Parson. For more information on Leon's beautiful work, contact: Leon Parson Studio, 298 S.W. 12th, Rexburg, Idaho 83440 (208) 356-4872 www.leonparson.com

Photo on inside title page: This remarkable 403-7/8 non-typical bull was taken by Fred S. Scott in Shoshone County in 1964. It is one of the most recognizable and unique bulls ever taken.

Photography by author unless otherwise noted.

Printed in the USA by Sheridan Books, Inc. Cover design by Julie Houk.

Published by: Ryan Hatfield
                Idaho's Greatest Big Game, Box 2, Council, Idaho 83612
                (208) 253-0002   idahohunting@hotmail.com

ISBN 13-digit: 9780974976617
ISBN 10-digit: 0-9749766-1-X

Copyright 2006© All Rights Reserved, including the right to reproduce or display this book or portions thereof in any form or by any means, electric or mechanical, including photocopying, recording, scanning, or by any information storage and retrieval system, without permission in writing from author.

The purpose of this book is to preserve a very important part of Idaho's history, and to pay tribute to some of the more amazing animals ever encountered in Idaho's mountains. It is not to promote or sensationalize the trend toward bigger is always better or more important. There's more to hunting than big antlers. It's all about memories and heritage.

Idaho's Greatest Elk

by

Ryan Hatfield

Cover and Drawings by
Leon Parson

About the Author

Ryan Hatfield was born in Council, Idaho in 1972. He attended school at Council High School, where he graduated in 1990. He has a Bachelor of Science in Forest Resources from the University of Idaho. He has worked in the commercial fishing industry in Alaska, and in the forest industry in Idaho and Oregon.

Being fascinated with both hunting and Idaho history, it seemed a natural fit to do something to preserve much of Idaho's historical hunting heritage. In 1998, Ryan embarked on a journey that is still very much in progress – the attempt to preserve all possible stories, photos, and memorabilia associated with Idaho's hunting past. The first product of this "hobby" was *Idaho's Greatest Mule Deer*, which was the first book in the Idaho's Greatest Big Game collection.

Upon the completion of his first book, Ryan was fortunate enough to be offered a position with the Boone and Crockett Club – the first hunter-based conservation organization in North America. Working for B&C now enables Ryan to work in the hunting and conservation realm as a career.

Ryan spends as much time as possible enjoying the outdoors. Whether chasing elk, deer, or a mountain view, he is completely fascinated with Idaho's limitless beauty, rugged landscape, and history. He hails from a hunting and outdoor family who has roots in western Idaho since at least 1870.

When not working, writing books, or exploring the outdoors, Ryan competes on the professional lumberjack circuit. He has been a perennial member of the United States National Team since 2000 and competes all over the western United States, Canada, and Australia, both as part of the team and individually. He can occasionally be seen on television in various lumberjack competitions.

He is married to his wonderful new bride, Kylee. Kylee, owner of the world's biggest smile, is very supportive of Ryan's dreams and work, and accompanies him on many of his hunting adventures. She also travels with him to lumberjack competitions, where she competes in the women's events.

About the Artist

Leon Parson moved to eastern Idaho when he was a young boy. There he developed a deep insight and love for wildlife, the outdoors, and all nature offers.

Although being involved in art and biology since childhood, he is, nevertheless, a firm believer in education. With nine years of formal art training he earned three degrees; an Associate in Art and Science in 1974 from Ricks College, a Bachelor of Fine Art in Illustration in 1977 from The Art Center College of Design, and a Master of Fine Art in Illustration in 1985 from Syracuse University.

He is currently a member of the art faculty at Brigham Young University-Idaho in Rexburg, Idaho, where he has taught drawing, design, color, illustration, and oil painting for 27 years. He has served the last three years as Chairman of the Department of Art.

Leon is among the top wildlife artists in the world and has received numerous regional, national, and international awards and honors. He was honored as Artist of the Year for the Mule Deer Foundation in 2005.

He is a member of two prestigious international wildlife guilds: the Society of Animal Artists, and the Worldwide Nature Artists Group. Throughout his career, he has produced magnificent works of art that have endured in collectibility and popularity. More than 50 of them have become limited edition lithographs and giclees. His artwork has been featured on the covers of nearly 100 magazines and publications, both wildlife and religious.

Leon feels that true art should communicate both intellectually as well as emotionally. "True art must stir the heart and reach deep into the soul of the viewer if it is going to last. Emotions are what make art live."

Leon currently resides in Rexburg, Idaho with his lovely wife, Kathryn. They have been married for thirty-three years. They have seven children and eight grandchildren.

Table of Contents

Introduction............	15
Swan Valley Elk Patrol.....	19
The Carlin Hunting Party of 1893.......	29
Clearwater Elk Encounter in the 1880s..........	46
Evolution, Life Cycle, Characteristics, & More.....	49
Elk Reintroduction Efforts.......................	57
Rise and Fall of the Clearwater Elk Herd..........	66
The Future of Elk in Idaho............................	75
Idaho Elk Management 101.....................	78
A Brief Synopsis of Big Elk in Idaho...............	86
Idaho's Greatest Non-Typical Elk......................	89
Idaho's Greatest Typical Elk.........................	137
Unofficial Trophies........................	284
More Great Bulls...........................	305
Freak Antlers & Rare Occurrences................	334
Great Days in Elk Country............................	354
The Golden Era & Other Days Gone.............	369
Packstrings & Elk Quarters...........................	394

Introduction

In September of 2002, my friend Derek Pouchnik and I were out on a scouting trip in rugged Idaho elk country. We set up on a ridge and gave a few cow calls. It was long after "prime elk hours" and we weren't expecting much but, nonetheless, we were quickly answered by a faint bugle. Cow call by cow call, the bugling came closer. Finally, as we squatted down behind a big yellow pine, he came into view. It was a nice five-point bull, and he was undeniably feeling his oats that day. We watched in awe as he mutilated a small white fir tree a mere twenty yards from us. He tore that poor little tree up to the point that it was entangled completely in his antlers. Frustrated, he gave one monstrous yank of his head and uprooted the entire sapling.

That minor obstacle out of the way, he continued on. Toward us he came, step by methodical step, confidently and patiently making his way toward the source of his interest. With only four yards separating us, he suddenly stopped. Derek and I were in awe of his regal and majestic form, now a little more than an arm's length away. We were pinned down and remained squatted, now looking squarely (and very much up) at the powerful profile of this imposing animal. Then, in a slow and deliberate but focused move, he swung his eyes and battle-ready headgear our way. He stared us straight in the eye, with now only a matter of inches remaining between his newly polished antlers and our ill-defended bodies. Our impending drubbing now seemed a mere formality. It was the longest three seconds either of us had likely ever experienced. It was so intense that I could no longer stand it. I burst out loud in laughter and, in an instant, the bull was gone.

Such is the intensity of hunting elk. Only a bull elk can give as dramatic an encounter as can ever be experienced in the wild. Only a bull elk can sing a melody in the pre-dawn darkness that can send chills to the deepest recesses of your soul, while the next minute coming into the scene with the confidence that he is about to wipe the forest floor with you. That is what, to me, makes elk hunting so unique. Answered challenges, keen wit and senses, unbelievably graceful for their size – that is what elk are about.

Hunting these magnificent creatures is far from the serene encounter a non-hunter might imagine. Elk hunting is not about ease, nor simplicity, nor leisure. It is not about guaranteed success or easy packouts.

What elk hunting is about is bad backs, sore knees, dull knives, and tested wills. It's about packstrings, wall tents, pack frames, and campfires. Bugling bulls, aspens, cold mornings, panoramic views, and lifetimes of memories are what make elk hunting one of life's great pleasures.

No friends are as close as those who have packed elk quarters together. Head to the bar or for a round of golf with a friend and you likely won't remember it a month from now. Pack elk quarters with a friend, and you will remember every detail for the rest of your life – and so will your knees!

Elk hunting is more than a pastime. It is a heritage. Once it's in your blood, there is no getting rid of it. Time spent in the elk woods are some of the best spent times you will ever have. These times, through tens of decades and millions of hunters, has created a history. It is Idaho's legacy of pursuing elk on frosty mornings in the fall while those not fortunate enough to know the bounty slave away at their jobs.

This book is an attempt to capture what is left of a fading history of the first few generations of elk hunters in Idaho – harrowing adventures such as the story of the Carlin party, great story tellers like Fred Scott, or great emotions, like Art Day, who describes the taking of his prized 385-5/8 bull from 1971 as "…one of the saddest moments of my life. Here was this magnificent animal that was dying, and there was a tremendous sadness on my part. I had killed him, and there was nothing to be said."

For the first part of the 20th century, there were very few elk in Idaho, and even less elk hunting. Slowly but surely, through the efforts of hunter-conservationists and a few massive wildfires, elk habitat and surging elk populations were created. The hunters that stalked these trophies in the 1950s encountered some wildly large bull elk. They also did it in a time where there was a little more magic and a lot more mystique to elk hunting.

As with old-time deer hunters, many of that generation talk much more about the weight of the animal than the antlers. And, as with the deer hunters, most of those big elk antlers rotted back into the soil. There just wasn't much point back then in packing out thirty pounds of bone that was likely to hook onto every last tree limb available on the way out.

In the old days, if you wanted to hunt elk, you headed north into the world-famous Selway region, or other parts of northern Idaho. The wildfires that devastated the entire north half of the state three decades earlier had, inadvertently, opened the forest canopy and created a wealth of elk habitat.

Four decades further yet, the situation has changed (see page 66 - "The Rise and Fall of the Clearwater Elk Herd".) Several decades of a wildland firefighting strategy of nearly total suppression has taken its toll, incidentally removing a major portion of the elk population in the Clearwater drainage. Anti-logging sentiments among extreme environmental groups have also hurt. With no healthy manipulations of our forest to set back succession, a situation has developed where there are insufficient openings in the canopy to provide adequate grazing to support a decent elk herd. The Clearwater drainage is quickly on its way to becoming a very beautiful wasteland, void of any decent big game populations. This is a situation that is being mirrored across much of the West. If our policies on fire suppression continue, look for this situation to spread like a plague over the next 50 years.

But while elk currently suffer in the Clearwater region, elk populations in the mountains that frame the Snake River Plain are burgeoning. In fact, serious efforts continue to be made to simply keep their populations in check. While many sportsmen have issues with the number of cow tags offered, elk populations in many areas of southern Idaho continue to do nothing but grow or, at worst, hold steady.

Today's hunters in Idaho enjoy a luxury that didn't exist in that bygone Golden Era – something that many hunters in Idaho currently take for granted. It is the ability not only to hunt elk every year, but also to have a legitimate chance of harvesting a bull elk every year.

Such was not always the case. In the 1920s, for example, the Idaho hunter's options to pursue elk (taken from the 1922 regulations) were: Clearwater and Idaho Counties - October 1 through November 15; Fremont, Clark, Bonneville, Teton, and Bingham Counties - November 15 through November 30. That was it! Elk were scarce, and not well distributed. The efforts of sportsmen, legislators, Fish and Game, and conservation groups helped over the next several decades in making sure their grandchildren (you and me) had better hunting opportunities than they did.

My uncle, Henry Daniels, tells me of a hunting adventure he had with George Green, a hunting buddy of his in the old days. They were hunting bucks in the mountains of western Idaho. As they pushed through the snow, Hank recalled seeing what appeared to be the biggest buck track he had ever seen in his life. He followed, full of anticipation, until he found their maker. It was no mule deer buck; it was the first elk he had ever seen in western Idaho. That was around 1950. That was only fifty-six years ago! Elk were only beginning to penetrate the area, and hunting seasons for them were just in the process of being established. Now, in that exact same area, I am able to take a bull elk annually, with minimal effort. Elk are literally overrunning the country. In their wake, their surging numbers are pushing out mule deer.

Idaho's elk hunting really seems to have two different types of "Golden Eras." The first was similar in time frame to the Golden Era of mule deer hunting – the mid-1950s thru the mid-1970s. This first wondrous time was not a time for abundant elk hunting opportunity, but a much better time in which to harvest an extremely large bull. Limited access, lower human population, and units that had just recently been opened for hunting had allowed for some incredible hunting opportunities for mature bulls. Many game preserves in the state had been closed to hunting for decades. Now, suddenly, there was opportunity to harvest elk there. Mature bulls in the 10 to 12-year-old age class were represented in these areas in numbers that had never been seen before nor will be seen again.

The second Golden Era is - (don't blink) - right now! While significant numbers of large bulls are not likely, the sheer opportunity to go out and harvest a bull elk in a general season for any common hunter has never been greater than in the mid-1990s thru today. Many general season Idaho elk hunts currently are pushing the 25% mark for success rates. This seems like an almost mythical number, but yet there it is, in black and white.

This second era may be coming to a close, however. A massive influx of Canadian gray wolves into Idaho is quickly changing the dynamics in the areas they are occupying. The next ten years, in regard to the state of Idaho's attempts to take over management of the species, will hold much of the fate of our elk herds in the balance. And with that fate will follow your future hunting opportunities.

If you are a trophy hunter, Idaho is unfortunately not the elk state for you. Idaho's bulls just don't have the overall genetics to really produce much for record book elk. Take a look at enough elk antlers from Idaho and you will quickly understand why. They have nice mass, but unfortunately also have famously (and somewhat notoriously) short G-3s. Idaho elk antlers have great main beams and typically develop strong back tines, given the chance to express their genetics, but the unfortunate dependability of Idaho bulls to have weak third points will keep most mature bulls out of the Boone and Crockett Club Records Book. I harvested a bull later in that season of 2002 mentioned earlier that had a rack weight of 30-1/2 lbs., yet the animal only scores about 315 on the B&C scale. Many bulls pushing the magical 375-mark from other states often have rack weights that only approach the 27 lb. range. This same bull had a verified skinned quarters weight of 510 lbs, translating into a live weight of right at 1000 lbs on the hoof (see p. 56 for a ratio of field-dressed weight to live weight, etc.).

So, Idaho is not much of a trophy elk state; no big deal. What we do have is one thing that is becoming increasingly rare in western states these days. We have an elk hunting heritage. Hunters in many western states must wait a decade or more before they are lucky enough to draw a tag. Most Idaho hunters are fortunate enough to have elk meat in the freezer almost every winter.

Recording Idaho's elk hunting history is a daunting task; one that would fill the pages of many books, if done properly. This book will only highlight some of its brightest and most amazing moments.

I consider myself a very privileged person. During the course of writing this book, I have had some wonderful opportunities. I have been privileged enough to do something that to me is of the utmost importance and significance. It is the preservation of a large part of our elk hunting legacy. I have also been able to meet some wonderful old-timers that can truly spin some yarns. I am fortunate to be able to call these people my friends.

One thing should be made abundantly clear. This is not a records book. This is a history. It is _our_ history. It is the preservation of stories that are beyond priceless. Some of these stories even I thought were gone. Fortunately, persistent digging and a few good strokes of luck produced the stories found in these pages. As each generation passes, more stories, history, and legacy are lost.

Internet auction forums and some antler dealers threaten to ruin the reliability of documenting our history. Precious details are lost every time a set of antlers changes hands. To some of these people, making a buck is the only bottom line, and the history that accompanies those great heads just goes by the wayside.

The history of these great trophies is priceless. The story written by my great-grandfather Lewis Daniels, in the next section of the book, is also priceless. Those written words are simply irreplaceable. I urge each and every one of you to make whatever efforts you can to help preserve any and all history you can, whether it be by sending in old photos and stories to us for inclusion in future books, bugging your elders for stories of their hunts in the old days, or simply by writing down your own personal adventures for your family. I hope this book will encourage everyone to write down his or her own personal hunting experiences, even if only for your great-grandchildren.

I hope you will truly enjoy and appreciate the history represented here. It was a pleasure and an honor to be a part of it.

I would also like to thank Leon Parson for being a part of this series. Leon's work in wildlife art is simply unparalleled. I consider it an honor to have had his paintings on the cover of the first two books in this series. As well as a gifted artist, Leon is also a true gentleman. As an added bonus, eight of Leon's most outstanding elk paintings, in full color, are included in this book as a special collection – something he and I affectionately call "dessert." Leon's current fans will find this especially exciting, as will his new fans, of which he will have many more after they have seen this collection. Enjoy!

Swan Valley Elk Patrol

In our first book, *Idaho's Greatest Mule Deer*, you all got a chance to meet my great-grandfather Lewis Daniels. As mentioned in that book, Lewis was the essence of old-time Idaho. He was practical, self-sufficient, tough as nails, and loved to explore the wilds of the great state of Idaho.

Later in his life, he took to writing many of his memoirs. Some of his writings are priceless not only to our family, but to the history of the state. His writings give insight into the reality of what things were like in the first quarter of the 20th century. They are not sanitized, politically correct, or the way people would like to "think" things were. They are just simple cold facts by a man who lived it. Some of his details may be slightly off, as science and history will prove discrepancies in some minor details, but this is not a textbook. For his time, most were probably widely held beliefs of the time.

What the following stories do tell is much of what eastern Idaho had for an elk population, what the prevailing attitudes were like at the time in regard to conserving precious resources, and the uphill battle he and others faced in helping in their own way to turn the tide. I hope you will all enjoy these short stories, as well as be educated by them.

Subsistence & Lack of Game Laws

The recent winter migration of elk to the vicinity of Iona, Idaho, and the Willow Creek area brings to mind the history of elk in eastern Idaho since the late 1880's and 1890's, much of which I have first-hand information on.

To begin with, records show that elk were not adapted to the high mountains, but rather frequented the foothills in summer, and in winter migrated to the Snake River desert in Idaho and to the Red Desert in Wyoming, where there was plenty of available feed, and they could winter nicely, as long as there was snow for water.

This past winter there was less than one foot of snow, and plenty of bunch grass, with sage and buckbrush to browse on. In the past, thousands of sheep were wintered on the desert, but now only a few antelope have access to the feed.

In the early spring in May, the cow elk had their calves in the aspen patches from the Willow Creek area to Gray's Lake and the Blackfoot area. The bulls shed their horns in March.

As the country was settled in the late 1880's and 1890's, the elk were forced to change their habits and winter in the mountains, principally on timbered hillsides where they would paw the snow down and eat the pine grass, which was not very palatable in summer until the fall and winter storms soaked it up. Domestic animals seldom ate any of it. The elk also browsed on mountain myrtle and huckleberry brush on the north slopes with timber, and on mountain mahogany and bunch grass on the south slopes.

As the country was taken over by settlers, the elk and deer were a necessary food item. They were also killed for their hides and tallow. Elk were also killed for their teeth. The Elks Lodge in early times used the elk tusks for watchfobs and tiepins. After the game laws came into effect, the lodge no longer used them.

It was common knowledge when I was a boy that one man sat in one place in Star Valley and killed over 70 head of elk for their hides and teeth. He was later apprehended and served one year in prison. As late as 1902, hide buyers came to Swan Valley to buy hides and tallow of big game animals and fur-bearing animals. I can remember two buyers who came to buy hides and furs, who stayed at our ranch many nights while scouring the country for hides. They each had a team and hay rack; the dried hides were stacked like a big load of hay, eight feet wide, sixteen feet long, and four feet high.

At that time, the only way to cross the South Fork of Snake River was to ford it. The ford was located just east of the present Caribou Ranger Station in Conant Valley. The hide buyers left our house near Irwin in the early morning. A little later on the same day, my father and brother-in-law started to Idaho Falls with a bunch of steers to sell. When they got to the river at the regular ford, they found the one hide buyer on the shore with his team tied to a cottonwood tree. They noticed piles of hides all down the river bank.

They asked the buyer, "Where is your partner?"

He replied, "Oh, he's gone. He pulled his team down river into the deep water and all were drowned; they disappeared in the deep water." Then breaking into a weak smile, he said, "I saved all the hides."

The settlers killed only for meat to eat, while others killed for the hides and tallow as a livelihood. There was no effective game protection in the Swan Valley area until about 1903. By that time there was very little game left in eastern Idaho.

My father had a large family, and came to Swan Valley in 1892. The first winter, '92-'93, he fed his family of seven on a total of twelve dollars cash. He had raised some wheat during the summer, which he threshed by hand and cleaned by separating the chaff in the wind. He took the grain to Afton, Wyoming, by team and wagon, and had it ground into flour, by what was known as a burr mill. This produced coarser flour than that made later by roller mills.

My father liked the white tail deer; therefore he hunted in the aspen patches and low hills, which was their favorite range both winter and summer. He would wait until the snow came and the weather grew cold, about November; then he would kill about 20 head of white tails, before they lost too much tallow. He dressed them and hung them in a shed to freeze, with the hides on, then brought them into the house one at a time as needed. Some of the hams were cured in salt for summer. None were ever wasted.

I recall as a very small boy seeing my father ride in on his favorite mare, Old Betsy, with a calf elk, and a mountain lion, or cougar, tied to her tail, and dragging in the snow. The thumb claws of the lion were kept in the old Seth Thomas clock until I was married; then Mother gave them to me. I had them mounted in silver for watchfobs for my brother Edward and myself.

From that time until the late 1920s the wild game continued to diminish. Any elk which came over the divide from Wyoming was considered to be a Wyoming elk, and was fair game for anyone who could get them. At one time in the early '20s, a bull elk appeared on Johnny Miller's cattle feed ground near Rainey Creek canyon. Two or three men started out to get him, shooting as he ran. He took the main road, going north toward the mouth of Rainey Creek canyon. Some more men with rifles met him there, and he turned down Rainey Creek toward the southwest, where he was finally brought down. There were 14 men to divide the meat.

Patrolling the Line

In the late 1920s, I worked summer times for the forest service, both on the Targhee and the Caribou forests. There was pressure from the Bonneville Sportsmen's Association to protect the drift of elk from Wyoming to re-populate eastern Idaho with big game. Peder Pederson was president of the BSA; he and his son Eddie, later the mayor of Idaho Falls, and the Swan Valley forest ranger Lyman Richwine were instrumental in getting the country closed, and protected against poaching.

Ranger Richwine persuaded me to form an N.R.A. club in Swan Valley and bring the elk protection program to the Swan Valley people to get their support, which we finally got from a great majority of them. Then the forest service decided that inasmuch as I had worked for the service for two summers, I would be the ideal one to do the patrolling of the state line in winter. Having been assured of the support of all the interested people in eastern Idaho, I accepted the job.

Lewis Daniels was one of the first game wardens of any type in Idaho. From 1929-1933, if you were an elk poacher in eastern Idaho, this is who you had coming after you.

The depression was on, and jobs were hard to get; thus I continued to work for the forest service for the next four years, wintertimes as patrolman, with Federal authority to make arrests anywhere on federal lands. I didn't like the idea of taking the job; but it was up to me to take it if I was to continue working for the forest service. The Swan Valley Rifle Club had also agreed to support the plan to protect the drift of elk to the Idaho side of the line, so there would be hunting for everybody.

In the fall and winter 1929-30, I was put on patrol of the Idaho-Wyoming state line to prevent poachers from driving the elk back over the divide. During the open season in Wyoming the state wardens could not handle it because they couldn't cross state lines. I was given federal authority with a deputy appointment from each state so that I could operate on state lands as well as federal lands. My area to patrol was from Grand Canyon to the Teton Mountains, covering all the country from Swan Valley to Jackson Hole. I rode horseback with a pack horse carrying my tepee, tent, bedding and groceries. I traveled this way until the snow got too deep to travel with a horse, then I checked the Idaho side of the line on skis.

Lewis Daniels (left) and forest ranger Lyman Richwine, with a nice six-point bull elk taken by Richwine in Dog Creek Basin in 1929.

This was the beginning of the depression, so there was no money to hire state game wardens. I was the only one in south Idaho except the State Game Warden, Amos Eckert of Boise. There was only one deputy game warden in north Idaho.

Up until this time, everyone who wanted an elk would kill them anywhere they found them, some going into Wyoming to get them. I had killed as many as most, but they were considered to be Wyoming elk and fair game for anyone who would take the trouble to hunt. The Wyoming state line was several miles west of the divide between Swan Valley and Jackson Hole.

It was common practice for people living near the mouth of Elk Creek to go up the creek on skis when the snow got deep. The elk used the creek and its tributaries for trails when the snow got deep because the creeks never froze over near the headwaters.

Ray Nickerson and Lewis Daniels (right) take a break for a photo on Elk Creek, Bonneville County, in the winter of 1930. Lew Daniels was the first, last, and only line of defense against poachers in eastern Idaho. He patrolled the Idaho-Wyoming line on horseback, skis, and snowshoes from 1929-1933.

Four men could go up Elk Creek - one would go up on the mouth of Sidoway Fork, another at the mouth of the South Fork, and the others would go up on the main creek. They would chase the elk into the creek, which they headed for readily to get away. With no one at the creek forks to stop them they would go back up the other creeks and get away, but with a man at the mouth of the other two forks, the elk continued on down the main creek, the men on skis staying close so the elk couldn't go back up and when they got close to the mouth of the creek would kill all they had brought down. I had known as many as twelve head to be killed in this way at one time.

The Swan Valley Rifle Club had also agreed to support this plan to protect the drift of elk to the Idaho side of the line so that there would be hunting for everybody. I had attended their meetings and told them that I had poached elk and that I was going to do the patrol job to the best of my ability. They all agreed to back me.

There were a few hardened poachers who still tried to operate, so some arrests were made, and we got some convictions. It was hard to get a conviction in Idaho because the poachers were paying off the judge and the prosecuting attorney with elk meat, but when I apprehended them in Wyoming there was no trouble getting convictions.

One poacher who didn't care whether he had killed an elk, moose, deer, or someone's fat steer continued to poach. He had killed a moose, but I hadn't caught him doing it. I got a search warrant and found the moose meat salted down in a barrel. I also found two wild geese, which were out of season. I took this evidence to Idaho Falls, where he appeared for trial.

There was moose hair among the meat, and I had a chemist take a blood test, which was positive on the moose meat, but the judge said "not guilty." This incident made the man very brave about poaching. He told me I had better not follow him into the mountains, so I didn't.

I found out he and two others had gone up Indian Creek. I waited one day, then I went up. I had Deputy Game Warden Wolfley from Wyoming with me. When we arrived on top of the divide of south Indian Creek and Wolf Creek, we could see the poachers' trail in the snow down through the dry fork of Wolf Creek into Dog Creek Basin. We rode north a short distance, looking down into Coburn Creek, then tied our hoses up in a brush patch, where they could not be seen, and walked down to their tent. There was a cow elk quartered and lying in the snow. The poachers were down below, trying to find more elk. We sat down on their bed in the tent, and waited.

It wasn't long until they rode up in front of the tent, so I stepped out and put them under arrest under Federal Regulation T-7, Occupancy Trespass. This meant being on federal lands for illegal purposes. The main poacher who had threatened me just turned pale, and told me they didn't know they were in closed territory – in fact they didn't know where they were. I took his rifle out of the scabbard in the saddle and Wolfley got the other two guns. The main poacher had thought that if I followed his trail to find him, he might fire a few shots warning me not to come closer, but when I stepped out of his tent not ten feet from him, wearing a 9mm German Luger Pistol, he could see no chance to get his rifle out of the scabbard even though he had it loaded. I didn't draw my Luger, because my old Uncle Charley Howell, who was a sheriff for thirty years, told me never to draw a gun unless I meant to use it. He said drawing a gun might scare some young kid into shooting in his own defense.

We brought our horses and came down and stayed all night at their camp. The next morning I told the poacher to pack up camp and elk to go to Jackson, Wyoming. He said, "If you want the elk packed, pack it yourself."

I told him if I packed the horses, of which he had eight, I would continue the federal charges and take them all to Cheyenne, Wyoming, to a federal judge. But, if he would plead guilty to a state charge of illegal possession of elk, I would dismiss the federal charge. At that point, he packed the camp and the elk, but Wolfley and I kept all the guns.

We came down Fall Creek to the Snake River, and forded the river. I hired a farmer with a truck to take us to Jackson. The attorney for Teton County was a young man from Star Valley named Wilford Neilson. The forest ranger and supervisor for Teton forest were also there. The poacher asked if it was true that he could be prosecuted on the federal charge for just being on forest land. The ranger said, "Yes, it's true, and if you don't plead guilty to a state charge here and now, then we will go to Cheyenne tomorrow morning, and we will take all your horses, your camp, every damned thing." The poacher slid back into his chair and said he would plead guilty.

The other two were just old farmers, who had no record of poaching, so I recommended leniency for them. On my recommendation, the poacher got the limit of the fine; the court confiscated his rifle and the elk meat. He had no money to pay his fine, so he stayed in jail. The others paid their fines of $50 and costs and went back to their farms.

On my trip back down Indian Creek, I found signs nailed to trees which read: "L.D. and E.W. were here." The poacher's wife had posted the signs. When I got to Alpine, I put up a sign in the store which read, "J.G. is in jail at Jackson."

That was the end of his poaching. He moved away and I never knew where, but the prosecuting attorney and judge at Idaho Falls had lost that source of supply of elk meat.

Some time later, I found the remains of a cow elk on little Elk Creek. I served a search warrant on a place near there and found three quarters of cow elk fresh killed with the hide still on it. This was in closed season and closed territory. I again took the case to the probate court in Idaho Falls, but they found the man in the case not guilty. I had given him a receipt for the meat and in the case of a not guilty decision was supposed to return the meat where I had found it, but the meat stayed in Idaho Falls.

Too Close for Comfort

The fall and winter of '30-'31, I again patrolled the Idaho-Wyoming line riding horseback until the snow got too deep, then going on skis or snowshoes the remainder until spring. On one occasion, Clon Jacobson, my nephew, skied up Elk Creek with me to count the elk and to check on their condition. It was late February, and the elk had congregated in the south hillsides and snowslide canyons, which were bare so feed was easier to get.

We were up the creek several miles when an old bull elk got excited above us on the hillside and tried to keep ahead of us going up the canyon. He was bucking deep snow, trying to get to the creek, which was not frozen over. We continued on, faster than the bull could travel; then he took off down the sidehill behind us and into the creek.

We continued for some distance until we had checked most of the open ground where the elk were congregated, then came back down the way we had gone up the creek. We were almost down to the Nickerson ranch when we came upon the old bull in a group of cottonwood trees. He had become exhausted with bucking the snow and traveling down the creek, and I thought I had better send him back up the creek before someone made stew out of him. We got below him and came up close in the grove of trees, but he just stood still and would not move.

Clon said he would like to have his picture taken with the elk. I said o.k. He moved quietly to about two rods of the bull. I had the camera ready, but just as I snapped the picture, the bull lowered his head and came after Clon. He tried to move quickly, but slipped and fell in the snow. He managed to roll over just as the bull buried his horns in the snow right beside him. The bull backed up and opened his eyes ready to charge again, but Clon made it to a tree and got behind it. I had dropped my camera in the snow and pulled my Luger pistol. I thought I would have to kill the elk to save Clon's life, but the bull stood with his head lowered ready to charge if we came near. We moved away slowly, keeping trees between the bull and us. He followed us a short distance, then stopped, as he was very tired. I checked the next day, and he had gone back up.

"Bull Elk tired of bucking snow." This photo was taken by Lewis Daniels on one of his adventures circa 1931. This is shortly before the bull charged Clon Jacobson.

"Elk at bay – Little Elk Creek." Photo from Bonneville County, in 1930.

There were numerous occasions when elk were tired from traveling in the snow, and then stood ready to fight. I would take their picture, and then go my way. There are a dozen or more pictures in my album to prove my statement, including one with his head lowered to jump at Clon Jacobson.

Frozen Solid

One December Sunday while living on the ranch in Swan Valley, four of us rode horseback up Palisade Creek to hunt elk just for the day. The weather was clear and cold. We took lunches and tied a small bag of oats on behind our saddles for the horses. The snow was about sixteen inches deep.

We hunted all day before we found where the elk were. It was nearly dark so we decided to stay overnight and try for elk early the next morning. We fed oats to the horses, left them tied to trees, and built a fire a few feet out from a big log that lay on the ground. We spread our wet saddle blankets on the ground between the fire and the log and tried to sleep.

Some of the boys could sleep longer than I in the cold as the fire died down. I had to get up every hour or so to build more fire. When daylight came, we went after the elk. We got close to them and tried to shoot but our cartridges would not fire as the powder had frozen so none of us fired a shot. If we had thought about it we could have warmed the cartridges but we had just left them in the rifle magazines. We then had to go back down to the valley where we found out that it was forty below zero that night. It was perhaps much colder up where we were.

Four poachers (and inexperienced woodsmen) in eastern Idaho circa 1930. Lewis Daniels came across them after they had poached this elk and were making a miserable attempt at field-dressing it. He showed them how, after he arrested them and took this photo.

Adventure, Desperation, & Tragedy: The Carlin Hunting Party of 1893

> *"Poor Colgate was so far gone that he could not remember his family, nor did he make any remarks or request concerning them. We made him as comfortable as we could, left him what necessaries we though he might require in the brief period he had yet to live and, shouldering our packs, we started sadly down the river. Although Colgate's head was turned toward us, he made no motion or outcry as he saw us disappear, one by one, around the bend."*

Abraham Lincoln Artman Himmelwright wrote that account of leaving George Colgate to die on a riverbank in the Idaho wilderness in 1893. Published in 1895, *In the Heart of the Bitter-root Mountains – The Story of the Carlin Hunting Party* was penned by Himmelwright using the pseudonym of *Heclawa*, and published by G.P. Putnam's Sons and The Knickerbocker Press. Within the pages of this amazing account is one of the most harrowing, intriguing, and controversial happenings in Idaho history.

Before delving into the details, it is important to put oneself in the proper perspective. Some of the men in the story were from New York, which was vastly different in 1893 than Idaho.

The decade of the 1890s in Idaho was a period of extreme transition and disparity. On one hand, statehood had just recently been granted, and the University of Idaho had just recently been founded. The sport of baseball was growing, and technology was beginning a fervent pace that may never be equaled again. On the other hand, the Nez Perce War had ended less than two decades previous. Idaho's oldest town was only forty years old, and the lack of human permeation into the wilds of Idaho could easily suggest it was the 1490s rather than the 1890s.

Such were the diverging situational aspects of a hunt undertaken by what would later become known as "The Carlin Party". This tragic journey into the deepest reaches of a relatively unknown wilderness known as the Clearwater would leave this hunting expedition in the highest annals of infamy in Idaho's hunting lore.

Several things about this tale make it extraordinary. First, two different members of the party (Abe Himmelwright and Will Carlin) actually took the time to write down their accounts of the story, in the form of the book by Himmelwright and as a diary for Carlin. These personal accounts of the events of their trek are priceless. Secondly, cameras were just being made available, and actual photographs of the expedition were taken. This in itself is simply amazing. Thirdly, death, desperation, and controversy, three main ingredients in any decently thrilling story, seemed to be rampant at every turn for this ill-fated crew.

The party consisted of three hunters and a total of five men. The first was William E. Carlin (the 27-year-old son of Brigadier General W.P. Carlin). Will Carlin had done a fair bit of exploring into the wilds of the west, and was anxious for more. The second was Abraham Lincoln Artman Himmelwright, a civil engineer in New York and good friend of Will Carlin. The third member of the actual hunting party was John Harvey Pierce, who was Carlin's brother-in-law and was also from New York.

Carlin, Himmelwright, and Pierce hired a man named Martin Spencer (originally from Iowa) as a guide and packer. Spencer, to his credit, had eight years worth of guiding experience. Still needing a cook, Carlin insisted on taking a 52-year-old man named George Colgate, from Post Falls, Idaho. Carlin had been on "safaris" with Colgate in previous years, and felt he would be a good fit for the expedition.

The country they were headed into was aptly described by Captain John Mullan, whom Himmelwright quoted in the book he wrote of their tragic journey. Mullan said, "I have traveled over much of the Rocky Mountain region from the 39th to the 49th degree of latitude north, and from the plains of the Missouri to the plains of the Columbia, but nowhere did I ever meet with so difficult, rugged, severe, and broken or mountainous country as that situated between the Tinkham route of 1853, and the Coeur d'Alene route (by me) in 1854."

Himmelwright wrote his own poignant description of the area where he almost lost his life:

> Sixteen years have elapsed since the Nez Perce outbreak, and the Lolo Trail, becoming yearly more and more obstructed, exists now only in history, for it is almost obliterated and practically abandoned. The region it traversed has relapsed again into its primitive state – a vast unbroken wilderness, thrillingly interesting in its history and traditions and impressively beautiful in its bold, majestic scenery. Far removed from the outposts of civilization; the watercourses impracticable for boats or canoes; and the region practically inaccessible except by the difficult Lolo Trail – the basin of the Clearwater River, with its vast forests, dense thickets, and innumerable streams, will remain for many years to come a natural and ideal home for large game – a safe and quiet retreat – a haven where the denizens of the forest need have no fear of molestation.

The Equipment

Spencer and Colgate prepared a list of the following food provisions for the trip:

125 lbs. flour	30 lbs. sugar
30 lbs. breakfast bacon	1 lb. tea
40 lbs. salt pork	8 lbs. coffee
20 lbs. beans	2 doz. cans cond. milk
40 lbs. salt	3 lbs. baking powder
10 lbs. oatmeal	citron, sage, mace, thyme
10 lbs. cornmeal	10 lbs. alum
5 lbs. dried apples	5 lbs. raisins
5 lbs. dried apricots	½ lb. pepper
1 gal. maple syrup	½ gal. vinegar
2 doz. tallow candles	block matches
3 lbs. laundry soap	1 gal. brandy
½ doz. cakes toilet soap	40 lbs. potatoes

Spencer, Carlin, and Himmelwright prepared the following list of camp equipage:

1 10x12 ft. wall tent	½ doz. knives and forks
1 7x7 ft. A-tent	9 tin plates
1 large wagon cover or fly	9 tin cups
10 double blankets	½ doz. teaspoons
2 heavy quilts	2 butcher's knives
½ doz. towels	2 large spoons
3 canvas pack covers 4x6	1 large meat knife
5 yds. Crash	1 4-lb. axe
5 yds. heavy unbleached muslin	1 2-lb. axe
3 camp kettles (nested)	1 8-in. flat file
2 gold pans for use at dishpans, etc	1 box assorted copper wire rivets
1 granite stew pan	2 10-yard coils wire
2 frying pans	2 lbs. assorted wire nails
1 reflector (for baking bread)	1 ball coarse twine
1 rubber airbed	1 ball light twine
1 coffee pot	50 ft. extra rope
	1 doz. extra cloth sacks

To pack this immense load (and the five men), they needed a large amount of stock. *"Spencer estimated that five packhorses would be necessary to carry the provisions and, as there were five persons in the party, five saddle horses with complete trappings were also required."*

On the Lo-Lo Trail

On September 19th, 1893, they started out, completely outfitted for the hunt. *"The whole party was in excellent spirits,"* wrote Himmelwright.

The following, in italics, are chosen excerpts of their personal accounts of their infamous visit into the *Kooskooskee region*, or the Lochsa River as it is known today.

September 21st – In about an hour's time Will returned to the cabin with fifty-three trout, a quarter-pound to one and a half pounds in weight, and reported rare sport in taking them. The stream was so small that he had cut a willow switch about seven feet long and, with only four feet of line, had been able to take in an hour all we could use. Abe and John returned to the cabin at noon with only two grouse each...

...At about ten o'clock on September 22nd, we crossed Musselshell Creek... Here, however, was the terminus of the wagon road. Forming in single file, with Spencer in the lead, the pack animals were distributed between the riders, and the train continued the journey eastward into the mountains along the Lolo Trail...

...The character of the country soon changed... At about three o'clock we reached the top of a high ridge called Snow Summit. Here we found six inches of snow on the ground...Here we made camp. The snow was about eight inches deep...

...September 24th was the hardest day we experienced until we reached our destination. The trail zigzagged up and down steep hillsides, crossed rocky gulches, and skirted or "cross-cutted" steep slopes of loose rock. Occasionally the horses would refuse to go, and it became necessary to dismount and lead and drive them...

The horses' legs became so badly scratched and bruised that they left bloodmarks in the snow...That night we reached and camped on Bald Mountain.

...On this occasion Spencer picketed his powerful white horse with a rope about thirty feet long, tying the end of the rope to a stump. After supper it was quite dark, and all were gathered around the fire. Suddenly a loud tramping was heard, and our hearts almost stopped beating at the thought that the horses had stampeded. Then Spencer's white horse rushed out of the darkness, passed within thirty feet of the campfire and tore at breakneck speed straight down the steep mountainside into the gloom and darkness below, a piece of the stump skipping and bounding after him at the end of the rope. In a moment all was still. In the excitement we had imagined the stump to be a cougar in pursuit of the horse, and Will had grabbed his gun to shoot it. Will and Spencer immediately started down the mountain to see what had become of the horse. In about fifteen minutes they returned and reported him safe and sound. He had succeeded in tearing loose from the stump and miraculously escaped a violent death. Fortunately none of the other horses stampeded, and congratulations were in order on our good fortune in avoiding a stampede, as well as for the opportunity of witnessing the fastest time ever made down so steep an incline. It was a spectacle never to be forgotten by those who saw it.

September 26th – Returning to the trail the next morning, we followed it only a short distance and then turned to the right and took an old Indian trail leading along a burnt ridge down to the Kooskooskee [now the Lochsa River]. *The last portion of the descent was very steep, the trail zigzagging down the nose of a spur, the altitude of which was at least three thousand feed above the river. During this descent Colgate became exhausted, and Will dismounted and assisted him down. On our arrival at the foot of the descent, Colgate's feet and legs were found to be considerably swollen. His condition alarmed Will very much, and on inquiring into the cause of the swelling and his weakness, Colgate insisted he was simply tired out and would be all right in a day or two after having a little rest.*

On reaching the river, all were surprised to find a cabin nearly completed and four men encamped. Spencer went over to the camp and soon returned with the information that a prospector whom he had known for years, named Jerry Johnson, and a trapper, Ben Keeley, had built the cabin in partnership, packed in plenty of grub from Missoula, and were going to spend the winter there. The other two men had come in for a few days' hunting and would return shortly to Missoula...

...On the north bank of the Kooskooskee, we made our camp...Unfortunately, it continued to rain...

September 28th – Colgate was now a trifle improved but not strong enough to attend to his duties. We all thus helped do the cooking and the work about camp.

Day after day it rained....

JERRY JOHNSON.

Jerry Johnson was a Prussian by birth. He emigrated at an early age to New Zealand, where he became interested in mining. He eventually made his way to north-central Idaho. Johnson chose wild, unfrequented country in which to search for precious metals, a habit that brought him to the Clearwater. He was around sixty years old when he was visited by the Carlin Party.

The First Elk

We had been in camp for over five days, and had as yet not been fortunate enough to secure any fresh meat. It had rained every day. The game moved about but little, and visited the licks and their drinking-places at night. Will, who was the most experienced hunter of the party, felt assured of this fact, for he had hunted at all times of the day about the springs; and while there were fresh signs, they had evidently been made the night before. On the evening of the fifth day, several fresh signs of elk (Wapiti) were seen along the hillsides, and we felt pretty certain that they had either commenced coming down from the high ranges, or that those already in our vicinity had begun to move about regardless of the wet weather. Accordingly, Will determined to visit the lower lick at daylight the following morning, and spend the day in hunting the adjacent sidehills.

He started for the lower lick just at dawn, and returned to camp at about eleven o'clock, carrying a large heart in his hand. The others had been busy all morning making camp more comfortable; but as soon as Will was seen approaching, every one became at once deeply interested and came forward to meet him. Seeing the heart, Abe asked, "Well, what is it?"

"Bull elk," said Will, laconically.

"The d---l! said Abe, taking Will's hand and giving it a warm squeeze of congratulation. "Luck at last, and fresh meat in camp!"

After congratulations all around, Will went into the tent, laid the rifle on the blankets, and began to change his wet clothes.

"But tell us something about it. Has he a nice set of horns?" asked John.

"Six points, and full grown," said Will briefly; adding, "say, out there, I want you people to know I'm hungry!"

By the time Will had changed his wet clothes and hung them on a line near the fire, a hasty meal had been prepared, and when Will seated himself at the table, he gave the following account of his morning's experience:

"As it was raining when I started, and considering the chances of seeing game very slim, I decided to take the 40-82 instead of my paradox. I started on a rapid walk for the lower lick, but the brush along the trail was 'sopping' wet, and I got wet to the skin before going half a mile. On arriving at the grove of cedars in which the spring is situated, I used the utmost caution in approaching the lick, but found it empty. As I stood debating a moment as to what I should do, I heard the clear whistle of a cow, which I judged must be about a hundred and fifty yards below me, on a small flat skirting the river. Slipping quietly along the brow of the hill, I had hardly emerged from the timber when the cow trotted slowly past me, not more than thirty yards away, without seeming in the least disturbed by my presence. Hastily getting behind a large tree, I waited for the bull, which I felt confident would follow her. I had not been there more than half a minute when I saw a pair of magnificent antlers moving slowly from right to left in front of me. The head and body were hidden from view, as the bull was walking up a little gully eighty yards away. I did not dare move, for a few jumps would take the bull out of sight in the timber. Although I did not stir, and he could not possibly have scented me, the bull seemed aware that there was some danger at hand, for he suddenly sprang up the side of the gully and stopped in an open clump of trees, and stood as though trying to decide in what direction the danger lay. His neck and shoulders were hidden by intervening trees, but I felt that I must make the best of the shot offered me, and aimed for the liver. At the report of the rifle, he gave one bound and disappeared over the brow of the hill. Hastening to the spot, I found his tracks following a well-worn game-trail, which led, slanting, down the hill. There were no signs of blood, but I felt sure that I had hit him. Walking with extreme caution and peering into all the little ravines and thickets, I had gone about half a mile, when, on stooping down and glancing ahead, I saw the elk lying behind a log seventy-five yards distant and looking directly at me.

"Sitting down quietly, I took careful aim at his neck and fired. The elk staggered to his feet and made for the river. Hastily throwing down the lever and inserting a fresh cartridge, I fired for his shoulder. At the shot he went down on his breast, but regained his feet and started off on three legs. The next shot struck him in the neck, and he went down all in a heap. He was not dead, however, and for fear that he might in his struggles break his antlers on the rocks, I finished him with a shot in the neck. My first sensation was a feeling of great satisfaction at killing the finest elk that I had ever seen; my second was a feeling of disgust with the gun for doing it in such a bungling manner. One shot from a proper rifle in the neck or shoulder, where these miserable little hollow-pointed bullets had struck, would have killed him outright. For fully five minutes I sat and admired the fallen monarch; his magnificent curving antlers; his splendid form and sleek, yellowish sides; the fine, long, reddish-black hair of his scalp and neck. Then, on preparing to bleed and dress him, I found that I had forgotten my long-bladed knife in my haste to get away early this morning, and had only a large pocketknife with me. With this, however, I dressed the elk and hastened back to camp."

THE FIRST ELK (*Wapiti*).

Will Carlin takes a moment to enjoy a successful hunt on the Kooskooskee (Lochsa) River in 1893. These two photographs are among the very oldest hunting photos ever taken in the history of the state of Idaho. What a tremendous bull, and what incredible history preserved in these images.

After congratulations a second time, we went down with horses to bring up the meat and antlers. Keeley accompanied us to get some fresh meat, of which he and Jerry were in need. On our arrival, we found the usual number of magpies and ravens rapidly making away with the entrails amid a perfect pandemonium of harsh sounds. When they saw us, they flew into neighboring trees and watched our proceedings.

After photographing the elk, we skinned and cut him up, and at four o'clock we were ready to start back to camp. The first bullet had cut his liver almost in two and had lodged under the skin on the other side. The second bullet had barely broken one shoulder and smashed into bits on the big bones, failing to penetrate farther. None of the last three bullets had passed through the neck, which was very thick even for this time of the year.

We started for camp and were overtaken by darkness half a mile beyond the lick. Keeley's horse slipped and rolled down a slippery sidehill, but my dint of considerable swearing and work on the part of his master, the horse was brought back to the trail. The darkness became so intense when a mile from camp that we were forced to build a fire, unpack the horses, and leave the meat and antlers under a tree till morning. While the fire was being built, one of the horses clumsily struck a dead tree, about eight inches in diameter. The tree fell and just grazed Will's arm – a very fortunate escape from a broken shoulder. All the matches were used in trying to start the fire, and we had a miserable time stumbling about in the darkness. After we had floundered around for an hour or so, Keeley came along with a torch made from cedar shavings, and we reached camp about eight o'clock. It took us four hours to go less than four miles. We secured the meat and antlers the first thing the next morning...

Snowed In

After we had been in camp nearly a week, a swelling in Colgate's hands was observed, while that on his feet and legs had increased. These swellings caused considerable alarm, and Will, taking Colgate aside, questioned him very closely about the new trouble. Colgate insisted that he would be all right in a little while, but Will, knowing that he was accustomed to hardship and exposure, rightly attributed the cause of his ailment to something more than fatigue. After being questioned further, Colgate at last revealed the true cause of his disability, admitting that he was suffering from a trouble with which he had been afflicted for a number of years, that he had been compelled to use instruments for a long time in performing the functions of nature, which he had failed to bring with him. Will, much surprised, then asked him why he had not brought the instruments, to which he replied that he did not like to use them and thought he could do without them. From the nature of the complaint, it was evident that Colgate must have known that he did not have his instruments the very first day out from Kendrick. Yet he had persistently journeyed for eight successive days, deeper and deeper into the woods, without acquainting anyone with the fact, and knowing at the same time that the instruments were indispensable to him. Will was dumfounded. When the facts were made known to the others, all realized the serious predicament in which they were placed. What was to be done? It did not seem advisable to start him back in the rain, which was probably snow in the mountains, so it was decided to make him as comfortable as *possible in camp and await fair weather. Exercise had, apparently, a bad effect on him, and we persuaded him to relinquish his duties and remain quiet, as we wished him to start out as strong as possible on the return trip. About this time, October 2nd, Spencer expressed fears that we might be snowed in, but no one deemed the danger from that source sufficiently serious to devote a day in climbing to the top of the burnt ridge to investigate the matter. The rain still continued. Colgate grew worse daily. By October 6th his legs had swollen to nearly twice their natural size, and he was barely able to move about camp without assistance. Spencer began to urge our return, and John, who did not care to hunt in the rain, vigorously seconded the motion. Abe insisted that the Indian summer and milder weather must yet come before winter would set in, and that the return in the rain and snow would be undertaken under the very worst conditions for Colgate.*

Debate followed as to what to do. Abe and Will tried to send the party back without them, as they had not yet had enough hunting. That didn't sit well with the rest of the party, however.

…Finding we could wait no longer for clear weather, and Colgate's condition becoming daily more and more serious, it was finally decided to leave for Kendrick…

Their attempt to return via the mountain (trail) route ended abruptly, after they were forced back when encountering snow depths already approaching four feet. They were forced back to camp (and square one).

…What would become of Colgate? He could not walk, and in the soft snow, even if we could make crude snowshoes, it would be impossible to carry him. The trail led along steep hillsides, often overgrown for great distances with thick brush and obstructed with thousands of boulders and fallen trees. If we should attempt to pull or drag him after us under these conditions, even if there should be a crust on the snow, our progress would be necessarily so slow that several weeks would be consumed in the journey…

The party surveyed every available option, both mentally and by personally inspecting routes and ideas. No matter what they chose, they knew now it would test them as nothing had ever tested them.

…We knew search and relief parties would be sent out at great expense, and that in hazarding a trip down an unknown river we were taking desperate chances with our lives; but on the river there was little or no snow, and since it offered the most feasible means of getting Colgate out, we considered it our duty to forego all other considerations and attempt a passage down the river…

…Will arranged with Ben Keeley, the trapper, for the sum of two hundred fifty dollars, to sell us his share of the grub in the cabin, help build our rafts, and accompany us down the river. Keeley was an excellent chopper and had considerable experience in rafting sawlogs in Minnesota and Wisconsin waters. He was, in consequence, a very valuable acquisition to our party in the emergency.

In most descriptions (and perhaps future justification) of their situation and the events that would transpire, they seemed desperate to get themselves (and more importantly Colgate) out. But then Himmelwright tells of how the group spent the next four days finishing Jerry's cabin, so that they could store all their unnecessary provisions. With Colgate worsening daily, some of these actions seem questionable at best. Further complicating matters was that Himmelwright and Carlin seemed to spend a fair amount of those four days hunting, rather than helping finish the cabin.

Building the Rafts

On October 15th, the party began to search for suitable timbers to build rafts. Again, considerable time had elapsed before the actual attempt to get out began.

In the afternoon Abe went down the river to see what success Spencer and Keeley had met with in their search for timber. He found them near the lower warm springs, where a bunch of dead white cedars of suitable size had been located, some of which had already been felled and peeled. Abe took a block of the wood, and after ascertaining its specific gravity by use of a small fish scale belonging to Will, he calculated the number of cubic feet each of the two rafts should contain in order to carry their respective loads. The object was to avoid unnecessary and superfluous weight, which would make the rafts more difficult to handle in the swift water.

That night quite a debate was indulged in concerning the rafts. Abe and Will insisted that a long, narrow raft was the only form that could possibly pass through the numerous projecting boulders in the river, while Keeley and Spencer were equally sure that a wider raft of less length was best. Keeley and Spencer were, however, won over and the dimensions of the rafts were finally fixed at four and a half to five feet wide and twenty-six feet long…

…Colgate required considerable nursing, and fires had to be kept going for his comfort. John and Abe were consequently kept busy most of the time cooking and getting in necessary firewood. Every afternoon, however, Abe would go down to the other camp and help for several hours on the rafts, carrying such additional provisions as the other camp required along with him. About this time myriads of snow geese passed over us daily as they migrated southward…

"Building the rafts."

...The building of the rafts was no small undertaking. The river was full of boulders, and the shores were a mass of jagged rocks. The heavy rafts in the swift water could not be so completely controlled that they would not strike the boulders and ledges occasionally, and for that reason had to be built very strong and firm. Having no spikes or bolts, we had to resort to framing and dovetailing methods in their construction.

On account of its lightness, dead cedar was selected as the best timber available for the purpose. Straight trees, sixteen to twenty inches in diameter, were chose, felled, and peeled. As the horses could not be utilized on account of the rough ground, fallen timber, and want of suitable harness, the work of collecting the logs on the riverbank was a difficult job and involved some heavy lifting. With skis, rollers, and handspikes, we moved the logs of the first raft in one day to the riverbank and placed them side by side on top of two crosslogs.

With the aid of a wooden square and a scribing awl, made by Abe, the logs were marked and the work of fastening them together begun. Our tools consisted of two axes, two hatchets, a broken crosscut say and an inch auger, the last two belonging to Jerry Johnson and having been borrowed from him...

...After October 22nd, when we moved Colgate to the lower camp, he failed rapidly. Liquid had collected in his lungs, which choked or smothered him when he assumed a horizontal position, and he was thus unable to lie down. Spencer made him a chair out of a block of wood, upon which he sat day and night. His legs were swollen enormously, and although a small man when well, he then weighed fully two hundred pounds. He was perfectly helpless and had to be assisted when he wished to move the smallest distance about camp. He was very sensitive to cold, and we constantly kept blankets around him. We were, besides, compelled to divide the night into watches and sit up with him, maintaining fires all night long for his comfort. Scarcely an hour passed that he did not require assistance, but not withstanding the most careful nursing and attention to his requirements, he grew steadily worse. On the 2nd of November the swelling on one of his legs broke. Considerable liquid was discharged, after which he felt somewhat relieved.

Knowing that we could return over the trail on snowshoes if disencumbered by Colgate, someone suggested that Jerry Johnson take care of Colgate until we could return to Kendrick, when a relief party could be sent after Colgate, with additional supplies for Johnson. Old Jerry refused to agree to this, however, on account of the uncertainly of a relief party being able to reach him at that season, and asserted that the remaining provisions were barely sufficient for himself during the winter. Colgate was, besides, afraid of Johnson and was unwilling to stay with him.

Colgate's rapidly sinking condition argued strongly against such a course. It was doubtful if he could survive the journey out, and it was almost certain that he could not live until rescued by a relief party, even if such a party were to start back for him immediately after our return to civilization. The only humane course left us, therefore, was to attempt a passage down the river and restore Colgate to his family before his dissolution, if possible...

...Everything being ready on the night of November 2nd, we decided to start the following morning as early as possible...

Up until this point in the book, all of the written account has been Himmelwright's. From this point forward through November 22nd, the details are taken from Will Carlin's diary.

The men instantly encountered difficulties. They struck two large rocks and jammed one of the rafts. Water came rushing over, instantly swamping it. John Pierce was thrown, and George Colgate sucked under water. They finally got the rafts righted, and the wet passengers to shore.

We all made as comfortable a camp as possible, hustled in firewood for the night, and cooked supper. It continued raining and sleeting. All in all, we'd had a rough sort of a day. The night was divided into watches so that a fire could be kept up for Colgate...
...We decided to leave our antlers and all other unnecessary things with Jerry and lighten our loads as much as possible...

For the next few days, Carlin gave description of one bad experience after another of trying to both raft the river and walk the river in advance to scout it. The beleaguered party kept on, but were becoming weary quickly.

...We had been out four days now and had not made much more than ten miles. Keeley was anxious to turn the rafts loose and trust to luck in running through, but the others did not consider it safe at all, as we didn't know what was below us...
...Wednesday, November 8th – ...Four of us went down to examine Abe's bad rapids, and John stayed with the rafts. We found by far the worst rapids we had yet seen. The current was extremely swift for a mile, and the river full of boulders. Then the river narrowed, and in the center was a very large rock which left narrow channels on each side, and these were full of rocks. Below, it was still worse – more boulders and worse water. It was clear that we would upset a good many times before getting through this rapid if we were to try to run it, and should we fail to make a landing, we would be carried into a row of rocks that would smash us up completely. We cannot lower the rafts by ropes from the right hand shore owing to perpendicular banks in many places. It would be unsafe to leave Colgate on the raft while passing through the worst places, and the right-hand bank was so steep and rough that he could not be helped along it at all. We returned toward evening and made camp. Tried fishing, but got only one strike. Some of us think we are at the canyon, but Spencer thinks not...
...John and I unloaded our raft, got in wood for the night, and tried to get a fire going for Colgate. Everything was soaked, and it took us over an hour to get the fire started. Colgate was so stiff that he could not move...

As they continued, Spencer nearly drowned when they lodged one of the rafts severely. They eventually freed the raft. During this time, as the rain continued incessantly, it also began to get much colder, to the point that the men had much difficulty sleeping. They had also reached a point that much of the raft movement would have to be done using ropes to carefully lower them through dangerous stretches – a danger in itself due to the ropes becoming considerably more damaged daily due to this practice.

...Upon their return they reported the water tremendously swift and that the rocks were more numerous and dangerous than any we had yet seen. In fact, they saw one place ahead that looked impassable, but did not have time to get down near it. This was very disagreeable news, for our ropes were becoming frayed and weak

from constant contact with sharp rocks and would not endure much more work of this kind. If they should break while we were letting a raft through a bad place, it would mean the probable death of those on board and the certain loss of the provisions. We were also worried about Colgate, who seemed to be failing very rapidly in strength and in mind. He hardly said a word all day except when spoken to, or at mealtime when he was given his food. He sat and gazed for hours with a vacant stare at the river or the rocks. His legs look very bad indeed and are evidently mortified from the knees down. We found today that our flour is getting very low; only about forty pounds are left. We've decided to eat no more of it at present, but to live on cornmeal and beans as long as they last. We are out of fresh meat. I tried to catch some fish, but they would not rise. We hope this might be the much talked of canyon and that we will soon be through it.

Saturday, November 11th – It is still cold and clear. We went down the river a long way this morning and were horrified to find that we are absolutely stuck. Half a mile below camp is a ledge of rocks and a rapid through which we cannot take a raft. Below this are two more places still worse. Everyone gave his opinion of his own accord that we cannot get our rafts farther down the river.

Our position is as follows: we have barely one week's short allowance of flour left. All our other provisions, except a few pounds of cornmeal and beans and a handful of salt each, are exhausted. The shores of the river are a mass of irregular rocks. Numerous ledges or cliffs, some of them hundreds of feet high, rise vertically above the river and project into it. The hillsides adjacent are steep and rocky and covered with dense brush. Many of the ledges are so precipitous that it is all an able-bodied man can do to hang to bushes and climb around them on narrow clefts or steps in the rock. Most of us are considerably weakened from exposure and are not in a fit condition to walk. Owing to the character of the country and our enfeebled condition, we cannot hope to accomplish more than four or five miles a day on foot. As nearly as we can estimate, we are fifty or fifty-five miles from civilization (Wilson's ranch, twenty miles below the forks). We know nothing whatever of the river ahead of us, of the obstructions we will meet with, or even if we can get through at all by this route. The dreaded Black Canyon is yet before us. Worst of all is the fact that Colgate cannot possibly walk, and it is absolutely impossible to help or carry him around the bad places along the river. His condition grows worse hourly. His legs are in a frightful condition, and the odor that comes from them is almost unendurable. He is perceptibly weaker than he was yesterday, and his mind is so far gone that he has lately appreciated no efforts to make him comfortable.

On our return from camp at half-past two p.m., we drew to one side and discussed every plan that could be thought of – not a stone was left unturned. If we stay with him, we can do nothing but ease his last moments and bury him, because it is impossible for him ever to get well again. His sickness is, besides, of such a character that he might linger in stupor or semi-conscious condition for several days, during which a large portion of our remaining provisions would be consumed. We cannot even take him back and leave him with Jerry Johnson while some of us go on our snowshoes for assistance. With no sight of game in the neighborhood and the river full of floating ice so that the fish will not rise, were we to leave half our provisions here and one man to care for Colgate, he would probably starve before succor could reach him, while such a drain on the meager supplies would render the chances considerably less of the others ever reaching civilization. We all feel that it is clearly a case of trying to save five lives or sacrificing them in order to perform *the last* sad rites for poor Colgate. To remain longer with Colgate is to jeopardize to the very doors of folly all our lives – not in the cause of humanity, for Colgate is beyond any appreciation of such kindness – but for sentiment solely. We have exhausted every resource and feel that we have gone to the extreme limit of duty toward Colgate in our endeavors to get him back to civilization. Our own families and friends have now a just claim upon us, and we have to save ourselves if possible. We therefore have decided to strike down the river, and, with luck, some of us may get through unless we encounter a bad snowstorm. Everyone feels very much dispirited at having to leave Colgate. There is hardly a word spoken by anyone tonight...

...We start on our tramp tomorrow, taking nothing but provisions, guns, and the clothes on our backs. Colgate is very bad tonight. He has great difficulty in breathing. It would not surprise me at all to see him collapse at any moment. I told him today that we could raft no farther and would have to walk, but it seemed to make no impression on him.

Monday, November 13th - ...Poor Colgate was so far gone that he could not remember his family, nor did he make any remarks or request concerning them. We made him as comfortable as we could, left him what necessaries we though he might require in the brief period he had yet to live and, shouldering our packs, we started sadly down the river. Although Colgate's head was turned toward us, he made no motion or outcry as he saw us disappear, one by one, around the bend...

...Wednesday, November 15th – The lack of nourishing food, loss of sleep, and exposure are beginning to tell on us all; we are very weak and unsteady on our feet. Everything that will lighten our load has been thrown away...I feel that our chances are rather slim of getting out of the mountains. Everyone is tired and miserable...

Thursday, November 16th - ...Following the ridge for a quarter of a mile, we made a descent to the river again when, on turning a small point, we came upon the Black Canyon. There was no mistaking it this time! I do not think any view in the mountains ever impressed me as this one did. The view did not impress me so much with its grandeur as with an indefinable dread weirdness. It immediately associated itself in my mind with death...

...Our camp is dismally cold and wet, but luckily we have plenty of wood near at hand. We made a big fire for the night. We saw that our best chance for food was fish, and after supper we hunted for something from which to make a spoon. Spencer produced a piece of copper wire, which he used to clean his pipe. Keeley made one spoon from the bowl of a teaspoon, while I made another by hammering out a silver half dollar. Money is some good in the mountains after all. They looked very good when finished and will undoubtedly attract the fish, but we still have to rely on the small hooks to hold them. Upon counting the hooks, I found that we have twenty-four left.

Friday, November 17th - ...The black dog looked so miserable tonight that I thought it the kindest act all around to kill her. This I did by shooting her in the head with Spencer's revolver. We then hung her up and skinned her, and when the flesh got cold, we cut off the best portions and made a strong broth – strong in every sense of the word. Into the broth we put a tablespoonful of flour. The soup was good, but the flesh was tough and strong. Although nearly starved, only one of the remaining dogs would touch the meat...

Saturday, November 18th - We started out by climbing up the side of the canyon, taking every available chance to get forward. The walking was harder than any we had yet had. Many times we were stopped by high perpendicular faces of rock. We had to go up or down for considerable distances to get around some of these; others we had to cross and trust to luck not to fall. Keeley is particularly good at finding all available footholds and paths. He has been a splendid fellow all through, doing all he could and not grumbling at all...

Sunday, November 19th – John decided to abandon his gun, so he left it hanging to a tree in camp. We felt that we must work hard today, which we did. We found occasional old game trails, and the walking improved. We lost much valuable time, however, by following one which took us up into the hills. We passed many bad places, and it is a wonder to me that no one slipped and fell, all being so weak. Two of us have no hobnails left in our boots, and three of us are very footsore...

...We have only enough flour left for one more meal. Not being able to sleep from weakness and cold, I sat thinking of what our friends were doing in the outside world, when my attention was attracted by the two little dogs, Idaho and Montana. Poor little Montana is very far gone, and so weak and thin that it is a surprise to me that she can keep up with us. All the hair is worn from her legs by the sharp rocks. Tonight she lay down as close as she could to the fire and extended her four legs, to keep them warm; still she shivered, I suppose from weakness. Idaho, her mate, is much stronger, and seemed to realize Montana's condition, for she came and lay partly on top of her and partly on the outside of her, so as to protect the side exposed to the cold. I do not recall ever having heard of a similar case of animal sympathy...

Tuesday, November 21st – We had a little piece of bacon, weighing about one-eighth of a pound, which we used to grease the pan with in baking bread. The flour being exhausted, we made a broth of the bacon this morning. Abe went for deer, but got none, as it began to snow. Most of us were too weak to walk without breakfast and could barely stagger around. Keeley caught three fish which we ate, and we started down the river at eleven o'clock, walking very slowly and often stumbling and falling down. After going about a mile we found a nice fishing hole. Keeley caught four and I two, making six fine fish in all – a veritable feast. I had no control over my arms. When I whirled the spoon around to throw it into the river, it was just as likely to fly back of or above me. We soon made camp and stewed the fish. The dogs got quite a meal of fish bones and seemed to feel relieved.

Wednesday, November 22nd – it snowed about two inches during the night...We tried hard to catch fish, but did not get a strike. One small fish kept following Keeley's spoon to the shore but would not strike. Getting desperate, he shot at it with his revolver but missed...

The men were eating some hawberries and began to discuss what might be going on in terms of any rescue attempt for them. Abe's thought on the matter was that they were probably another three or four days out from receiving any help. That would change in a mere matter of moments.

...On turning the next point, we saw two men hurrying toward us. Thinking they were of our party I said, "I wonder what's the matter? Perhaps they have seen a deer and want us to shoot it!" But he replied, "I am afraid someone has fallen into the river." As they approached nearer, we saw they were not of our party, and a moment later Abe recognized our old-time shooting chum, Sgt. Guy Norton of the Fourth Cavalry. With him was Lt. Charles P. Elliott. It expresses it mildly to say we were overjoyed to see them.

Much discussion ensued over how to proceed with George Colgate. Worsening weather, tired men, and rough country all weighed in the loudest, and it was decided not to attempt to retrieve Colgate's body until the following spring.

Shortly after their return to civilization, Dr. W.Q. Webb, George Colgate's physician, was found. After hearing of the specifics of his patient's ailments, he issued the following statement in writing:

> Mr. Colgate came to me from Post Falls last summer and I placed him in the Sacred Heart Hospital, where he remained about three weeks and then returned to Idaho. Early last fall he again came to me to be examined and said, if he was well enough, he would start on a hunting trip as cook. Mr. Colgate was troubled with an enlarged prostate and chronic inflammation of the bladder and had been for twenty years compelled to use catheters to relieve the bladder. I told him he could make the trip but to continue the use of the catheters, and from the history of the case and symptoms described by the Carlin party, I am satisfied Colgate's illness would have resulted fatally under any circumstances, and when he was left behind in the condition described, he would not have survived twenty-four hours.
>
> W.Q. Webb
> Spokane, Wash., December 4, 1893

The first reaction of the public was celebration the party had been rescued. Jubilation was brief, however, as newspapers across the country carried the story and blasted them heavily for abandoning "poor Colgate." Immeasurable controversy ensued. The rescued party attempted to justify their desperate actions, but a public reading the story from their easy chairs were very judgmental of the affair.

Matters were made worse when Keeley (according to Himmelwright) began to make up vicious rumors of the circumstances after Carlin wouldn't give him more money for his efforts and further loss of equipment once the journey turned for the worse.

Unbelievably, to make matters even more bizarre, the New York World ran a story that December of how two trappers had found Colgate alive, wandering in the mountains, and almost dead. This story was obviously never substantiated.

The following year, several independent attempts were made by several different parties to retrieve evidence, a body (or parts), and other items. One such party met with a similar fate as the Carlin Party itself. Two of the four men on the expedition drowned in a rafting accident, their bodies subsequently being found downriver – one near Kooskia and the other near Lapwai.

A group of Army regulars headed by Lt. Elliott, who found the ill-fated party, found the only human remains. A thighbone and a few of Colgate's shreds of clothing were about all that was turned up. The rest appeared to have been packed off by scavengers.

This was but a small glimpse into a much larger story that totaled 259 pages in the original book. A reprint, by Mountain Meadow Press (208-926-7875), is still available. This book is a must-read for anyone that enjoys hunting and history.

KEELEY. SPENCER.
PIERCE. CARLIN. HIMMELWRIGHT.

The members of "The Carlin Party", minus George Colgate and with the addition of Ben Keeley.

Clearwater Elk Encounter in the 1880s

The following account of an elk encounter in Idaho's deep woods was written by G. O. Shields. It was from a book titled, *Cruisings in the Cascades and Other Hunting Adventures*, written in 1889. This particular excerpt was taken from Chapter XXII - titled "Elk Hunting in the Rocky Mountains." It is a classic story of the adventure and innocence that was hunting in the 1800s. The old language and descriptions are so much more poignant than we seem to be able to capture today.

Of all the large game on the American continent, the elk (Cervus Canadensis) is the noblest, the grandest, the stateliest. I would detract nothing from the noble game qualities of the moose, caribou, deer, or mountain sheep. Each has its peculiar points of excellence which endear it to the heart of the sportsman, but the elk possesses more than any of the others. In size he towers far above all, except the moose. In sagacity, caution, cunning, and wariness he is the peer, if not the superior, of them all. He is always on the alert, his keen scent, his piercing eye, his acute sense of hearing, combining to render him a vigilant sentinel of his own safety.

His great size and powerful muscular construction give him almost unbounded endurance. When alarmed or pursued he will travel for twenty or thirty hours, at a rapid swinging trot, without stopping for food or rest. He is a proud fearless ranger, and even when simply migrating from one range of mountains to another, will travel from seventy-five to a hundred miles without lying down. He is a marvelous mountaineer, and, considering his immense size and weight, often ascends to heights that seem incredible. He may often be found away up to timber line, and will traverse narrow passes and defiles, climbing over walls of rock and through fissures where it would seem impossible for so large an animal, with such massive antlers as he carries, to go. He chooses his route, however, with rare good judgment, and all mountaineers know that an elk trail is the best that can possibly be selected over any given section of mountainous country. His faculty of traversing dense jungles and wind-falls is equally astonishing. If given his own time, he will move quietly and easily through the worst of these, leaping over logs higher than his back as gracefully and almost as lightly as the deer; yet let a herd of elk be alarmed and start on a run through one of these labyrinthine masses, and they will make a noise like a regiment of cavalry on a precipitous charge.

I have stood on the margin of a quaking-asp thicket and heard a large band of elk coming toward me that had been "jumped" and fired upon by my friend at the other side, and the frightful noise of their horns pounding the trees, their hoofs striking each other and the numerous rocks, the crashing of dead branches, with the snorting of the affrighted beasts, might well have stuck terror to the heart of anyone unused to such sights and sounds, and have caused him to seek safety in flight. But by standing my ground I was enabled to get in a couple of shots at short range, and to bring down two of the finest animals in the herd.

The whistle of an elk is a sound which many have tied to describe, yet I doubt if anyone who may have read all the descriptions of it ever written would recognize it on a first hearing. It is a most strange, weird, peculiar sound, baffling all efforts of the most skillful wordpainter. It is only uttered by the male, and there is the same variety in the sound made by different stags as in different human voices. Usually the cry begins and ends with a sort of grunt, somewhat like the bellow of a domestic cow cut short, but the interlude is a long-drawn, melodious, flute-like sound that rises and falls with a rhythmical cadence, floating on the still evening air, by which it is often wafted with singular distinctness to great distances. By other individuals, or even by the same individual at various times, either the first or last of these abrupt sounds is omitted, and only the other, in connection with the long-drawn, sliver-toned strain, is given.

The stag utters this call only in the love-making season, and for the purpose of ascertaining the whereabouts of his dusky mate, who responds with a short and utterly unmusical sound, similar to that with which the male begins or ends his call.

Once, while exploring in Idaho, I had an interesting and exciting experience with a band of elk. I had camped for the night on a high divide, between two branches of the Clearwater river. The weather had been intensely dry and hot for several days, and the tall rye grass that grew in the old burn where I had pitched my camp was dry as powder. There was a gentle breeze from the south. Fearing that a spark might be carried into the grass, I extinguished my camp-fire as soon as I had cooked and eaten my supper. As darkness drew on, I went out to picket my horses and noticed that they were acting strangely. They were looking down the mountain side with ears pointed forward, sniffing the air and moving about uneasily.

I gave their picket ropes a turn around convenient jack pines, and then slipping cautiously back to the tent, got my rifle and returned. I could see nothing strange and sat down beside a log to await developments. In a few minutes I heard a dead limb break. Then there was a rustling in a bunch of tall, dry grass; more snapping of twigs and shaking of bushes. I ascertained that there were several large animals moving toward me and feared it might be a family of bears. I feared it, I say, because it was now so dark that I could not see to shoot at any distance, and knew that if bears came near the horses the latter would break their ropes and stampede. I thought of shouting and trying to frighten them off, but decided to await developments. Presently I heard a snapping of hoof and a succession of dull, heavy, thumping noises, accompanied by reports of breaking brush, which I knew at once were made by a band of elk jumping over a high log.

The game was now not more than fifty yards away and in open ground, yet I could not see even a movement, for I was looking down toward a dark canyon, many hundreds of feet deep. Slowly the great beasts worked toward me. They were coming down wind and I felt sure could not scent me, but they could evidently see my horses, outlined against the sky, and had doubtless heard them snorting and moving about.

The ponies grew more anxious but less frightened than at first, and seemed now desirous of making the acquaintance of their wild visitors.

Slowly the elk moved forward until within thirty or forty feet of me, when I could begin to discern by the starlight their dark, shaggy forms. Then they stopped. I could hear them sniffing the air and could see them moving cautiously from place to place, apparently suspicious of danger. But they were coming down wind, could get no indication of my presence, and were anxious to interview the horses.

They moved slowly forward, and when they stopped this time, two old bulls and one cow, who were in the front rank, so to speak, stood within ten feet of me. Their great horns towered up like the branches of dead trees, and I could hear them breathe.

Again they circled from side to side and I thought surely they would get far enough to one quarter or the other to wind me, but they did not. Several other cows and two timid little calves crowded to the front to look at their hornless cousins who now stood close behind me, and even in the starlight, I could have shot any one of them between the eyes.

My saddle cayuse uttered a low gentle whinny, whereat the whole band wheeled and dashed away; but after making a few leaps their momentary scare seemed to subside, and they stopped, looked, snorted a few times and then began to edge up again – this time even more shyly than before.

It was intensely interesting to study the caution and circumspection with which these creatures planned and carried out their investigations all the way through.

The only mistake they made, and one at which I was surprised, considering their usual cunning and sagacity, was that some of them at least did not circle the horses and get to the leeward. But they were in such a wild county, so far back in the remote fastnesses of the Rockies, that they had probably never encountered hunters or horses before and had not acquired all the cunning of their more hunted and haunted brothers. After their temporary scare they returned, step by step, to their investigation, and the largest bull in the bunch approached the very log behind which I sat. He was just in the act of stepping over it when he caught a whiff of my breath and, with a terrific snort, vaulted backward and sidewise certainly thirty feet. At the same instant I rose up and shouted, and the whole band went tearing down the mountain side making a racket like that of an avalanche.

As before stated, I could have had my choice out of the herd, but my only pack-horse was loaded so that I could have carried but a small piece of meat, and was unwilling to waste so grand a creature for the little I could save from him.

Evolution, Life Cycle, Characteristics, & More

Evolution of the American Elk, or Wapiti

*A*rcheomeryx, from the Eocene Period (55.6-33.4 million years ago), is considered the beginning of all cerviforms. From that line, what is considered the first true deer emerged about 14.5 million years ago. It was Dicrocerus, and likely resembled a muntjac. Fossils of Dicrocerus have been found in Mongolia. The genus *Cervus* comes into the fossil record in the Pliocene Epoch (5.2-2.4 million years ago) in Eurasia. *Cervus* evolved and diversified in Eurasia during the Pliocene (4.5-1.8 million years bp).

It is hypothesized that elk may have entered North America as many as 500,000 years ago, but a concrete fossil record can only reliably prove, at this point, that elk were here 40,000 years ago. By 10,000-8,000 years ago, *Cervus elaphus* was fairly well distributed across most of North America.

While elk were fairly well distributed by then, it should be noted that evidence suggests that their populations were likely not significant until the post-Columbus era. In other words, not until European diseases had decimated Native American populations did elk populations become significantly large.

The American elk, the Tian Shan elk, and the Altai elk (the latter two of which are from eastern Asia) are all closely related subspecies that originated from one species that occupied the area known as the Bering Sea land bridge. As the land bridge disappeared, and the populations became isolated, they slowly evolved into separate subspecies. The megafaunal collapse during the last ice age created an herbivore vacuum. This new niche was soon filled by many of the large herbivorous mammals that we know today in North America, including the American elk.

When discussing the evolutionary history of the elk, it should probably be noted that not all scientists and taxonomists agree on whether or not the North American elk is even a distinct species. Those that believe that they are distinct classify them as *Cervus canadensis*. The majority of the scientific community believes that all red deer in the world (of which elk are a part) are the same species, and classify them as *Cervus elaphus*. The official name change from *canadensis* to *elaphus* took place in 1973.

There are obvious phenotypic differences between red deer in different parts of the world, but all red deer can and will readily interbreed when the opportunity is presented. The North American elk's counterparts in other parts of the world include, but are not limited to: The maral (Asia), red deer of various subspecies in Europe (from Norway to Scotland to Spain), hangul (Kashmir), Manchurian elk (Siberia, Mongolia, Manchuria), Altai elk (China, Siberia, Mongolia, etc.), Corsican red deer, shou (Tibet), M'Neill's deer (China), Gansu deer (China), Alashan elk (Mongolia and China), and Tien Shan elk (China and Kazakhstan). Of these, the Tien Shan elk and the Altai elk probably most resemble the overall look and appearance of Rocky Mountain elk, especially in the antlers. As mentioned, they are North American elk's closest cousins, having come from the same strain of animal that inherited the Bering Straits area before the two populations diverged.

It is agreed, however, that within the North American elk realm there have been six different subspecies. Two of these, the Eastern and Merriam's elk, are extinct. The Eastern elk was first described by Giovanni da Verrazano in 1524. This deciduous forest dweller proved no match for early encroaching settlement. By the mid-to-late 1800s, the last remnants of Eastern elk, which had taken refuge in the Allegany Mountains, had vanished from all of their original range, which stretched from near the East Coast all the way west to Minnesota and Arkansas. The Merriam's elk fell to the same terrible fate. The Merriam's, which inhabited the arid regions of the American southwest and northern Mexico, is believed to have gone extinct around 1905.

The four remaining subspecies are Roosevelt's elk (coastal Oregon, Washington, and British Columbia including Vancouver Island, and Afognak Island in Alaska), Manitoban elk, Tule elk (central California in more arid habitats) and the most obvious and well-known Rocky Mountain elk (most of the western United States and western Canada as well as transplants now located in such places as Arkansas, Pennsylvania, and Kentucky).

Annual Cycle

Elk in Idaho, on average, shed their antlers from mid-March thru mid-May. Big bulls are the first to shed, usually the last week of March and the first two weeks of April. Most raghorns will shed throughout April, and many spikes will still be packing into early May. Some of this, in regard to bigger bulls shedding earlier, may have to do with varying testosterone levels by age, but the simple physics of leverage probably contribute significantly as well. There just isn't thirty pounds of beam pulling those little spikes off like on the big boys.

As spring settles in and fades to summer, bulls will often form bachelor groups, although not to the degree of mule deer. It is much more commonplace to see small 2-3 year old bulls hanging with a herd of females than is seen with their smaller deer counterparts.

Cows will form fairly large and protective matriarchal groups in the summer as they head to their time-proven calving grounds. Safety in numbers is the goal, and all mothers new and old help to watch newborn calves. Elk seem to have very specific areas they prefer in which to calve, and it is not unusual to see the same elk come back to the same area annually.

Only a small percentage of yearling cows will breed in their first year. This appears to be a function of body weight and proximity of that weight to their expected size at full maturity.

A mother will give birth to one calf, which usually weighs between 30-40 pounds, usually in late May or early June. Twins account for less than 1% of all births. A soon-to-give-birth mother will seek isolation, having her calf on her own. A normal birth will result in the front forelegs emerging first, followed by the head. This is known as an anterior birth.

As soon as the calf is born, the new mother will consume all possible evidence of it, including licking the calf completely clean. This, of course, is to rid all possible smell from the area that could attract potential predators. She will then hide the calf, which will remain almost completely still until called by its mother. The call, a nasal whine, is nearly the only sound or action the young calf will respond to. This short phase of motionless hiding will last only a few days. It will be after about two weeks that the calves will be more active and visible, at which point they are potentially able to use a more escape-style defense.

A newborn will begin suckling right away. A fascinating fact about the first day of a calf elk's life is that it is the only day it can readily absorb the colostrum without worrying about digestive breakdown. The colostrum is the first milk produced by the mother, and is extremely rich in immunological components, such as antibodies and phagocyte cells. Some of the immunity this colostrum provides to fight disease may be effective for a period of up to a month.

Once the mother feels that she and the calf are both ready to be slightly more mobile, they will rejoin their matriarchal group on the summer range. This might be in just a few days, but it will be about six weeks after birth before the nursery herd is at its largest. This time alone has provided mother and calf a chance to heal, bond, and strengthen. For the next two months, the growth of the calf will be almost completely and directly tied to the physical health of its mother. For the first few months of life, a calf elk will put on nearly two pounds per day, potentially turning from a 35-lb. calf at birth in June to a 270-pounder by the 1st of October.

Elk, like deer, are ruminants. They have multi-chambered stomachs that allow them to eat massive quantities of food in a short time. This allows elk to retire to the relative safety of cover and shade during the day. There they can pass the previous evening's and that morning's bounty through the digestion process at a slowed rate that can last until the following evening.

Elk are, by nature, grazers, and will concentrate more on grasses than forbs. This, however, is a generalization. They are actually considered intermediate feeders, meaning they will eat significant percentages of forbs, shrubs, and grasses. Studies done in Idaho and Montana have shown a propensity for elk to select sites proportionately higher in succulent forbs and shrubs during the late summer period. Elk, like all wildlife that have to find a way to survive, are opportunists. Studies have also been done that show that forbs can constitute 80-90% of an elk's diet, particularly in the winter months when food supply is limited. These studies are important, because they help to show that elk can and do outcompete deer for winter food sources, a problem currently hurting deer populations in all of southern Idaho.

As summer nights begin to get colder, the elk rut will begin to pick up. Bulls will strip the velvet off their antlers in late summer in preparation for future battles and advertisement of their status. Branch bulls will peel first, usually from August 10th-25th, with spikes often waiting into the first two weeks of September to join the club.

Myths still seem to surround elk bugling, in that many believe elk only bugle during the rut. In fact, it is not completely uncommon to hear an elk bugle at practically any time of year, although much less frequently and heartily.

The rut usually begins to warm up in the first week of September, with the peak likely coming the last full week of September. It will, however, usually be fairly solid from mid-September thru the first week of October in Idaho.

Bulls will begin serenading, both to attract mates and to call out their rivals. The testosterone levels of bulls skyrocket during this time and they become uncommonly aggressive. Bull elk, like whitetails, will make scrapes. These scrapes are a few feet in diameter, and consist of the bull scraping the ground with his antlers and then urinating in the furrowed ground. Often, this happens at the same time, as while his head is down performing the scrape, you can witness the palpitation of the penis as he sprays both on his underbelly and the scrape itself. This fluid does contain sperm. Wallowing also becomes a mainstay at this time.

All the while, these displays (along with direct interaction and bull-to-bull contact) allow bulls to establish pecking orders. Most times, eye contact and body posture are enough to determine the dominant bull. Some playful and half-hearted sparring will also help to distinguish dominant, sub-dominant, and inferior males. The prime example of when you actually see serious and intense fighting is when you have two fairly equal-sized bulls, or two on the same level of the pecking order, who show no sign of submission to each other. In this case, a true fight is often the only way to determine the answer of who is dominant.

Eventually, the herd bull (which will do most of the breeding) is determined. This bull will run himself ragged through the course of the rut. Half the time he will be trying to keep control of his cows, check their state of estrus and do the actual breeding; the other half of the time he will be fending off potential rivals or satellite bulls attempting to get a "freebie." During this intense rutting period, it is not uncommon for a breeding bull to lose 20% of his body weight.

Elk, like deer, will sense a mate's receptiveness by performing a lip curl. This is performed by using an organ located in the upper palate as its sensory receptor.

It would be logical under most circumstances to think that the bull is the one to initiate the copulation. This is and is not true. When the bull starts to sense a cow's state of receptiveness, he initially makes the first move and show willingness and interest. The cow will most times show lack of interest in the relationship in the initial stages. This, however, can change dramatically when she really decides she is ready. I can distinctly remember watching a cow one time that was extremely ready – more ready at that moment than the bull. Her behavior turned from one of complacency to one of sheer desperation. She began to squeal, bite playfully at the bull's ears, and rub her neck desperately on his neck, attempting to get him aroused. Needless to say, it worked like a charm. When a cow is at her prime moment of readiness, she will often become the aggressor.

When a bull and cow copulate, it will be surprisingly brief. The bull will attempt to mount the cow, and upon his eventual success in "finding the right spot" will give one major thrust and practically launch himself in her direction and upward. It is not uncommon for this effort to lift the bull completely off of the ground. The one thrust is the entire copulation.

A cow elk will often only be in estrus for a period of one day. As such, not all cows will be bred in the first go-around. Therefore, a smaller secondary rut is common. It is not at all unusual to see the rutting action picking up again the last week of October, as all cows not impregnated the first time around come back into cycle. Once successfully bred, the average gestation for elk is 250-255 days.

The timing of the elk rut has everything to do with proper timing of birth for calves the following spring. They need to be born late enough in the spring to withstand cold nights and late freezes, but early enough to build as much weight and strength as possible before the onset of the following winter. This is a critical period. Bulls lose huge amounts of fat reserves during the rut, and many are injured as a result of struggles with other bulls. Antler tine punctures (some of which become badly infected) are not uncommon. Bulls that are unable to heal and regain body fat sufficient to endure extended periods of near-starvation are unlikely to survive through long winters and tough wet spring weather.

Following the rut, filling their bellies will be precisely what most bulls will have on their mind throughout the fall, when not busy eluding arrows and bullets. A good portion of the mature and semi-mature bulls will commonly rejoin each other again, leaving the cows behind in order to fatten up before significant snowfall makes it impossible.

With their longer leg length and ability to survive in much harsher and deeper snow conditions, they need not usually migrate as far to acceptable winter grounds as mule deer. They can often survive in much more marginal habitats and tolerate much deeper snow. This is a calculated risk. By staying away from lower elevations, elk can select areas where feed is more abundant, where competition for feed is reduced, and where potential predators are scarce. Severe and/or prolonged storms may, however, trap these animals for an extended period, with eventual starvation being a likely outcome.

Throughout winter and spring, bands of elk can often be seen throughout the state that number in the hundreds each. They often congregate in large numbers in their favorite winter range haunts. This helps to break trail through deep snow as well as provide safety in numbers. The cost is greater competition for limited food supplies, and greater attraction of predators such as wolves.

As winter gives way to spring, elk will retreat, following the snow line to better cover and fresher, newer browse. Soon, they will be dropping their antlers again, and continue on with the previous year's routine.

Physical Characteristics

A mature bull elk will weigh between 600 and 1000 pounds, and stand 4-1/2 to 5 feet at the withers. Chest height of an average mature bull is 35 inches. Mature cows will be slightly less, on both counts, weighing between 400-600 pounds and standing 4 to 4-1/2 feet.

For their size, elk are astonishingly agile. Many a hunter has been left speechless after witnessing the ease with which a half-ton bull with antlers stretching four feet wide can navigate through thick timber and brush, all the while never missing a stride. Elk seem to have an uncanny ability to reshape themselves and their antlers to fit through the most minor of cracks in vegetation with speed and ease.

An elk "coasting" on a run might resemble a toned down version of a mule deer stot, with legs going in the same direction, whereas when an elk is accelerating or running full, its legs (front and back) are in opposite motion.

Scent glands occur on the lower hind legs (metatarsal glands), in the front portion of each eye (pre-orbital glands), and on the underside of the tail. In addition, males produce secretions at the base of the antlers and around the penis, while cows produce secretions in the vicinity of the vagina and anus.

Of all ungulates, elk are likely the most vocal. Much has been written about the bone-chilling, stillness-piercing screaming whistle of the bull elk. Simply put, it is likely the most beautiful sound in nature. A number of other sounds also convey meaning with elk. The distinctive mew of a cow elk, and the shorter, higher pitched version emanating from a calf are all common and easily recognizable sounds. Perhaps the one sound a hunter doesn't want to hear is the alarm bark. Made by either bull or cow, it is a short, choppy bark not unlike that of a dog. This sound is performed not only as a warning to other elk in the herd, but as a natural vocalization indicating frustration and nervousness generated from uncertainty. Uncertainty is the key word, because if they knew what you were, they wouldn't still be standing there worrying about you. You would already have heard the massive crackling and breaking of every tree limb on the mountain as they were leaving you in their dust.

Left alone to live out an entire healthy lifespan, bulls in the wild can live to be 14-16 years old, with females living up to 15-17 years. Unlike deer, whose best racks might be found between 6-9 years of age, elk generally sport their best racks between 8-10 years of age.

Another thing worth mentioning is the elk's incredible ability to withstand pain. Of all North American big game, elk seem to constantly top the list of amazing stories of physical toughness. Stories abound of bulls living through embedded arrows, broken and poorly healed legs, and other traumatic experiences. For their size, to watch a bull take a round from a .300 and not even wince never ceases to amaze.

How Antlers Grow – The Layman's Version

Elk antlers are some of the most fascinating and fastest growing of all antlers. While a mule deer may grow up to ten pounds of antler in approximately 7-8 months, elk can grow over thirty pounds of antler in five months.

We'll start at the point that the previous year's antler is shed. This date is generally pre-determined by photoperiod and the subsequent effects on the bull's testosterone levels. Things that can influence this and alter it include the age of the bull, its general health, and time spent through the winter with the opposite sex. The latter can have a huge difference in the shedding date due to increased cycles and amounts of testosterone following the rut.

Elk in Idaho, on average, shed their antlers from mid-March thru mid-May. As a general rule, big bulls are the first to shed, followed by raghorns and then spikes.

Once the antlers are cast, a scab will form on the open sores. These sores will heal in a matter of days and the new year's antler growth will begin immediately.

The interface of the scalp and the pedicle is where it all begins. Blood supply, through the porous pedicle, is supplied through a temporal artery. This blood supply transports all of the necessary ingredients to form the developing antlers.

During the first couple of months, the antlers only partially mineralize. Mineralization, which heads into high gear in the waning stages of antler growth, forms from pedicle to tip, the same as the original antler growth.

When the fall season approaches and the blood supply is cut off, the velvet will be rubbed of in short order. This leads one to believe that there is likely a sensible irritation in the dying velvet, perhaps causing the elk to rub the velvet off like one would scratch an itch. It is known that the velvet tissue is innervated and sensitive. Idaho branch-antlered bulls will often strip their velvet around the middle of August, while yearling bulls (carrying their first sets of antlers) will usually wait until early to mid-September. Note that as you head further south in North America, both rutting dates and annual antler cycles will be pushed back further into the year as a general rule.

Freshly polished antlers are dead bone with close to 50% water content. It is interesting to note that the chemical composition of antlers from the base to the tip varies wildly. The tips, which are by far the most dense and ivory-like, are the only area that has Chondroitin sulfate (one of the main ingredients in the glucosamine/chondroitin supplements used to promote joint health in humans).

An interesting thing to note about the pedicle (the base protrusions sticking up from the skull) is that they reach their maximum height in their first antler year, and continue to lose height in each successive year. Also, the diameter of the pedicle basically predetermines the diameter of the beam, as antlers only grow in length. A few things can slightly alter this assumption, but are somewhat incidental, such as juxtaposition of superficial arteries and their subsequent antler tines, along with significant antler beading, ridges, and curves. Also, on each successive cast of antlers, the outer portion of the pedicle is shortened at a greater rate than the inner portion, resulting in a basic formula for wider antlers in each successive year.

An elk antler as it lay. This nice 330-class antler was found by the author on a spring stroll in 2002. The best thing about looking for antlers in southern Idaho in May: Peace and quiet, arrowleaf balsamroot sunflowers, and nice weather. Worst thing: Mud and ticks!

Another interesting note is that the antler seal, which is the porous base of the cast antler, is a great indicator of the condition of the bull. A convex or bulbous base indicates that the bull's antlers are still in the upward swing of their "career". A flattened base indicates that the bull's potential for antler growth is tapering off or has peaked, and a concave seal often indicates poor health and/or a downward trend in antler production.

How Big Was He?

At campfires, cafés, and other places where hunters might brag, boast, or otherwise relate stories of bulls bigger than life or packouts too painful to remember, the discussion always comes up about how much a bull weighed, how much meat it yielded, or how much an elk quarter weighed.

An attempt to answer just such a question was done in Wyoming in 1973 (Field, R.A., F.C Smith and W.G. Hepworth.1973b. The elk carcass. Bull.594. Univ. Wyoming Ag. Exp. Sta., Laramie. 6 pp.) Below is a table showing the results.

Weight conversions for a 770-lb. bull elk

Component	Weight (in pounds)	Proportion of Live Weight
Live weight	770	1.00
Bled weight	750	0.97
Field-dressed weight (no viscera or forelegs)	503	.65
Clean dressed weight (no head or hide)	417	.54
Retail cuts (bone in)	269	.35

From this study, some easy rules of thumb can be used. First, field-dressed weight is roughly two-thirds of the total body weight. Second, the cleaned dressed weight (hide, forelegs, head removed) was 54% of the live weight. Therefore, you can roughly double the skinned, field-dressed carcass to get a very close estimate of live weight. Third, the live weight would be equitable to roughly three times the weight of your processed meat, assuming little to no harvest damage.

By Truck and Rail:
Idaho's Elk Re-Introduction Efforts

Attempting to tell the comprehensive story about all of the elk reintroductions is a nearly impossible task, as information is widely scattered and somewhat independent at times. As such, this chapter is, in the author's mind, incomplete. Hopefully, this will spur other individuals with knowledge of events not included here to come forward and help complete the story in a future book in the series.

Elk populations in Idaho have gone through some notable peaks and depressions. The great herds we see in Idaho today were not always so abundant. At the time of Lewis and Clark's arrival in Idaho, elk were extremely difficult to find. In fact, after several months of exploring in Idaho in 1805-06, they were unable to catch up with one. Multiple predators, including Native Americans, likely kept their populations artificially suppressed, as these predators were able to continue to survive on alternate food sources.

After 1806, not much changed in Idaho until the 1860s. With the discovery of gold in Idaho, miners and other explorers flocked into Idaho's rugged mountains. As a result, one elk predator was beginning to be replaced with another. With city-sized communities springing up over night in some areas, food sources were exploited to the fullest. This took drastic tolls on not only elk, but bighorn sheep as well. An estimated 15,000 hungry miners had to be fed somehow, and so Idaho's wildlife took a beating. Full-time hunters shot game year-round to keep up with demand.

The mining boom eventually receded, only to be replaced with a new demand on the resource – settlers. With no real system of game management, rules, or regulations in place, it was in many cases wanton slaughter. In a previous chapter, Swan Valley Elk Patrol, Lewis Daniels mentions one man slaying 70 head of elk in eastern Idaho just for the hides. Another incident mentions hide buyers leaving town with 4'x8'x16' loads of elk hides. It was becoming quickly apparent that if something didn't change, we would lose our wildlife.

Several things happened to help turn the tide for the future of Idaho's wildlife. One is the establishment of seasons, bag limits, and hunting regulations in effort to stem the slaughter. Another is how heroic legislators, sportsmen, and other advocates helped reintroduce elk back into our state on a monumental scale.

The First Territorial Legislative Assembly met in 1863, and the first attempt at wildlife management was taken. A statute created there stated, *"It is unlawful for any person at any time after the 1st day of February and before the 1st day of July to* *kill or have in possession any buffalo, deer, antelope, elk, mountain sheep, or goat."* In that era of selective abiding of the law, however, it was taken by much of the local populous as a "suggestion." Idaho didn't appoint its first game wardens until 1893.

The 1900 biennial report (three years before a fish and game department was created by legislature) says that "elk are becoming scarcer and scarcer every year." In 1909, State Game Warden J.B. Gowen estimated that elk were "fairly numerous in Bannock, Bonneville, Madison, and Fremont counties as a result of the protection provided in the Yellowstone National Park and the stringent laws in the state of Wyoming, a source of replenishment of Idaho elk herds." Warden Gowen added that "scattered bands" of elk were reported in Lemhi County, and an increase in the Payette Game Reserve herd of about 25 head when the reserve was created in 1909, to 150 head in 1912, and "at least 200 head" in 1914. Obviously, elk were bouncing back a bit in areas that afforded them some protection. Other areas were not so fortunate. In 1911, the season was closed in Bonner, Kootenai, Shoshone, Latah, Nez Perce, Clearwater, and Idaho counties. The 1912 regulations for elk stated that it was *"unlawful to kill Elk within the Counties of Bonner, Kootenai, Shoshone, Latah, Nez Perce, Lewis, Clearwater, and Idaho for a period of five years."*

According to a report, by 1914 only a few scattered herds existed, mostly in far eastern Idaho, portions of the Clearwater drainage, and along the upper South Fork of the Payette River. The first recorded estimate of elk numbers was published in the U.S. Forest Service census during 1918. It estimated 610 elk present on national forest lands – a dismally low figure.

In the early 1910s, opportunity knocked. Yellowstone National Park was being overrun with elk. A broadscale plea was sent out stating that elk were available to any agency that was willing to take them. Several different individuals, clubs, and agencies in Idaho responded, and a loose plan was hatched. With the approval of the state legislature, several game preserves were created, whereupon soon to be transplanted elk would receive refuge for a limited number of years. During this time, it was hoped that they would expand in numbers as fast as possible.

19 yearling elk shipped to Twin Falls Co. from the Yellowstone Region 3-5-16.

The Gardiner trap and chute, one of a few such facilities in Yellowstone designed for shipping elk out of the Park.

A translocation program was initiated in 1915 and proceeded through 1946. During that time, at least 675 elk from Yellowstone National Park and Jackson Hole, Wyoming were translocated throughout the state. Elk were eventually reestablished in 40 of Idaho's 44 counties. Some of the first transplants were to Adams, Bannock, Boise, Elmore, Idaho, and Minidoka counties. These areas would be off limits to elk hunting in order to hopefully let the newfound elk population acclimate and flourish. By 1925, there were 11 such game preserves in Idaho, along with sanctuaries created by the Idaho Fish & Game Department. Combined, they accounted for nearly 3 million acres

Warden Gowen wrote the following in the Fourth Biennial Report in regard to the first transplant:

> "Recently, this department made application to the Secretary of Interior for 70 head, or two carloads of elk, from the Yellowstone National Park. The application was passed on favorably for 50 head to be turned out on the Weiser National Forest providing the department would provide a deputy to be in charge to prevent the herd from being killed until such time as the legislature would pass a law making the Weiser reserve a permanent Game Preserve. This department has had the active cooperation of all the residents of Washington and Adams counties. They have agreed to furnish winter feed and corral for elk, and it is the intention to turn the elk loose in two bands, one west of Council and another west of New Meadows in the Seven Devils Mountains."

Another example occurred in 1930. Moscow-area representatives of the Isaak Walton League were instrumental in getting another shipment of 30-50 head of elk shipped via rail to the Bovill area east of Moscow. Volunteer donations by League members were taken to help curb the cost. Homer W. Davis wrote:

The look in this bull's eye says it all. Look carefully and you can see the man on the other side of the fence, and the saw going to work on the bull's antler.

> *"Both bulls and cows were included, and I remember that the antlers of the bulls had been cut off before the shipment to prevent injury in shipment, I suppose."*

In another letter received by the Department, Fourth F. Thomas, of Princeton, wrote:

> *"I well remember one incident in moving elk to the corrals. One truck was unloaded inside the confines of a corral. Although elk usually are not considered exceptional jumpers, one cow leaped up out of the truck, made a few running hops and sailed over the high board fence like a bird. She would have escaped but for the fact that surrounding the corral was a drainage ditch just outside the fence. She landed in the ditch and broke her back."*

Many elk were transplanted into the Shoshone County area, largely due to the sportsmen in the area. Donald E. Hill wrote a paper on the history of those transplants, which was given to the Idaho Department of Fish & Game. Some excerpts from that paper:

> *Shoshone County Sportsmen's Association planted 237 head of elk in the Coeur d' Alene River and St. Joe River drainages in 1925, 1936, 1938, and 1939. The total cost of these elk amounted to $2,298.00 not considering feed while they were held for planting. Records of hay purchases made amount to $191.45 just for the 1939 shipment of elk. Some of the feeding cost may have been paid by the Idaho Fish and Game Department, but there are no records that it was. All the money for these elk transplants were from private individuals in Shoshone County.*

"Ranger and worker dehorning elk at Blacktail Deer Creek Corral before shipment." **This photo was taken on January 23, 1936. This is possibly part of the shipment that went to the Grizzly Flats area near Coeur d'Alene.**

In February, 1925, two [railroad] carloads of 60 elk, mostly cows, were shipped from Yellowstone Park and planted near Grizzly Creek on the Coeur d' Alene River. Each elk cost $17.65 including freight for a total of $1,059.00.

In February, 1936, 41 elk, mostly cows, were trucked in and planted near Grizzly creek on the Coeur d' Alene River. These elk cost $7.00 per head for a total of $287. There is no record of where these elk were purchased.

In February, 1938, 60 elk were shipped in by rail from Yellowstone Park and planted near Herrick, which is at the mouth of Big Creek on the St. Joe River. These elk cost $7.00 per head for a total of $420.00. There were 37 cows, 17 female calves, 2 mature bulls, and 4 spikes in this group. It was noted that they crossed the St. Joe River and joined a small native herd of elk.

In April 1939, 76 elk were brought from Yellowstone Park by truck and planted at Montgomery Gulch, which is about halfway in between Wallace and Kellogg, and Steamboat on the Coeur d' Alene River. These elk cost $7.00 per head for a total of $532.00. This group were mostly cows and were kept in corrals and fed for some time before being released.

November 2, 1939, one of the cows planted at Montgomery Gulch was killed by a hunter in the Clearwater River drainage. The hunter turned the ear tag in to the Forest Service. The Forest Service had copies of all ear tag numbers of the elk planted by the Sportsmen's Association so wrote to the Sportsmen's Association to report the kill. This cow had traveled about 75 air miles after being released. How many elk of the Clearwater herds were from the Shoshone County Sportsmen's efforts? We will never know, but it makes you wonder.

(Above Left) An interesting (and unhappy) bull elk, awaiting shipment from the Mammoth Trap in Yellowstone. (Above Right) Antlers were sawn off before transporting elk, to save them from injuring themselves, other elk, or workers.

Table 1. An incomplete list of elk transplants in Idaho, 1915-1946

Year	# animals	County	Location
1915*	50	Adams	Rubicon area
1915	65	Boise & Elmore	Arrowrock Dam
1916**	19	Twin Falls	
1916	17	Bannock	Pocatello
1917	18	Bannock	Pocatello
1918	200	Adams, Bannock, Boise, Elmore, & Minidoka	
1919	21	Shoshone	Boyhill Creek
1925 or '26	58	Kootenai	Grizzly Flats
1930	30-50	Latah	Bovill
1930s	?	Lemhi	Unit 28, Panther Creek
1930s	?	Lemhi?	Camas-Cache Creek
1935	19	Bonner	Hope
1936	41	Kootenai	Grizzly Flats
1936	17	Bonner	Hope
1937	15	Bonner	Hope
1938	60	Shoshone	Herrick
1939	74	Shoshone	Kellogg
1944	50	Owyhee	
1946	56	Owyhee	
1946	19	Owyhee (from Bannock)	
1946	40	Bannock	Pocatello

All non-asterisked information taken from Idaho Wildlife Review, Jan.-Feb., 1975, "*Modern Day Elk More Plentiful*" by Jim Humbird.
*Info from Adams County Leader   **Info from Bisbee photo (ID State Hist. Soc.)

An elk being loaded into the truck for shipment, likely via rail. This photo was taken on March 4th, 1936. This is possibly the shipment headed to Hope, Idaho in Bonner County.

An incomplete list of Game Preserves, with varying inception and ending dates, included the Warm Springs Creek Game Preserve, Big Lost River Game Preserve, Soldier Mountain Game Preserve, South Fork of the Payette Game Preserve, Selway Game Preserve, Pocatello Game Preserve, Ashton Big Game Refuge, Rock Creek Game Preserve, and many others.

According to 1923-24 biennial report, there were 5200 elk in Idaho. The preliminary statement in the report reminded readers that Idaho is a vast area with only a few men to check remote regions. By 1924, the estimated elk population in Idaho was 5900, with an estimated harvest of 350. Less than thirty years later, in 1943, the estimated elk population was nearly 30,000, with a harvest of 2400, nearly a 700% increase!

Transplants continued, however. In 1945, 19 head were removed from the Pocatello herd and transplanted to Owyhee County, along with 56 head from Yellowstone and 49 from Jackson, Wyoming. An additional forty bull elk calves were released in the Mink Creek area to offset inbreeding in the Pocatello herd.

The magnitude of effort and expense had been immense, but the results would prove that it was all not only worthwhile but also highly successful. Elk populations would continue to skyrocket over the following decades, filling Idaho's mountains with a bountiful elk population.

Table 2. Elk populations, elk harvest, and licenses issued.

Year	Estimated Population	Harvest	Licenses issued
1923	5,200		
1924	5,900	350	
1929		778	
1935	16,000 (1934)	1,821	3,758
1943	30,000	2,398	
1945		4,392	12,752
1950		7,165	33,855
1955		15,799	52,257
1960		16,545	58,717
1965	60,000 (1963)	14,064	59,177
1968		17,064	
1970		14,146	72,793
1973		12,287	76,800
1975		8,981	49,427
1980	90,000	8,300	79,000
1985	110,000	15,550	85,000
1990	115,000	21,500	98,000
1994	**Peak year for harvest**	**28,000**	
1995	116,000	22,437	114,300
1998	124,000	18,750	
2000		20,200	
2004		20,800	

Numbers taken from a variety of sources including biennial reports, other Fish & Game reports, and "Elk of North America." Note that "licenses issued" does not necessarily correspond directly with actual number of elk hunters.

From 1956-1971, the average annual harvest was 14,500 with 1968 being the top year at 17,000. Many thought that this number would never be beaten, and that the 1960s was the Golden Age of elk hunting in Idaho.

Increased access by hunters using newly pioneered logging roads established by a booming timber industry began to take its toll on elk populations. Simultaneously, the continuing degradation of the Clearwater drainage in terms of browsefields being reclaimed by vast overmature forests was taking its toll on Idaho's crowned jewel, its Clearwater elk herd. By 1972, the harvest was down to 9,000, and the ten-year average from 1972-1981 was only 8200.

New measures had to be taken. Deer and elk seasons became separated in many units and, in 1976, 57 units became bulls only. Elk numbers rebounded and, by 1988, the harvest was a staggering 20,400. Much of this population increase that continued up through the 1990s is a result of expansion of elk into southern Idaho, a situation that has had detrimental effects on mule deer in those areas.

Over the past 100 years, Idaho's elk history has been one of replenishing, fostering, and perpetuating elk to make sure that future generations (that would be you and me) would have good elk hunting. For that, we owe them a tremendous debt of gratitude. It is one of the true success stories of wildlife conservation.

Theodore Roosevelt once said, "*It will be a real misfortune if our wild animals disappear from mountain, plain, and forest, to be found only if at all, in great game preserves. It is to the interest of all of us to see that there is ample and real protection for our game as for our woodlands. A true democracy, really alive to its opportunities, will insist upon such game preservation, for it is to the interest of our people as a whole."*

Idaho's elk reintroduction efforts proved to be an effective endeavor. Idaho currently has the second-largest elk population of any state or province in North America, next to Colorado, and is one of the few states left where anyone can buy an over-the-counter tag and enjoy a fall full of chasing elk. ⚜ ⚜

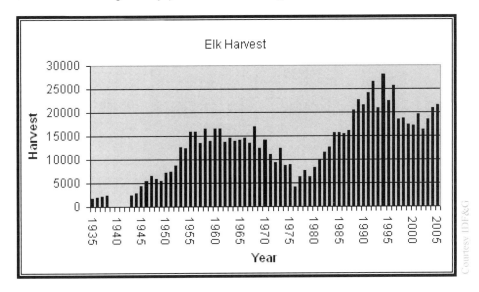

Information in this chapter was taken from a large variety of sources. The following sources provided many specifics:

    Humbird, J. 1975. Modern day elk more plentiful. Idaho Wildlife Review. (Jan./Feb.):16-17
    Edson, M.A. 1963. Idaho wildlife in the early days. Idaho Wildlife Review, 16 (1); 8-13.
    Toweill, D.E. and Thomas, J.W. North American Elk: Ecology and Management. Smithsonian Institution Press, 2002.
    Robbins, R.L., D.E. Redfearn, and C.P. Stone. 1982. Refuges and elk management.

The Rise and Fall of the Clearwater Elk Herd

Most any elk hunter who has been around for any period of time can remember the legend and fame that accompanied the Clearwater elk herd and the Selway-Bitterroot Wilderness. During the 1950s-1980s, the reputation, mystique, and romanticism of that country and that elk herd was unparalleled by any other in North America. Countless articles appeared in Outdoor Life and other publications remarking of the amazing hunting opportunities that awaited every hunter there. Without major change, those days could be over forever. The rise and fall of the Clearwater elk herd, in North American game management history, is a worthy comparison to that of the rise and fall of the Roman Empire.

The history of the Clearwater is one of big and dynamic changes. For example, when Lewis and Clark first passed through the Clearwater region, there were few elk to be found anywhere. Meriwether Lewis wrote the following on August 20th, 1805:

> "I now asked Cameahwait by what route the Pierced nosed Indians, who he informed me inhabited this river below the mountains, came over to the Missouri; this he informed me was to the north, but added that the road was a very bad one as he had been informed by them and that they had suffered excessively with hunger on the rout being obliged to subsist for many days on berries alone as there was no game in that part of the mountains which were broken rockey and so thickly covered with timber that they could scarcely pass."

Captain Clark followed that entry in June of 1806 with this statement, summing up their return trip through the region:

> "Descended the mountains to Traveler's Rest, leaving those tremendous mountains behind us – in passing we have experienced cold and hunger of which I shall ever remember."

That was only 200 years ago. That trend seemed to continue until some specific catastrophic circumstances and events changed everything.

Two major components are largely responsible for the Rise. The first is the inaccessibility of the region. The Clearwater, in that era, was very difficult to get to. This, in itself and by default, helped the area become a superior hunting ground.

But remoteness in itself cannot grow elk. There has to be a base potential for feed and habitat. That base was created by the most influential event in the region's history - the Great Fire of 1910, along with large subsequent fires in 1919 and 1934.

The gigantic catastrophic fire of 1910 was the most destructive and far-reaching fire in our nation's history. During a short period in August of 1910, this fire burned 3.3 million acres in four northwestern states. Idaho alone had 1.7 million acres go up in smoke (one-sixth of all its national forests in northern Idaho). Most of this unthinkable damage happened in a short two-day flare-up with hurricane-force winds. Several communities burned, including a third of the community of Wallace, and smoke was reported as far east as Boston. Seventy-two firefighters lost their lives in the 744 recorded blazes. The fires of 1919 and 1934 added hundreds of thousands of charred acres more to the newly available openings.

While tragic in a multitude of ways, there were some large positive implications. Those 1.7 million acres that burned in Idaho had opened the seemingly impenetrable forest canopy and eventually created a wealth of new wildlife habitat. Now that the habitat was created, all that needed to happen was for it now to be filled with animals to occupy it. Such things take time.

Ralph Space, supervisor of the Clearwater National Forest many decades ago, started working for the agency in 1919. He wrote the following about elk in the Clearwater region (taken from: Edson, M.A. 1963. *Idaho Wildlife in the Early Days*. Idaho Wildlife Review, 16 (1); 8-13.)

> *My father came to the Pierce country in 1891. He never saw an elk and knew of only one being killed before 1930. The diary of the men who died of scurvy at what is now Cayuse landing field shows that they killed two elk near there in 1907. One of the earliest maps of the Clearwater shows elk "yards" near Cold Spring. A few elk may have wintered there about 1912.*
>
> *From 1919 until 1923, I traveled a lot in the Deadhorse, Elk Mountain, Freezeout and Stocking Meadows area and never saw an elk track. I saw my first elk in 1923 on Meadow Creek and saw where several head wintered on Glover Creek. In May, 1924, I saw a number of elk between Selway Falls and the Old Meadow Creek ranger station. In late August the same year I found a small band of elk on Doubt Creek, which is a branch of Hungry Creek. This was the first time we knew of elk in the Fish Creek drainage and concluded that elk were spreading.*
>
> *Albert Cockrell started work on the Clearwater in 1918 and reported much the same thing. He said the first open season was in 1919, and he killed a bull elk on Elk Mtn. in November of that year. One other was killed on the Orogrande. These were in all probability the only elk killed on the Clearwater that year.*

This individual statement is not necessarily completely accurate, but simply one person's observation of much time spent in the Clearwater. There were other elk in the Clearwater. The infamous Carlin party did, after all, kill elk in the Clearwater in 1893, and dispersed bands of elk occupying the huge watershed was certain.

However, a second observation, made by Charles Gallagher (a conservation officer in Grangeville) noted that while on a 1930 hunt between Ditch Creek and Moose Creek they saw an estimated 665 deer and only one bull elk.

The change was coming fast, though. The additional fires that had charred the watershed in 1919 and later in 1934 further enlarged the new areas that would soon be open for browse. By 1934, the Clearwater range report said, "Elk were becoming so numerous that they were depleting their winter range."

For decades to come, early successional species of flora and quality, young, succulent browse would fuel a newly burgeoning elk herd that would continue to grow as fast as the newly sprouting vegetation. Sunlight was now reaching the forest floor in places that hadn't received it in decades or maybe even centuries.

In 1939, a study was conducted on what was then the Selway Game Preserve. Vernon A. Young (professor of Range Management at University of Idaho) and W. Leslie Robinette (Junior Range Examiner, Region 4, USFS) conducted the study, titled *A Study of Range Habits of Elk on the Selway Game Preserve*. It stated, among other things:

> "The Selway Game Preserve, located in a large wilderness area of north-central Idaho, is a big game haven because of its partial inaccessibility to hunters and the luxuriant growth of forage. The dense vegetation composed of browse, weeds, grasses, and grass-like plants have come in since the severe forest fire of 1910 as a successional development.

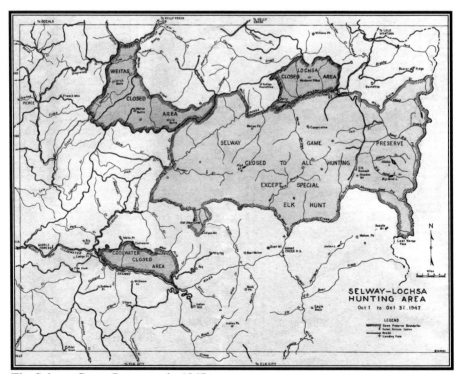

The Selway Game Preserve, in 1947.

Another passage stated:

> "The great amount of highly palatable forage that has come in as seral communities as a part of the succession following the 1910 fire, plus the inaccessibility, has introduced an elk and deer "heaven" in this region. These animals are not required to compete with domestic stock because grazing is prohibited on the game preserve. As a result, elk have steadily increased during the last two decades. Completely forested areas, such as the Selway region prior to the fire of 1910, are not desirable as big game range because of the scarcity of forage. Such a condition may again prevail on the burned areas when plant succession has approached a climax [condition]."

As the heyday continued, write-ups and ads far and wide proclaimed to sportsmen around the globe of the burgeoning populations and abundant hunting opportunities to be had in the Clearwater region. Just one of many examples, the following excerpt appeared in the 1962 Idaho Fishing and Hunting Guide:

This old ad from the 1960s shows what could be expected for any hunter heading to north-central Idaho. It was a time of bounty that hunters thought would last forever.

> As in the case of fishing, hunting opportunities are varied in the Clearwater country. The magic word is "elk." It's estimated that the Clearwater drainage elk herd numbers between 35,000 and 40,000 animals, one of the largest concentrations in the nation.
>
> Year by year the elk and deer herds have increased – and are threatening to over-populate their range. In the 1940's the annual harvest of elk was around 5,000 and this harvest has steadily grown since then. Upward of 2,500 elk per year have been taken in the North Fork district the past few years – and the figures are almost as high for the Lochsa and Selway districts.

Unfortunately, the times of a bountiful surplus in the region are coming to a disastrous downturn. It's not a new observation. Jack O'Connor, Idaho's most famous outdoor writer, saw it coming as early as the mid-1960s. In the October 1965 issue of Outdoor Life, he made the following observations:

> Probably the lush days of Clearwater elk hunting are drawing to a close. In many areas, the brush is growing out of reach of the elk. The winter range in creek and river bottoms is badly overbrowsed, and in years of great cold and deep snow many hundreds of elk perish. A recently completed highway across the mountains along the Lochsa to Missoula, Montana, will greatly interfere with wintering elk. A dam to be built near the mouth of the North Fork will destroy most of the winter range of the North Fork herd. The dam is a pet project of that most powerful of all lobbies – the U.S. Army Corps of Engineers. To get it authorized by Congress, the corps enlisted chambers of commerce and powerful lumber interests. Sportsmen and conservationists fought it but, as generally happens, they eventually ran out of wind and money. What will eventually finish the great Clearwater elk herd is another dam the Army Engineers are planning on the Middle Fork at a spot known as Penny Cliffs. This will flood out most of the winter range along the Lochsa and the Selway, but by that time those hills will be too steep for me.

O'Connor's casual and informal observations, in regard to browse, echo Young and Robinette's findings on the devastation that could occur should we allow the browse conditions to reach climax. He correctly identified an aging forest understory that was losing its potency, and the potentially devastating loss of winter range associated with the construction of Dworshak Dam on the North Fork of the Clearwater River near Orofino.

Jim Humbird, in a 1975 article in the Idaho Wildlife Review, made the following observations:

> Wildfire in the 19th century burned considerable summer range. Later conflagrations early in the 20th century burned large blocks of timber destined to become extensive winter range areas for elk. Mountain slopes formerly in timber became, in a few years, solid stands of shrubs.
>
> The mature forests were reduced to the early stages of plant succession and the seral shrub stage occupied hundreds of square miles. Highly palatable shrubs such as willow, red-stem ceanothus,

mountain maple, serviceberry, and chokecherry provided an almost unlimited supply of food.

Elk numbers in the Clearwater River drainage have peaked and have started to decline in recent years. This has been caused mainly by the natural progression of vegetation – the extensive brushfields on which wintering elk feed are growing out of reach. Plant succession gradually is advancing toward conifers, too, and thus reducing that carrying capacity of the ranges.

Man's activities, such as the construction of the Lewis-Clark highway from Lowell to Powell along the Lochsa River, have also had some effect on wintering herds.

Observations such as those by O'Connor, Humbird, and countless biologists are also unbelievably keen for the time period. The key issue was obviously maturation of vegetation, but they also mention the construction of Highway 12, which all but opened the floodgates to mass droves of hunters that had never before been able to access the area. They even talk about the adverse effects that could and would happen to various areas of their winter range. But even these bright and observant men could likely not foresee the degree of the devastation that two heavy-hitters would have on the fate of the Clearwater, as well as other areas of Idaho.

The first is the devastation that has happened to base habitat in the Clearwater. The Forest Service began aerial firefighting techniques in 1938. This has shown to be so effective that there hasn't been a major fire in the region since. This policy of nearly total fire suppression, in combination with the environmental movement, timber sale litigation, and the standstill it creates in regard to forest managers being able to thin and battle the closing forest canopy, has created a habitat nightmare. With the fundamental paralysis that is the current standard, there is no way for any successional setbacks to re-invigorate the region with browse and other important components of elk habitat. And thus, without fire, logging, and other tools that could create more elk habitat, we can have few elk. Blanket anti-logging sentiments without reasonable rationale continue to degrade the western landscape. These anti-logging sentiments and the subsequent lawsuits are indirectly promoting decadent forests void of legitimate food sources and vigor in entire fauna classes.

The second, and perhaps eventually even more directly devastating in the short-term, is the evolving predator situation. Seemingly everything possible that could go against elk in the Clearwater is happening. This would include a curious phenomenon in regard to bear predation on elk calves. With the habitat disappearing rapidly in the region, openings are a rare commodity. Pregnant cows seek out openings in which to calve, for two reasons - more room to watch their calves and spot predators, and a more abundant food source.

Coincidentally, and somewhat tragically, bears coming out of hibernation are seeking these very same precious few openings. The original intent of this is to seek out lush new grasses to fill the void created by several months of hibernation. Unfortunately, this creates a focused concentration of fresh elk calves and hungry bears in the same narrow belt of habitat at precisely the same time. Bears come into these rare openings looking for grass, and coincidentally find an abundant and tasty new food source. Bears in the region, over time, have adjusted to this change in habitat and the newfound prey source, and thus now concentrate on patrolling these meadows, picking off calves at a rate that is beyond unnatural.

Schlegel, 1976, reported that 38 of 53 (72%) of marked calves in north-central Idaho were killed by bear and 11% by cougar. Most all mortalities occurred when calves were 3-42 days old. Over time and further study, average for bear predation on elk calves in the Clearwater seems to be hovering at an astounding 50%.

What the bears are not taking could soon be falling to the wolf. Reintroduction of the gray wolf into Idaho is currently helping to further decimate game populations. Of course, O'Connor never could have seen that coming. After all, it was the generation before his that had purposefully eradicated wolves from Idaho. Wolves will likely have a hard impact on calf recruitment in the decades to come, and without recruitment, we will have no population. It is already happening.

Fish and Game population estimates for the region tell the final tale. In the 1980s, there were an estimated 36,000 elk roaming the Clearwater Basin. Unit 10 had an estimated elk population of 11,507 in 1989. That number had plummeted to 2643 as of 2003. Unit 12 mirrors the same situation. In 1985, that unit's population was estimated at 4787. As of 2002, it stood at 2048.

The winter of 1996-97 didn't help an already bad situation. It is estimated that winterkill pushed the 50% mark in some areas of the region.

Is the sun setting on the Clearwater elk herd? Lack of allowing fire to play an adequate natural role, along with inability of forest managers and wildlife professionals to do their jobs without fear of lawsuit, means our elk grounds are giving way to an encroaching canopy and predator population that could soon choke the life right out of the Clearwater.

But who knows; something's got to give. Every year, the threat of catastrophic fire increases. In areas that have a high component of dead and down timber, natural "loading" ranges from 10-30 tons/acre. In the Clearwater, fuel loading in some stands is an astounding 50-200 tons/acre, suggesting that if natural fires ever start, they may be difficult, if not impossible, to control – and the risk is increasing. Lodgepole stands average 80-year life cycles, and with no fire to cleanse the forest, stands are being infested with disease and insects that kill trees and add to the fuel base. Some areas of the Clearwater are a ticking time bomb. When it does go, it will likely burn so hot that sediment loading could damage the Clearwater River, the soil will be sterile in some places for decades, and habitat will be void. As in 1910, it will likely require decades to restore vegetation – and elk – to the area. In time, the Clearwater could become the most beautiful wasteland you ever drove through, as you search in vain for a remnant elk population that has all the cover it needs, but either starved to death for lack of browse or has been devoured by the bear or wolf.

So what can be done to save it? With regard to the predator situation, Idaho Department of Fish & Game has attempted to address the bear situation by offering reduced price bear tags to non-residents in hopes that additional "incidental" hunting might keep bear populations a bit more in check. This may have a small net effect, but until that narrow belt of elk nurseries and spring bear feeding grounds is increased, concentration of predator and prey into small areas will likely still keep the remaining bears in good food supply.

With regard to habitat, more broad-scale education is the start, and understanding the importance of productive habitats vs. decadent habitats is the key. Fire needs to be adequately reintroduced at a much larger scale, and forest managers must be allowed to do their jobs without lawsuits, or the situation is unlikely to change enough to make a substantial difference.

Humbird noted, "Continuing range studies including controlled burning are underway to find workable solutions to this problem. Controlled burning shows great promise. Study area results indicate an immediate increase in available browse production during the first growing year, especially from willow. Redstem ceanothus seeds germinated after burning and populated the area with new plants. The young redstem are just beginning to add to the browse production on the study areas."

According to University of Idaho wildlife professor Jim Peek, the tide is turning in regard to letting a more natural fire regime regain a foothold. Fire is now being allowed to burn under prescribed conditions. Somewhat of a landscape-level experiment, much of this is taking place on the North Fork, where the potential is there to do the most good. Peek said, "We haven't ever been able to substantially affect an elk population by doing enough to its habitat to be meaningful, so we have a substantial amount of uncertainty involved in whether we can burn enough habitat to stabilize an elk population at some higher level than it currently is."

The Rocky Mountain Elk Foundation has been a key player in helping to promote over 40,000 acres of prescribed burns in the area, which is a good start. Government agencies also seem to be taking a positive step forward.

A change in policy regarding natural wildfire and allowing successional setbacks to reinvigorate browse and reduce fuel-loading is a key factor not only for elk, but in struggling mule deer populations in southern Idaho as well. Fire must be allowed to perform its natural function at a rate beyond the current pace. The future health of our entire state, as well as the health of the entire West, depends on it.

Jim Peek might have summed up the current situation the best. He says, "The battle has at least been joined, and that deserves recognition, whether it leads to significant elk population change or not.

Courtesy of Roland Wilson

Roland Wilson, who graced the back cover of Idaho's Greatest Mule Deer, holds a fine bull taken in the Selway region in the mid-1960s. Roland is from Idaho Falls, where elk populations were not high at the time. Like many Idaho hunters of his era, they trekked much further north in search of good elk hunting. The Selway, in the middle of its heyday, had plenty to offer.

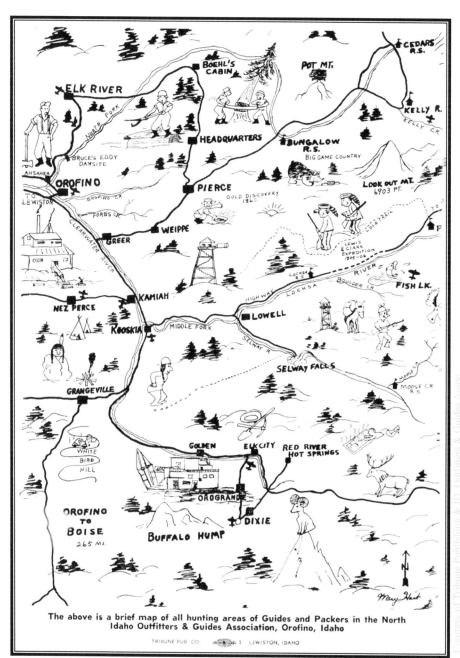

This unique map appeared in a pamphlet promoting guides and outfitters in the north-central Idaho area in 1960. It's really an informative and entertaining map.

The Future of Elk in Idaho

The future of elk in Idaho seems very mixed. Elk are thriving and pushing populations to new levels in some areas. The opportunity to hunt elk has never been better in many of those same places. Unfortunately, there are threats coming fast that could change everything. The following are just a few of the potential problems that could impact elk in the next few decades in Idaho.

Wolves. Wolves are fascinating and beautiful animals. Seeing one is a unique experience. With that said, reintroduction of the wolf into Idaho has had major negative consequences on elk in some areas.

Most big game managers would like to see the calf to cow ratio somewhere in the range of 70 calves per 100 cows. At a minimum, 30 calves to 100 cows is considered necessary just to keep a population stable. Following the reintroduction of the wolf, some areas in Idaho where wolves are prevalent currently have declined in ratio to 13 calves to 100 cows. In the short term, what this means is that the elk population is rapidly aging, even though herd size has not necessarily begun to decline. When this happens, there is high potential for later catastrophic decline, since recruitment for younger age classes may result in reduced production and survival of calves.

From a handful of wolves reintroduced in 1995, the population has exploded to 565 confirmed wolves in Idaho ten years later – far past projections and expectations. The population, in all reality, is likely higher. The jury is still out as to what degree wolves will permanently affect elk populations. Should the decline due to wolf predation be significant, it could potentially negatively affect not only elk populations, but also tourist dollars and hunting opportunity.

Chronic wasting disease (CWD), or spongiform encephalopathy. CWD was first found in Wyoming and Colorado in 1980. It is in the group of diseases that includes Creutzfeld-Jacob disease in humans, bovine spongiform encephalopathy (Mad Cow Disease) in cattle, and scrapie in sheep and goats. In elk, it can be seen easily in the advanced stages and is marked by drooling, an emaciated appearance, severe weight drop, low-hanging head, and wobbliness. It affects the brain and central nervous system. Prions are extremely resistant to any sort of eradication treatment, including intense heat, and no way to rid an infected area has yet been found.

Some selfish private individuals are doing everything they can to introduce bills to bring domestic cervidae (privately owned moose, whitetail, and more elk) into Idaho in high-fenced breeding and shooting operations. Not only does this stand in direct opposition to Idaho's hunting heritage and what Idahoans believe in with regard to fair chase hunting, it also threatens to bring CWD into our state.

Once that happens, we could lose everything. Varying opinions exist on how to deal with CWD once it infiltrates an area. Drastic measures, such as ones taken in Wisconsin, involve eradicating all live cervids within miles of the source in efforts to reduce the spread. This means killing every live elk and deer within "X" miles of the outbreak – a wildlife "ground zero."

In September 2006, the scenario that elk breeders insisted would never happen happened. Over 100 domestic elk escaped from a canned hunting operation in eastern Idaho. Not only did this happen right in time for the breeding season, but the owner of the escaped elk also never notified the authorities. The confusion and inefficiency that ensued in attempting to rectify the situation shows that Idaho is not ready to deal with this nightmare. Historic genetic pools could be permanently tainted, disease is at least a possibility, and for the next few years, Idahoans will wait on pins and needles to find out the long-term ramifications.

We can't afford to let selfish individuals, who want to profit off of domesticated wildlife, to ruin all that we hold dear. Idaho needs to push legislation prohibiting all game farms and domestic cervidae from coming into the borders of our great state. Several western states, including Montana, have banned all canned hunting of mammals. Idaho is seriously lagging behind on this and should have made this happen long ago.

Will Idaho's elk legacy be wild, free-ranging, native elk? Or will it be privately owned domesticated elk, like this bull in a pen near American Falls?

Fire suppression, the logging slowdown, aging understories, and lack of browse. This was touched on in the chapter "Rise and Fall of the Clearwater Elk Herd". Habitat is the most crucial component needed to have wildlife. It's also the component in the most trouble in Idaho. Seven decades of intense fire suppression, coupled with efforts of some Environmental groups to stop nearly all logging no matter the reason, have succeeded in stopping successional setbacks from reinvigorating the flora of the West. Trees per acre have skyrocketed, choking out understories, and even brushfields and general plantlife are aging and becoming less potent and succulent. This is not jut a problem statewide in Idaho; it's a problem clear across the entire West.

A major swing is going to be needed in how we as a public view differing types of vegetation setbacks and disturbance. If we don't reintroduce fire, responsible logging, and other types of scarification on a much broader and more frequent scale, our wildlife habitats are going to continue to become much less productive, and in turn will support much fewer elk, mule deer, and most all other wildlife.

Elk vs. mule deer? In southern Idaho, the future of elk seems to be more a function of how many elk we *want* to have. Populations and overall biomass of elk are currently fairly high. The downside is that more and more opinion seems to be unifying that this increase in elk is more of a direct problem with displacement of mule deer than most ever wanted to admit. With the newly started Mule Deer Initiative, Idahoans will soon have to be making decisions on whether or not they are willing to significantly reduce elk populations in order to once again favor mule deer.

Idaho Elk Management 101:
It's Not Just Biology Anymore

Guest Chapter
by Dale E. Toweill
Idaho Department of Fish and Game

Whenever hunters gather, few topics generate more discussion than the decisions made by wildlife management agencies – particularly when setting hunting seasons. During the past 25 years, I've listened to hunters talk about big game regulations in forums ranging from public agency meetings to private telephone calls and through public media ranging from 30-second news spots to letters to the editor of local newspapers.

In my case, the topic is often elk management. As author and editor of the *Elk of North America* (Stackpole, 1982) and more recently *North American Elk* (Smithsonian Press, 2003), I have heard from thousands of elk hunters. I've heard numerous hunter-derived management philosophies and dozens of elk management conspiracy theories (some downright bizarre). It has become obvious the rationale behind many wildlife management decisions is not well understood by a whole lot of folks. So when Ryan provided me this opportunity to provide a "short course" in how the Idaho Department of Fish and Game really *does* manage elk, I jumped at it.

The Law

The very first thing to understand about elk management is that the elk don't belong to the wildlife management agency – they belong to everyone in the state. Hunter, non-hunter, anti-hunter, it makes no difference. The wildlife resource and its management were given to each state when statehood was granted. In effect, state government became a trustee for maintaining wildlife as a valuable resource for all of the state's citizens, a legal obligation in the same sense as a lawyer assigned as a trustee for the money in an estate. The state's obligation for wildlife (written into state law) is a mandate that wildlife be "preserved, protected, perpetuated and managed" for the benefit of all citizens – a mandate called the Public Trust Doctrine. Idaho's obligation goes even further and requires that wildlife be managed for "continued supplies of such wildlife for hunting, fishing, and trapping." The Department of Fish and Game, and the legal mandate for wildlife management, was created by a citizen's initiative in 1938.

The Public Trust Doctrine identifies wildlife management as a responsibility of governance, just like its responsibility to ensure public safety and well-being. Wildlife management must co-exist with other activities: ranching and farming, road construction, housing development, and so on, but it cannot be ignored. As a trustee for the public resource, the state has an obligation to "preserve, protect, perpetuate and manage" elk, and that responsibility demands that the employees of the Department of Fish and Game work with farmers and ranchers, highway engineers, land developers and others to try to find solutions that will accommodate elk as Idaho grows.

Population Growth and Challenges of Elk Management

Idaho *is* growing, and at an unprecedented pace. The number of people living in Idaho doubled during the four decades from 1960 (667,000 people) to 2000 (over 1.2 million). Most of that growth (over 28%) occurred in just the last decade of that period, between 1990 and 2000. Idaho was the fifth fastest growing state in the U.S. in 2000. Since 2000, Idaho has been among the top ten fastest-growing states *every year* and was the third-fastest growing state in 2005, when *annual* population growth exceeded 2.4 percent. This rate of growth in human populations puts a tremendous strain on wildlife habitat, as new housing developments gobble up critical winter ranges and as ever-more-distant communities become bedroom communities for commuters as well as those trying to escape the hubbub of city life.

When the focus is on elk management, losses of habitat quickly become critical. Elk are big animals, requiring a lot of room to move about. Nearly all elk herds in Idaho are migratory, to a greater or lesser degree, and those that are not now migratory probably were before human development boxed them into fragments of their former habitat. Fortunately, elk are also very adaptable, and can learn to live near humans – a benefit that also creates additional problems for elk managers, constantly struggling to balance the biological needs of elk and increasing demand for elk hunting opportunity.

The challenges of elk management are daunting – human development inevitably squeezes elk populations into smaller and less productive habitats at the same time as hunter numbers increase and increasing numbers of rural residents find elk less than desirable neighbors. Hunters find themselves hunting smaller and more fragmented habitats more intensively than ever before. Some areas that formerly supported elk populations are being lost forever, as elk herds can no longer compete with human activities.

Economic growth in Idaho means that more people have time to hunt elk, many of them equipped with better and better equipment – off-road vehicles, telescopic hunting sights that automatically adjust for distance, better firearms and archery equipment, bigger trucks and better camping equipment. In a state that's two-thirds public land, that means that elk not only have fewer and fewer places to live, they have fewer and fewer places to hide during hunting seasons.

Nearly twenty years ago wildlife managers were struggling to maintain elk populations and general season hunting opportunity. The traditional season framework allowing hunters to harvest any elk during a long season that started early in the fall had resulted in over-harvest of bulls in some areas, and declines of elk populations in others. Bull-only hunting was initiated in 1976 (when statewide harvest of elk was less than 8,000 animals). Elk populations responded, and began to increase. Additionally, vacant habitats in southern Idaho were being discovered by elk and populations grew as these elk herds responded to uninhabited islands of suitable elk habitat.

While elk populations in southern Idaho were experiencing rapid population growth, populations in the heart of historic north-central elk country were showing signs of being habitat limited. To understand the ebb and flow of elk populations, one must understand the changes in their environment. There were relatively few elk when Lewis & Clark crossed through Idaho. Many of the forests were made up of mature stands of trees. Mature forests do not provide optimal elk habitat. Elk need nutritious supplies of grass, forbs, and shrubs. Large fires between 1910 and 1934 created an unprecedented quantity of elk habitat throughout much of north-central Idaho, and elk responded. However, Smokey Bear and fire suppression have begun to take its toll. What were once young productive habitats are quickly becoming stagnant stands of mature timber providing little forage for elk. One of the first signs of habitat becoming limited is declining calf production and survival. As early as the mid-1980s, elk biologists in north-central Idaho detected declining trends in calf recruitment.

The bulls-only hunting framework adopted in the mid-1970s resulted in increasing populations. However, focusing the majority of harvest on bulls, combined with declining calf recruitment, resulted in declining bull:cow ratios and bull numbers in portions of Idaho. In 1996, the Department recommended and the Commission adopted a minimum bull:cow ratio of 18:100 based on research at Starkey Experimental Station in Oregon. Research at Starkey identified the minimum bull:cow ratio necessary to maximize pregnancy and birth synchrony. Synchronization of birth is important to minimize predation risk and allow calves time to reach adequate body weight in order to survive an Idaho winter. Beginning in the early 1990s, elk managers were concerned about declining calf recruitment and increasing bull harvest in certain areas of the state.

Because of declining calf recruitment in core elk populations, increasing hunter efficiencies, increasing bull harvest rates, and increasing elk populations in southern Idaho wildlife managers realized that something would have to change – and to help them determine how to make those changes, they turned to hunters.

Elk Hunters and Hunter Opinions

In 1988-89, the Idaho Department of Fish and Game conducted a broad-scale, intensive study of the characteristics of elk hunters using a very detailed questionnaire and profile of hunters. Although that project is now more than 15 years old, frequent mini-survey "checks" reveal that much of information gained is still valid.

Most of the demands facing wildlife managers come from elk hunters. Even though elk hunters comprise a fairly small segment of Idaho's citizens, hunters are typically the most concerned about the status of wildlife populations in general, and game animals in particular. Hunters are also the group that finances wildlife management, both directly (by the purchase of hunting licenses and tags) and indirectly (through a federal excise tax on sporting goods). In Idaho, tax dollars are not used for wildlife management.

The hunter questionnaire was both timely and fascinating. Some of the findings were obvious: elk hunters were primarily male, and employed full-time. Elk hunters included a true cross-section of Idahoans of all age and income groups, and most preferred to hunt with a rifle. Non-resident elk hunters tended to be more affluent and older on average than resident hunters.

Others were less obvious. For example, the catch-all term "elk hunter" actually encompassed at least five different groups of people, based on their reasons for hunting elk. Some just wanted a reason to get outdoors and enjoy nature and natural surroundings, while another group focused primarily on personal development of hunting and outdoor skills. A third group used hunting as an opportunity to get together in an outdoors social setting with friends or family. Then there were the two other, more commonly understood groups: one that hunted primarily for food, and another that hunted specifically for the opportunity to harvest older, 'trophy' animals. Each of these groups shared many characteristics with all of the other groups—and yet each group typically viewed hunting regulations differently!

It quickly dawned on folks analyzing these results why it was so difficult to formulate regulations, since each group wanted different things from their hunting opportunity. Even contacting the groups to get their opinions was difficult, since fewer than one third of Idaho elk hunters belonged to any hunting, conservation, or sportsmen's organization, and only a tiny percentage those participated in public hearings or meetings about hunting regulations. Often the *first* indication of the opinions of many hunters followed adoption of new hunting rules and publication of season brochure (which many hunters don't read until just before, or during, the hunting season).

Faced with these findings, Commissioners and wildlife managers realized that in order to provide the types of elk hunting experiences demanded, the emphasis would have to be on providing many different types of experience, so that hunters could choose the type of setting and opportunity most desired. Fortunately, the survey also allowed elk hunters to identify in some detail both the kinds of opportunity desired and potential trade-offs among season structure and success rates and other elements that the department could control—information very helpful as wildlife managers began to cope with changes in elk populations and other challenges.

The elk hunter survey also made wildlife managers more acutely aware that there a many other 'owners' of Idaho's elk resource whose interests must be considered. There were farmers and ranchers, with the legal option of excluding elk from their property, or allowing elk to mingle with their livestock on what is often critical winter range. There was (and is) the constant potential for new development of landscapes for summer homes and housing developments, actions that ultimately limit the amount of habitat available to support elk. There were small-town merchants (the owners of gas stations, hotel/motels, and restaurants) whose livelihood depended in no small part on hunters visiting their communities during the hunting season, and other businesses (such as some golf course operators) who believed elk to be a nuisance or worse. And there were citizens – more than those who hunt each year – who simply enjoy seeing elk in places where they could be watched and photographed seasonally or year around.

Faced with these competing social demands and the biological realities of elk management, wildlife managers set about crafting a framework for elk management for the future. The first task was to build a management plan that addressed both the needs of hunters and of elk. Elk managers crafted two alternative management approaches, first a framework that would maintain general hunting opportunity, and a second one that relied on implementing controlled hunts throughout the state. A survey of the public clearly indicated hunter's preference, 86% of hunters preferred the general season framework – preferring to accept some additional restrictions rather than rely on the luck-of-the-draw on whether or not they would hunt that year.

The General Season Framework

General season hunting is the key to allowing hunters to hunt elk every year. Long seasons are important, to allow hunters opportunity to spread out through both space and time, avoiding the crowding that most hunters found objectionable. The survey clearly showed that most hunters preferred to hunt on the opening day of the season, even if that opening occurred on a weekday – and that some would hunt successive opening days in different areas of the state, contributing to hunter congestion.

The obvious way to address this problem was to coordinate the opening of hunting seasons statewide to disperse hunters across the greatest geographic area. Years of day-by-day harvest data have shown that most of the elk taken were harvested the first few days of each annual season. When season opening dates varied around the state, hunters could maximize their likelihood for success by hunting only the first day or two of each season in different game management units. By adopting a standard season opening date hunter congestion was reduced.

This reduction in hunter congestion was reinforced by requiring hunters to choose to hunt in just one of 29 Elk Management Zones. Each zone included one or more Big Game Management Units with similar characteristics relative to elk management – characteristics like similarity of habitat, hunter access, or isolated elk herds. By adopting zone management for elk, wildlife managers could more closely monitor hunting pressure and harvest, while still allowing hunters the freedom of hunting every year within a general season framework. The number of hunters in each zone could be monitored annually and 'capped' with a limited number of elk tags if necessary. In addition, zone management allowed wildlife managers to closely track herd responses to hunting seasons, weather, and other factors.

There was another advantage to zone management: within certain limitations (primarily hunter and elk herd numbers) hunters within each zone could be afforded additional opportunity to match their desired style of hunting to the conditions specific to each area. Thus, nearly every zone has both an "A" tag (which provides the maximum number of hunter-days of hunting opportunity by limiting hunter to some of the less-successful but high-demand types of hunting opportunity, such as requiring primitive weapons or hunting at times, such as late fall, when weather condition might concentrate elk, making them more vulnerable) and a "B" tag (designed to accommodate the highest-demand rifle seasons). This also afforded additional opportunity—a second, different season opening dates for hunters who elected to hunt with primitive weapons, thereby reducing hunter congestion still further.

Hunter congestion wasn't the only problem that needed to be addressed for this approach to work, however. Wildlife managers also needed to rebuild elk herds where habitat was available. Wildlife managers knew that elk herds were most productive when each herd included a number of older, mature animals. The mating behavior of mature bulls tends to shorten the breeding period, resulting in most calves being born when conditions were most favorable in the spring, "swamping" potential predators with prey and maximizing the likelihood of a calf surviving the most critical few weeks after birth. Older cows were usually the leaders of cow-calf bands, having learned from years of experience where and when to lead their followers to find the best habitat, depending on the season and year-to-year fluctuations in weather. Managers established management guidelines for post-hunting-season bull-to-cow ratios after each hunting season to ensure that this older age segment would not be completely removed through hunting – and set about finding a way to achieve these goals within the elk zone management framework.

The solution was to move elk hunting later in the fall, further past the elk breeding season, or "rut." All bull elk, but especially the oldest bulls in any herd, were most vulnerable to hunters during the elk breeding season. Bulls bugle to attract cows, accumulating a harem that they then defend from other (usually smaller) bulls. The mating behavior of mature bulls and association with other cows tends to reduce the period of breeding activity. Unfortunately for the elk, however, some cows may not be bred during the peak of the rut, coming into breeding condition a second time about a month later, re-triggering mating behavior (and bugling) by bulls well past the September rut and into October. To help mature bull elk survive, the elk hunting season was pushed later into the fall, and the deer season moved forward. Surprisingly to some, this move did not significantly reduce the harvest of bull elk—but it did reduce the percentage of mature bulls harvested. Wildlife managers had predicted this, based on hunter questionnaire results that showed that while most hunters preferred to harvest a big, mature bull, few would pass up a legal spike, and almost none would pass a branch-antlered raghorn bull.

The Elk Zone Management System was established to allow the Department to continue to offer general season elk hunting in Idaho, and it is currently working well. Bull:cow ratios in most populations have stabilized, and even increased in a few areas. Additionally, the Zone System has allowed the Department to shift harvest to elk populations in southern Idaho in need of additional harvest because of agricultural concerns or concern over elk occupying crucial mule deer habitats. About three-quarters of all elk hunting in Idaho occurs within general season hunts. General seasons address the needs of hunters who want an opportunity to enjoy hunting as outdoors recreation, as well as those who want to develop outdoors skills, and those who view hunting as a social event to be enjoyed with friends and family. Even better, it has provided hunters opportunity to choose from areas well-distributed around the state, confident of an opportunity to pursue their sport close to home or in an area of their choosing depending on the type of experience they desire. The questionnaire revealed that the features most important to some hunters are landscape (forested or open, steep and rugged or more gentle, Wilderness or highly-roaded), while others focus more on weapons (rifle or archery or muzzle-loader), and yet others on distance traveled.

If elk hunter numbers increase, or elk populations in some areas dramatically decrease because of loss in habitat quantity and quality, wildlife managers could be forced to impose a cap on participation, displacing some hunters to other zones already near capacity. Fortunately, under the present system wildlife managers can shift hunting pressure between elk zones by using a variety of tools to make a particular zone more or less desirable to hunters. Tools include adding hunting days to the end of a season, allowing elk hunters to hunt deer during some portion of their season, or use of a wide range of other measures to influence hunter access.

Controlled Hunts

While the public clearly did not want all elk populations to be managed through controlled hunts, these types of hunts clearly serve a purpose and are an important tool for elk managers to use.

Controlled hunts account for about one-quarter of Idaho's elk hunting opportunity, with between 20,000 and 25,000 permits offered annually. These hunts are critically important to wildlife managers, allowing them to address specific management issues and offer unique hunt opportunities. The simplicity of controlled hunts is that hunter numbers can be limited (one hunt in 2006 offered a single permit), and since the number of participants is limited, season dates can be fitted to particular management challenges and opportunities.

One constant challenge faced by wildlife managers is the problem of elk being someplace where they're not wanted, often because of potential damage to growing crops or incursions into farm and ranch or rural areas. Controlled hunts can be used to target these problems, when and where they occur. Thus, it is common to see controlled hunts in August when crops are beginning to ripen, and many of these hunts will be limited to areas immediately around farm ground. Others may focus on moving animals away from livestock pastures and stored crops late in the fall. Often, these hunts occur on privately-owned lands, and many require landowner permission and limit vehicle access – limitations often offset by very high hunter success rates since these hunts target specific problem areas where elk are more concentrated than during most general seasons.

Controlled hunts are also used to allocate permits for specific purposes. Prime examples of this type of use include "Youth Hunts" designed to allow youngsters between 12 and 17 opportunities to hunt without competition with high numbers of more experienced hunters. Nearly 500 such permits were offered in 2006. Other examples are special, limited-entry hunts featuring archery or muzzleloader weapons, designed for primitive-weapons enthusiasts. These hunts are often highly sought, since hunter density is usually very low, giving the primitive weapons user an opportunity to pursue elk in an area where likelihood of disturbance by other hunters is minimal. Outfitter permit allocations also fit into this category. Outfitter allocations are permits set aside specifically for use by outfitters in areas where these businesses had operated under a general season-framework, prior to adoption of the Elk Management Zone system, and allocations are based on a formula dependent on the level of historic use.

Most hunting for antlerless elk are offered as controlled hunts. These hunts appeal primarily to resident hunters primarily interested in obtaining venison, and they are critically important to wildlife managers whose job is to maintain an elk population in balance with available habitat.

Finally, controlled hunts also provide a vehicle whereby wildlife managers can offer some truly unique hunts for those hunters seeking trophy-class mature bulls. While some mature bulls are available in most elk zones that include rugged terrain and forest cover, some areas are particularly noted for growing big bull elk, such as the country south of the Frank Church-River of No Return Wilderness Area, east of Hells Canyon, and near the Montana and Wyoming borders. Many of these areas provide excellent opportunities for a few lucky hunters to locate mature bulls, and hunts in these areas are in high demand.

Depredation Hunts

There is one final type of hunt opportunity in Idaho – the depredation hunt. Depredation hunts are used to resolve and unexpected, area-specific problem, such as a band of elk unexpectedly causing severe damage to the crops in a local area. These hunts by their very nature are unexpected events, and are offered to area sportsmen willing and able to respond to the situation on short notice when called by a Department representative. Hunters interested in participating must sign up for an annual 'call list' at the local Regional Office of Idaho Fish and Game.

Conclusion

Idaho's Elk Zone Management System has been successful in providing a framework that both maintains general elk season hunt opportunity in Idaho, and in allowing wildlife managers the ability to adjust seasons as needed to protect Idaho's elk resources for the future. Elk harvests in Idaho are near an all-time high, despite record-breaking growth in Idaho's human population over the past decade and more. Elk hunter success currently averages from 20 to 25 percent for approximately 90,000 hunters annually.

One of the key features of Idaho's program is an attention to the desires of hunters for a variety of different types of hunting experience. By maintaining a combination of general seasons and controlled hunts, Idaho can accommodate hunters seeking to maximize their opportunities for outdoor recreation, for hunting with friends and family, for developing outdoor skills as primary components of their elk hunting experience, for harvest, and for the pursuit of mature trophy bull elk.

A Brief Synopsis of Big Elk in Idaho

There's probably no sense in beating around the bush on this one. If you are looking for trophy-class elk, Idaho is not the state for you. Arizona, Utah, and many other western states routinely clobber Idaho in amounts of records book bulls, particularly in the last two decades.

Idaho doesn't manage their elk for quality; they are managed for quantity and opportunity. With elk, that doesn't have to be a bad thing. Knowing that Idaho's propensity for producing big bulls is somewhat lacking, the hunter opportunity scenario is not necessarily the worst scenario for Idaho's hunters. On the other hand, if you simply want a chance at a mature bull, Idaho offers you a reasonable chance. It remains one of the only states in the west that you can buy an over-the-counter tag, and Idaho hunters still have the opportunity to have a nice freezer full of elk meat every winter. In that sense, Idaho hunters have something that many other states are lacking – a genuine elk hunting heritage.

Beyond Idaho's hunter opportunity-focused management, Idaho simply does not have outstanding genetics to produce massive quantities of trophy-caliber elk. As mentioned in the introduction, they routinely produce very poor G-3s, and oftentimes stunted front ends. They do, however, typically have fairly outstanding "backs" if given the opportunity to mature.

The following table and map show Idaho's historical trophy elk distribution, by county. The data was compiled from four sources – Boone and Crockett Club, Pope and Young Club, The Longhunter Society, and Idaho Department of Fish & Game listings. Only elk scoring 360 and above (typical category) and 385 and above (non-typical category) were considered. Those listings with locations too vague to be accurately determined were not considered.

Note that there may be no correlation between numbers of record book bulls and mature bulls. For example, one of the top controlled hunt elk units in Idaho is in Blaine County, where the chance to take a big bull is as good as anywhere in the state. However, if you look at where it ranks in the record book listings, it is comparatively insignificant. The same could be said of Custer County, which has some excellent controlled hunt areas for bulls, but similarly has few bulls that have made the 360-mark.

Another note worth mentioning is that with many fewer elk entries in Idaho than, say, mule deer, the statistical significance of the following table and map is not nearly as reliable. This is true particularly in the areas with 0-1 entries.

Boone & Crockett-class elk by county (all-time)

County	Typicals	Non-typicals	Total
Shoshone	12	4	16
Idaho	8	4	12
Fremont	9	2	11
Adams	4	3	7
Nez Perce	6	1	7
Valley	7	0	7
Clark	6	0	6
Lemhi	5	1	6
Kootenai	5	0	5
Benewah	4	0	4
Bonner	4	0	4
Owyhee	4	0	4
Bonneville	3	0	3
Caribou	3	0	3
Clearwater	1	2	3
Washington	3	0	3
Blaine	2	0	2
Custer	2	0	2
Latah	0	2	2
Teton	2	0	2
Bannock	1	0	1
Bear Lake	1	0	1
Boise	1	0	1
Butte	1	0	1
Cassia	0	1	1
Elmore	1	0	1
Jefferson	1	0	1
Lincoln	1	0	1
Ada	0	0	0
Bingham	0	0	0
Boundary	0	0	0
Camas	0	0	0
Canyon	0	0	0
Franklin	0	0	0
Gem	0	0	0
Gooding	0	0	0
Jerome	0	0	0
Lewis	0	0	0
Madison	0	0	0
Minidoka	0	0	0
Oneida	0	0	0
Payette	0	0	0
Power	0	0	0
Twin Falls	0	0	0

Idaho elk record book entries, by county, all-time.

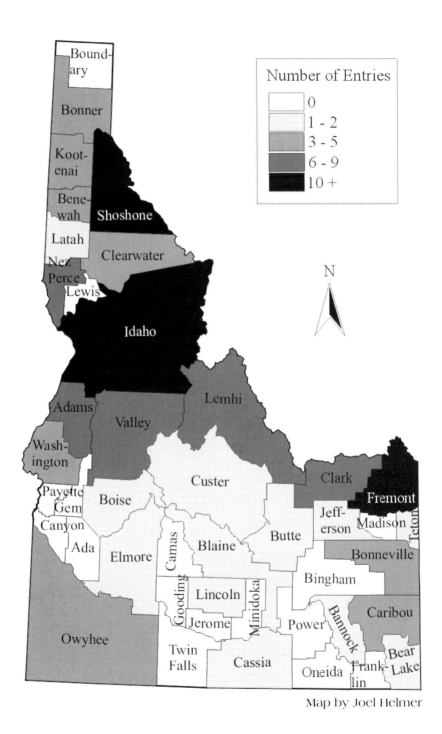

Map by Joel Helmer

Idaho's Greatest Non-Typical Elk

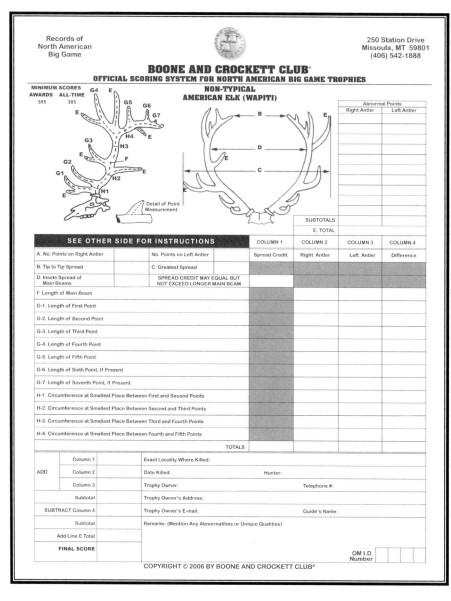

Idaho's Greatest All-Time Non-Typical Elk
(Boone and Crockett Club Scoring System)

Rank	Score	Year	Location	Hunter/Owner	Points R L	Main Beam R	Main Beam L	Widest Spread	Inside Spread	Bases R	Bases L
1*	430-4/8	1977	Latah County	Peter J. Orazi, Jr./Peter J. Orazi, Jr.	11,12	49-7/8	51-4/8	70-3/8	44-7/8	7-0/8	7-2/8
2	420-5/8	1981	Shoshone County	Steven W. Mullin/Bass Pro Shops	9,8	57-5/8	58-1/8	48-2/8	39-2/8	8-2/8	8-5/8
3	403-7/8	1964	Shoshone County	Fred S. Scott/Hollinger&Howard	8,9	46-5/8	52-0/8	43-5/8	32-4/8	10-3/8	10-6/8
4	402-4/8	PR 1960	Selway	Unknown/Cabela's	7,11	53-1/8	49-4/8	52-2/8	47-2/8	8-4/8	8-5/8
5	400-5/8	1964	Fremont County	Ernest Paskett/Ernest Paskett	8,7	52-5/8	51-3/8	53-0/8	44-0/8	9-4/8	10-1/8
6	400-2/8	1967	Lemhi County	Bill Kelly/Bill Kelly	8,7	52-7/8	52-3/8	51-4/8	42-1/8	8-0/8	7-6/8
7	398-3/8	1955	Adams County	Unknown/Delvin Watkins	8,9	52-2/8	51-3/8	44-0/8	37-6/8	8-7/8	9-3/8
8	395-5/8	1976	Fremont County	James E. Hoover/Hollinger&Howard	7,10	49-5/8	48-0/8	50-4/8	44-7/8	9-2/8	9-1/8
9	393-3/8	1974	Shoshone County	Hugh M. Kitzmiller/Robert Kitzmiller	8,7	50-2/8	48-4/8	70-1/8	41-2/8	9-5/8	10-1/8
10	393-2/8	1990	Idaho County	Johnny Bliznak/Johnny Bliznak	8,7	50-1/8	50-3/8	44-4/8	36-2/8	11-5/8	11-1/8
11	390-6/8	1973	Clearwater County	Gordon F. Larson/Gordon F. Larson	6,7	48-6/8	49-6/8	46-2/8	41-6/8	8-6/8	8-5/8
12	390-2/8	1995	Adams County	Robert F. Hughes/Robert F. Hughes	10,11	46-4/8	49-0/8	55-1/8	38-2/8	8-3/8	8-1/8
13	388-6/8	1978	Shoshone County	Roger R. Davis/Aly M. Bruner	7,7	50-5/8	48-1/8	51-4/8	45-0/8	8-6/8	8-1/8
14	386-2/8	2005	Idaho County	Daniel R. McClure/Daniel R. McClure	8,9	47-4/8	47-7/8	42-5/8	35-6/8	9-6/8	10-6/8
15	385-5/8	1977	Adams County	Richard L. Hansen/Richard L. Hansen	8,9	47-7/8	46-1/8	41-2/8	32-0/8	9-5/8	9-0/8
16	385-1/8	1985	Latah County	James A. Carpenter/James A. Carpenter	9,8	50-5/8	48-6/8	51-2/8	40-4/8	7-5/8	7-4/8
16	385-1/8	1996	Clearwater County	Tim Papineau/Tim Papineau	7,7	48-7/8	50-0/8	44-0/8	36-1/8	8-6/8	8-0/8
18	385	2001	Cassia County	John Spratling/John Spratling	7,9	55-0/8	56-4/8	54-7/8	47-5/8	8-7/8	9-2/8

*Pending verification at Boone and Crockett Club's 26th Awards Judges' Panel in April 2007.

Peter J. Orazi, Jr.
430-4/8 B&C Non-typical*
Latah County, 1977
Idaho State Record Non-Typical Elk
pending verification at B&C's 26th Awards Judges' Panel in 2007

Idaho Non-typical Rank: 1 *Length of Abnormal Points: 57-5/8* *Points (R,L): 11,12*
Inside Spread: 44-7/8 *Widest Spread: 70-3/8*
Main Beams (R,L): 49-7/8, 51-4/8 *Bases (R, L): 7-0/8, 7-2/8*

Finding places to hunt near the Moscow area can be challenging. Seas of wheat and other crops on the Palouse mean isolated and scattered timber patches and draws, and mostly privately owned ground, unless a hunter wants to take a major trek to the national forest lands to the north or east.

Peter Orazi had a spot near the Troy area he wanted to try, and it wasn't too far to drive, so despite a bit of a late start, he headed east on Highway 8. He turned onto a graveled county road, eventually pulling up not too far from a good timbered draw.

He had seen what he thought was an elk in this same draw a few days earlier, but couldn't make out a properly identifiable target. That's why the elk liked it here, of course – nice and thick, and easy to hide and escape.

Peter stepped into the cold morning air and was welcomed by a fresh blanket of snow. He hoped he might find some good tracking. He started toward the draw on a typical windy day on the Palouse. It was a weekday, and a guy could be doing a lot worse things than chasing elk, he thought to himself. He made his way into the second growth timber and hoped for something big and brown to cross his path.

He was about ten minutes removed from the friendly confines of the cab of his vehicle when he saw something he could hardly make himself believe. Bedded ahead of him, only 75 yards away, was the biggest elk he had ever seen. The bull was chewing his cud, half in a trance, with glazed over eyes.

The bull's vitals were covered by the brush, but the bull's huge head remained free of distraction or cover. Not one to question the circumstance or wait for a situation to deteriorate, Peter shouldered his .30-06 and aimed right between the eyes of the dozing bull. The simple twitch of a finger was all that it took. The bull never heard the shot, nor gained his feet. A few obligatory kicks and it was all over. With one squeeze of the trigger, Peter J. Orazi, Jr. had just made history. His 1977 Latah County bull would become the largest elk ever taken in the state of Idaho.

While visiting Kip Manfull (who will be in Idaho's Greatest Whitetails with a tremendous non-typical) in 2003, he gave me a photo of a man holding a monstrous elk. He also gave me Peter Orazi's name, but had long since lost contact with him. No matter how I tried to "shortchange" the bull when staring at the photo, I just could not imagine it would not be the new Idaho State Record non-typical elk.

For three years, I looked diligently for Peter with no luck, but then caught a lucky break and found him just before the release of the book. Pete had measured his big bull on his own years ago, but found it quite a bit short of the records book, as B&C did not have a non-typical category for elk at the time. Peter had not heard the news when B&C created one, so for decades the bull simply sat in his home, with no recognition other than an occasional houseguest.

This incredible elk is not only the largest bull ever taken in Idaho, but also the <u>widest ever recorded</u> by Boone and Crockett Club. If you are less than six feet tall, chances are you could fit right inside this bull's greatest spread.

Nearly thirty years after Peter took his prized bull, it was finally officially recognized as one of the biggest bulls ever taken in North America.

A slightly younger Peter J. Orazi, Jr. proudly poses with his outstanding Latah County bull from 1977.

A side view of Peter's wild 11x12 monster bull. Even being this large, it is amazingly symmetrical, including the two matched splitting cheaters.

Steven W. Mullin
420-5/8 P&Y Non-typical
Shoshone County, 1981
Idaho State Record Non-Typical (Archery)
Owned by Bass Pro Shops

Idaho Non-typical Rank: 2   *Length of Abnormal Points:* 23-5/8   *Points (R,L):* 9,8
Inside Spread: 39-2/8   *Widest Spread:* 48-2/8
Main Beams (R,L): 57-5/8, 58-1/8   *Bases (R, L):* 8-2/8, 8-5/8

I killed this elk in the rugged mountains of north Idaho in the fall of 1981. I was hunting with several friends, and had camped off of a logging road that ran along the spine of a long ridge. Canyons led off in both directions to roads miles away. The headwaters of the canyons were quite steep and the sunny exposures were thick with alders.

I had left camp early that morning with more gear than usual, since I wanted to be prepared to spend the night out. Getting out of the canyons in the dark took hours, and I preferred to do it every other day. So, in addition to my game bags and rope, I had a little food and a small sleeping bag and ensolite pad.

I spent the day hunting slowly down the canyon slopes. Late in the afternoon, I got to a spot at the head of the canyon where two creeks came together. At that point, there was a lot of elk sign and a fresh wallow in the soft dirt near the creek. On the far slope was a jungle of 10-foot alders, and the near side was covered with fir and pine. I found a spot in the "V" of the two creeks about 12 yards from the wallow and nestled in under some brush to wait out the twilight hours. Nothing stirred, so when it got dark, I rolled out my bag and went to sleep.

The next morning, I got up with the light and got comfortable sitting right there on my pad. I was using a Graham Dynabow with fiberglass arrows, and broadheads with inserts. I put one in my bow and had a couple more on the ground next to me.

It wasn't until almost 9 a.m. that I heard a noise. It sounded like a small herd of large animals coming from the direction of the alders. Soon, a cow elk appeared and headed down my way toward the creek. Moments later, an impossibly massive bull came out of the alders after her. I can't imagine how he was able to get that rack through the brush. I had poked around in there a little the day before, and it was barely penetrable for a human, let alone an animal the size of a horse with a small tree on his head. But, out he came.

He followed her down toward the creek, but she kept going. She then turned down and headed toward his wallow. By this time, I had my bow at full draw. I was in plain sight in front of the brush, but I was wearing full camo and my outline was broken up by brush all around me. The bull walked straight to his wallow with no nervousness.

As soon as he turned his right side broadside to me, I let the arrow fly. I made the usual neophyte mistake of getting excited and shooting at the whole animal rather than picking a spot. As the arrow flew, he took a step, so it ended up hitting him too far back in the ribcage and glancing off of a rib. Luckily, from there it angled back and into his liver, but it had only penetrated about nine inches.

At the sound of the bowstring, he bolted. This caused the cow that was nearby to bolt, also. She cleared out, but he ran only about 30 yards up the slope before stopping and looking back. He seemed undecided about what had spooked him; it was as if he hadn't felt the arrow at all!

He just stood there, and so I began debating whether or not to try another shot. My confidence had been badly damaged by my first attempt, so I decided not to test fate. He wasn't frightened and didn't seem to be going anywhere, so I just sat still and watched. He stood on the hillside 30 yards from me with the arrow going back and forth with each breath. We stayed that way for the longest 15 minutes of my life and then, without warning, he just toppled over and slid several yards down the hill toward me.

I can't describe the feeling at that moment, but I can describe the rest of the day – a lot of very hard work. I estimate that he weighed 1000 lbs., and he was in an awkward spot on the hillside. It took me all day to get him field-dressed and quartered. I cut off the legs, leaving the long bones in place, and boned out all the rest of the carcass. I left it all in game bags down by the creek in the shade. Taking the cape and heart, I headed back to camp on the ridge.

It was after 8 p.m. when I got back to camp. I had been gone nearly two days, causing my friends to go to the nearest town and report me missing. There was a search and rescue operation organized that was to begin looking for me the following morning. I was offended, but they went back and straightened things out.

The next day, we all got to spend the entire day in a brutal backpacking marathon getting the meat out of the bottom of the canyon. That's when friends come in handy, although a couple of horses would have complained a lot less.

Mr. Mullin no longer hunts, and was somewhat reluctant to tell the story of his encounter with this tremendous bull. We want to thank him for agreeing to let us record his story for future generations that will consider this story an important historical event in Idaho's hunting lore.

For years, Steve Mullin's fantastic bull – the second-largest non-typical ever taken in the state of Idaho – sat low in the records book, scored as a typical. No category existed back then for elk with non-typical antlers. When such a category was established, Steve's bull eventually became not only one of the biggest non-typical elk ever taken in Idaho, but also the Pope & Young Club's World's Record (the largest bull ever taken with bow and arrow). Its standing has since been surpassed, but its significance has not. Steve's bull is truly a rare occurrence.

Fred S. Scott
403-7/8 B&C Non-typical
Shoshone County, 1964
Owned by Hollinger & Howard

Idaho Non-typical Rank: 3 *Length of Abnormal Points: 49-5/8* *Points (R,L): 8,9*
Inside Spread: 32-4/8 *Widest Spread: 43-5/8*
Main Beams (R,L): 46-5/8, 52-0/8 *Bases (R, L): 10-3/8, 10-6/8*

I was up at 4 a.m., out of habit from work. My first task of the day was trying to decide whether I should go hunting or just stay home. I had injured my left hand in an accident at the silver mine, and I couldn't go to work yet because of danger of infection. It wasn't a hard decision; I decided to hunt elk. Now, I just had to gather my gear. I quickly grabbed all that I thought I might need for the day and headed out the door.

As I drove north out of Wallace, my destination on this beautiful fall morning was Sunset Peak. From there, I would take the trail out along the beautiful high alpine ridge to Pony Peak. Pony Gulch, whose headwaters are right up under the west side of Pony Peak, is a great place to hunt elk. There is plentiful water, feed, and bedding cover, which all makes for wonderful elk habitat.

My arrival at Sunset Peak left me plenty of time to await the sunrise. I sat there in the dark with the wind rocking my truck, as the cold night wind blasted gusts across the open peak.

Like all hunters who lust after big antlers, I sat there visualizing a great royal bull elk. This wasn't all fantasy, though, because the area where I would be hunting held such a bull. This bull was so big and old that he appeared almost white in color, especially when glassing him from across a canyon, which was how most hunters had seen him. He was well known in our area; everyone referred to this legendary bull as "The White Bull." He had eluded hunters from our local fraternity for many years now. Maybe today would be the day, and I would be the lucky one to harvest that big old "White Bull."

The cold was starting to creep into the truck cab, which brought me out of my daydreaming. It wasn't long and I was down the steep part of the trail off the peak. I had sped up into a jogging trot out along the flat ridge, trying to work some warmth into my chilled body.

Just then, a screaming bugle just off the ridge top to my left stopped me dead. My heart was right up in my throat; it had about scared me out of my wits. I knew he had to be close, because I heard him clearly even with my hearing impairment. I cupped my hand over my mouth and gave a short squeal from deep in my throat, trying to sound like a smaller bull elk.

I wasn't prepared for what happened next. Up onto the ridge top came a bull elk that could have been a cross with a caribou. His antlers were massive, with lots of points, and had points going in all directions.

This bull was mad as hell; his hair was standing the wrong way, slobber drooled down the corners of his mouth, his eyes were on fire, and he was going to whip somebody. Was this the White Bull? No! This bull was bigger! A lot bigger than you could imagine.

The bull didn't see me as he charged up onto the ridgetop only fifty yards away, standing perfectly broadside. I dropped on my butt in the middle of the trail, trying to swallow my heart down to where it wouldn't choke me to death. I could feel every beat, in my throat and in my ears. I just knew that anytime now, that bull would hear my heart thumping away inside my chest.

As I watched the bull walking across the open ridge in front of me, unconcerned and unaware, I was finally coming out of my stupor. Advice my dad had given me years before entered my thoughts. *Concentrate on where you want to hit, and forget about the rack.*

I raised my rifle and squeezed off a shot. The bull lunged forward, raking his antlers through a small evergreen tree on the ridge top. The tree exploded into a shower of branches and other miscellaneous debris. I shot again, and the bull lunged ahead, hooking at his shadow, and then turned directly away. I shot for his neck, and then the bull was out of sight – gone, like a poof of dust. I couldn't believe it. The bull of a lifetime had walked out of sight. He had been only fifty yards away. How could I have missed him?

I hurried over to the track, and quickly found droplets of blood in the frosted grass. I decided to back off and give the bull and myself an hour to settle down. At that point, I had a renewed hope, and also an increased sense of worry and anticipation.

This wasn't going to be easy. My bull had escaped onto a north slope that was a jungle of second-growth hemlock timber, with an understory of huckleberry and alder that you could barely crawl through.

After an hour, with the wind now in my favor, I started out on the bull's trail. Several times I lost the trail, flagged the spot, and then continued to circle until I found it again. I spent hours following that bull. He had to be hurt pretty bad because I kept jumping him. He wasn't traveling far, as the whole chase hadn't covered half a mile.

Finally, I spotted an antler tine sticking up above the brush 25 yards away. Right about then I asked for some help from above, as I believe He is the only one who regulates who kills whom, when, and why. I moved ahead very cautiously, watching for the opening that would end the drama. I finally had a shot and took it, only to see a piece of antler fly off. I readjusted my aim and managed to bring him to possession.

After it was over, I fell apart. My hands shook, my legs wobbled, and I broke out in a sweat. I smoked a cigarette as I examined this great bull elk. My .270 had done the job, but my first two hits had been too low in the brisket. The bull's antlers were truly out of this world. He was certainly one of a kind, with bases that seemed like bighorn sheep bases, and several points over 20" long.

It was starting to get sunny, so I had to get to work. I cleared away quite an area of brush, and tried to flatten my work area. In no time, I had the quarters hanging in a tree.

Now it was a 2000-foot climb back to the truck. I made that as quickly as possible, grabbed a beer, and headed to town to fetch some pack stock.

Back at the ranch, I found that the horse herd had been badly picked over. Evidently, I wasn't the only one who had been successful that day. I was stuck with two rank geldings to pack my elk. It was time for their crash course on elk packing.

After loading the horses and gear, I pulled into town to get help. After a quick and frenzied search, I ended up with my brother Don and a friend named Frank. We made good time back to the elk.

After we arrived clear back at the elk with the stock, we had to employ every trick in the book to get the quarters onto those horses. We tied each horse to a stout tree, blindfolded them, rubbed fresh blood on their noses, and tied up their hind feet. It was only then that we were able to load the quarters. Now believe me when I tell you that you had better get it right the first time! If you have to do it a second time, you can bet you are going to be in for one heck of a wrestling match, not to mention picking up all the scattered pieces.

Don and I led the stock, while poor Frank got stuck packing those antlers. Two long hours later, we staggered up onto the peak, just as the western horizon turned crimson and the wind began to start up again. We were a group of three very tired cowboys and two semi-educated packhorses.

Back in town, that set of antlers gathered quite a crowd wherever we stopped. Believe me when I tell you we made lots of stops to show off that trophy rack. I must have puffed up something terrible, because every time the story was repeated, the elk got bigger and further away, until I could hardly believe it myself!

Originally, when we took it to get scored, it didn't even make the minimum score for entry into the records books, because the Boone and Crockett Club didn't have a non-typical elk category. Finally, in 1987, when they created the category, my trophy became eligible. It was invited to the 20th Awards Program Judges' Panel, where it received its final score of 403-7/8.

The only thing I can guarantee you is that my bull elk will never be duplicated. He is and will always be "one of a kind." I can only hope that people enjoy reading this story as much as I have enjoyed reminiscing and writing it. I know that I will never harvest a bigger or more special bull than this one. Good luck, and goodbye.

Fred Scott's big 1964 Shoshone County bull tends to leave a person speechless. This bull has as much character and uniqueness as any bull that has ever existed. He is easily the most identifiable and recognizable bull of any bull in recorded history.

Fred Scott displays his trophy bull elk from Idaho's 1964 hunting season.

Unknown
402-4/8 B&C Non-typical
Selway, Prior to 1960
Owned by Cabela's

Idaho Non-typical Rank: 4   *Length of Abnormal Points: 28-2/8*   *Points (R,L): 7,11*
Inside Spread: 47-2/8   *Widest Spread: 52-2/8*
Main Beams (R,L): 53-1/8, 49-4/8   *Bases (R, L): 8-4/8, 8-5/8*

This great bull is currently without much of a history. Sometime in the 1950s, this massive elk rack was brought in to Barry's Taxidermy in Pocatello. William J. Barry owned and operated the business. Astonishingly enough, the man had brought the antlers in not to get mounted but merely to accompany the hide, which the hunter wanted tanned. Unfortunately, the man never returned to claim his goods. All that Mr. Barry could remember was that the man had said the bull was taken in the Selway region.

This gorgeous bull is the fourth-largest non-typical elk in Idaho history. Sadly, the lucky hunter may never be known.

Ernest Paskett
400-5/8 B&C Non-typical
Fremont County, 1964

Idaho Non-typical Rank: 5   Length of Abnormal Points: 18-5/8   Points (R,L): 8,7
Inside Spread: 44-0/8   Widest Spread: 53-0/8
Main Beams (R,L): 52-5/8, 51-3/8   Bases (R, L): 9-4/8, 10-1/8

In 1964, Ernest Paskett was working for the National Guard near Idaho Falls. It was fall, and someone in his group suggested a hunting trip. It didn't take much prodding to get an eager Ernest to go along.

He and five other men left early the next morning from Idaho Falls and headed north into a cold but snowless country, arriving at their chosen location around 8 a.m. It was just east of Mesa Falls and near the highway.

Ernest was concentrating on an area between the highway and the railroad. He was following an old wood road on that overcast day and packing his Remington model 721 .30-06. He recalls it was near an old railroad stop called Eccles.

Now, since most hunters ever faced with this particular situation prefer to call it temporarily misplaced, we don't want to even imply that Ernest didn't know where he was. After all, he was right there. Everyone else's location though, at that point, was undetermined.

Ernest was just sort of starting to wonder what had become of the rest of the world when he walked into a clearing. The only thing he had seen move up until this point was his frosted breath as it dissipated into colder, relenting air. But as Ernest peered into the meadow, there before him was the most immense and awe-inspiring animal he had ever seen. It was a magnificent, long-tined bull elk, and it was running right toward him. Ernest figures it must have been spooked by another hunter, as it was covering real estate at an alarming rate.

Just then, the bull looked up and saw Ernest. Almost like in a cartoon, the bull came to a screeching halt, plowing dirt as he slowed. The longest one-second stare down in history ensued as two brains raced in thought. The bull then took off just as Ernest raised his rifle and fired. The .30-06 barked and, very shortly thereafter, a bullet connected with the bull's massive chest. The bull turned away and a second shot followed, dropping the bull by a big log. Ernest walked up, expecting the bull to be dead. Instead, the mortally wounded bull whipped his head around, nearly scaring Ernest half to death. One additional shot put the bull to sleep for good.

Shortly after the shots, the hunter that had spooked the bull came into the clearing. He yelled over to Ernest, "Did you see that big bull?"

"Yep. I shot him." Ernest replied.

As they looked over the great elk, Ernest offered meekly, "Do you happen to know which direction it is to the highway?"

The other hunter pointed and replied, "It's right there."

Ernest looked over. Not two seconds later, he watched as a little blue car drove right by them! No one probably needs to go into how smart Ernest was feeling right about then.

The happy hunter walked back and got the pickup, which they were able to drive right to the bull. They loaded him whole, using rope to move the bull about an inch at a time.

Ernest, then as now, feels very fortunate to have taken such a beautiful animal. And so goes the story of the first and only bull elk Ernest Paskett ever killed.

Unknown
398-3/8 B&C Non-typical
Adams County, 1955

Idaho Non-typical Rank: 7   *Length of Abnormal Points: 40-1/8*   *Points (R,L): 8,9*
Inside Spread: 37-6/8   *Widest Spread: 44-0/8*
Main Beams (R,L): 52-2/8, 51-3/8   *Bases (R, L): 8-7/8, 9-3/8*

Not a lot is known about the circumstances that led to this bull's demise. For years, it hung on the front of an old sporting goods store in Council. Around 1960, it went out of business. Delvin Watkins, a local resident, asked if he could have the antlers. Delvin is quite the pack rat, and his request was granted.

It is currently not certain who the hunter was. Delvin seems to recall the owner of the sporting goods store telling him that a man named Wes Knee had taken the bull in October of 1955. He also went on to say that the bull had been taken in the Tamarack area. Another person believes it may have been taken by Buzz Shelton.

The antlers show a lot of cracking and bleaching from being weathered, but that takes nothing away from the character of this massive rack. The back half of the rack has some of the most massive tines of any bull ever taken, as well as some uniquely matched abnormal points coming off of the G-5s.

A few different angles of one of Idaho's biggest and most massive elk racks.

James E. Hoover
395-5/8 B&C Non-typical
Fremont County, 1976

Idaho Non-typical Rank: 8   *Length of Abnormal Points: 10-4/8*   *Points (R,L): 7,10*
Inside Spread: 44-7/8   *Widest Spread: 50-4/8*
Main Beams (R,L): 49-5/8, 48-0/8   *Bases (R, L): 9-2/8, 9-1/8*

As is too often the case, details are scarce on this big bull. James Hoover killed the bull in 1976 with his .270 in Fremont County. It hung in a taxidermy shop for over 25 years before it was sold, and most information has slipped away with time.

The following is all that could be found, and was reprinted with permission from Roger Selner, of *Trophy Show Productions*, who had it on one of his elk tours.

> *James Hoover hunted elk solely for meat. The antlers had no significant importance to him, other than a larger rack meant more meat. The outing in the mountains, seeing wildlife, and the experience with family and friends held the true meaning of the hunt. His favorite type of hunting was a horse pack trip into the mountains complete with tent camp.*

Hugh M. Kitzmiller
393-3/8 B&C Non-typical
Shoshone County, 1974

Idaho Non-typical Rank: 9 *Length of Abnormal Points: 106-5/8* *Points (R,L): 8,7*
Inside Spread: 41-2/8 *Widest Spread: 70-1/8*
Main Beams (R,L): 50-2/8, 48-4/8 *Bases (R, L): 9-5/8, 10-1/8*

Hugh Kitzmiller lived in the Post Falls area in the mid-1970s, working as a forester in the thick timber of northern Idaho for many years. In the summer of 1974, while doing some timber work, he spotted a huge bull elk from a helicopter. Hugh needed no prodding to go after the bull come hunting season; it was the biggest and strangest thing he had ever seen!

The exact circumstances of how the hunt unfolded are not known. Hugh took those secrets to the grave with him only a few years after he downed the big bull. He was the unfortunate victim of a helicopter crash in the late 1970s.

There are a few general details that family could recall, though. Once the season opened, Hugh drove up the mountain in his 1968 Ford pickup and headed into the vicinity of the Coeur d' Alene River near Pritchard. He was packing his .308 Winchester Model 100 semi-auto, chasing the bull he had been dreaming about. When hunter and hunted finally met, at about 75 yards, Hugh watched the bull materialize right out of the mist, giving him an image he would never forget, and the only opportunity he would ever need. He made good on the shot, and as he approached his quarry, there is little doubt he was overjoyed.

Hugh Kitzmiller's gigantic bull is unique for many reasons. First, it's one of only three bull elk ever recorded by the B&C to surpass 70" in width. Second, his antler formation is very bizarre, with long split main beams on both sides. This, coupled with double droptines off of both G-3s, gives this bull a breathtaking and jaw-dropping appearance. Third, this bull's left brow tine was almost completely broken off. Assuming it would have been similar in size to the right brow tine, this bull would have scored approximately 424 B&C, and would quite likely have been the second-largest bull ever recorded in Idaho. This lasting tribute to Hugh is, without a doubt, one of the most fantastic animals ever taken in North America.

It is also interesting to note that the two wildest sets of record book antlers, Kitzmiller's and Fred Scott's, were both taken within a short distance of one another. Whether it represents a genetic anomaly or some other undefined source is uncertain.

Robert Kitzmiller poses with his Uncle Hugh's tremendous bull. The two matched bulbous double-droptines are a rare circumstance, indeed.

Another view of one of the wildest bulls in North America.

Johnny Bliznak
393-2/8 B&C Non-typical
Idaho County, 1990

Idaho Non-typical Rank: 10   Length of Abnormal Points: 17-0/8   Points (R,L): 8,7
Inside Spread: 36-2/8
Widest Spread: 44-4/8
Main Beams (R,L): 50-1/8, 50-3/8
Bases (R, L): 11-5/8, 11-1/8

"*Elk!*" Someone had yelled the word I had been waiting for. I certainly wouldn't have recognized that stammering voice, which was one octave higher and 30 decibels louder than mine, as my own. There I was, though, stuttering and stammering, trying to tell my guide I had spotted an elk.

I was glassing a ridge over a thousand yards away, and he was spotting a ridge two miles away. There were two elk. The first looked as though he had pipes growing out of his head; the other was feeding next to him and was a magnificent six-point - two old bachelor bulls this October 30, 1990, feeding all by themselves, totally unaware of our presence at this hour of 7:45 a.m. "Let's go get 'em!"

We had about a mile and a half to go to sidehill around the bowl-shaped mountainside to get to their ridge. The wind was with us, and we had a chance to get to them if we hurried.

Jerry Jeppson, from Challis, was my guide and outfitter. At the time, he owned Mile-Hi Outfitters, with his base camp located in the Frank Church Wilderness. I had known Jerry for years, but this was my first time hunting with him.

After the 15-minute flight from Challis to the backcountry airstrip, Jerry met Troy McDaniel and I with a wagon and draft horses. After the gear was loaded in the wagon, we rode a mile over a dirt path through the timber to base camp. While Troy and I were eating lunch, Jerry and the guides and wrangler packed and loaded our gear for our 4-½-hour horse ride to Crescent Meadows hunting camp.

Troy and his guide and cook stayed at Crescent Meadows while Jerry, the wrangler, Darrel Kester, and myself packed up and headed another 4-½ hours into the wilderness to a remote camp at 8000 feet. At this camp, there was a 14x20 tent that served as both a cooking and sleeping tent. We arrived there the evening of October 29th. After getting the tent and gear in order, we had dinner and went to bed.

After a restless night in our sleeping bags, we awoke and had bacon, eggs, toast, and coffee. The three of us left camp before daylight and headed into the darkness, barely able to see our hands in front of our faces. We rode into the timber, tied off our horses, and started walking to a ridge Jerry wanted to glass. After 30-45 minutes of glassing, we spotted the bull.

Jerry and I started out at a fast walk. The country was relatively open with some trees, downfall, ravines, rocks, and other sundry things to fall into or trip over. I was very careful not to trip or bump into anything. I climbed over and under downed trees, navigated boulders, and crawled through brush. I knew this was the stalk of a lifetime, as the bull we had seen had seven or eight points per side.

While trying to be careful, I also hurried like never before. It was all I could do to keep up, but I pushed myself, knowing that we wouldn't have any time to spare. Ten minutes after we began, we were halfway there. I still hadn't slipped, and the wind was still in our favor, but I was barely able to keep up with Jerry.

Once we started, I never saw the elk again during the stalk, as they were behind the far ridge. To keep up with Jerry, I had to break into a slow trot occasionally, but the vivid picture of that magnificent bull drove me on in spite of the pain in my legs and my burning lungs.

As we approached the ridge where we had last seen the elk, we slowed down. Jerry took my coat, as it was noisy, cumbersome, and hot. We inched our way down the ridge from above to stay with the wind, and then looked where we thought the elk would be. *Oh, no! They weren't there!* I had a sick feeling in the pit of my stomach, and without anything better to do, I sat down, feeling mighty blue.

Jerry said that he had caught a glimpse of them when we were near the end of the stalk, and that they were feeding off to our left. He excused himself and said he would look for them. He returned shortly with a wild look in his eyes, and I knew that luck was still with us. Sure enough, off to our left I could see one bull feeding in the timber between stands of trees. He was 250 yards downhill to our left.

Shooting right-handed from a sitting position with my elbows on my knees was perfect for this situation. When I looked through the scope and could tell that my shooting position would allow me to hold very steady, I figured I had him. I shot once with my .300 Win.-mag. and could hear the whack of the bullet on elk hide. I reloaded and shot twice more before he fell and then slid down the mountain.

As I watched, everything was in slow motion. It seemed as if I was in a dream. We walked, slid, and stumbled down the mountain in our excitement. About 75 yards from him, when he was in plain sight, Jerry and I stopped, rested, and savored the moment. I looked at him through my binoculars and could hardly believe the mass. Only in pictures had I seen an animal like this.

After field-dressing, skinning, and quartering the animal, we packed the hide and antlers out from the bottom of the canyon. It took us five hours of hard climbing to get out of there. Pack animals were used later to bring out the quarters. Subsequently, Troy shot a nice 5x5 bull to complete the hunt.

When I think back on the hunt, I always figure I must still be dreaming. To take a trophy of this size is still overwhelming.

Courtesy of Johnny Bliznak

Gordon F. Larson
390-6/8 B&C Non-typical
Clearwater County, 1973

Idaho Non-typical Rank: 11 *Length of Abnormal Points: 10-2/8* *Points (R,L): 6,7*
Inside Spread: 41-6/8 *Widest Spread: 46-2/8*
Main Beams (R,L): 48-6/8, 49-6/8 *Bases (R, L): 8-6/8, 8-5/8*

Gordon Larson is just the type of older hunter you love to listen to when he tells a story. He tells it with no nonsense, just the way it happened, and with plenty of color. Just as he should be, he is very proud of his big bull he took in 1973, which has a proper place on his wall so he can retrace those steps daily.

He started hunting in the Clearwater drainage back in 1957, and by 1973 knew it quite well. He and hunting partner John Simpson were at it again that fall, hoping for another winter's meat supply.

Going into their last day, Gordon had still not punched his tag. That morning was nice and cool, but still with no snow. It was still early when he caught an undeniable odor. It was a rank, old, musky elk. Gordon continued slowly down the trail, much more carefully now. Soon, he saw a movement. To his amazement, the most massive bull elk he had ever laid eyes on stood up from his bed, only fifty yards away and right on the trail!

Gordon had little time to do anything but act, so he leveled his .30-06 and pulled the trigger as soon as he found the scope full of hair. The big bull swept the air with his stunning rack as he turned and went crashing down the hill and out of sight.

Gordon couldn't tell whether he had hit the bull well or not, so rather than risk moving in and spooking the bull, he sat down to have a cigarette and wait. Time has never before nor since gone by as slowly as it did for Gordon in those few minutes.

Eventually, he followed the blood trail and found his bull piled up dead. He was so excited he threw his hat up into the air, and with such vigor that he never was able to find it again!

The packout was nearly 2-1/2 miles, and tested their resolve, to be sure. They took a total of three trips each, using their old packboards. In addition, Gordon made one more trip to get the hide for John, who wanted to take it home.

As of this writing, Gordon has been hunting that area for fifty years. At 75, he doesn't appear to have much thought of slowing down. As we ended our conversation, Gordon stated, "I'm 75 and still hunting hard; gonna get one this year, too!"

We hope you do, Gordon. We hope you do.

Gordon Larson proudly shows his trophy elk from 1973. This is a great photo. It also shows the difference between a small to medium six-point and the behemoth bull he was fortunate enough to take.

Robert F. Hughes
390-2/8 B&C Non-typical
Adams County, 1995

Idaho Non-typical Rank: 12 *Length of Abnormal Points: 55-0/8* *Points (R,L): 10,11*
Inside Spread: 38-2/8 *Widest Spread: 55-1/8*
Main Beams (R,L): 46-4/8, 49-0/8 *Bases (R, L): 8-3/8, 8-1/8*

Their hunt began long before daylight in Boise. Robert Hughes, his dad Doc, and uncle Jesse Palmertree got up halfway through the night for the long drive from Boise and into the mountains to the north. Eventually they got on an old four-wheel-drive road and wound their way toward the top of a mountain.

Already tired, their reception was not very welcoming. They opened the doors to cold and nasty weather. On the bright side, there was new snow on the ground.

They walked out about a mile and a half to the trail's end, and then discussed who would go where. Robert walked out to a vantage point and sat, hoping hunters from below might push something his way. The draw he watched had average relief, and was full of buckbrush and mixed high-elevation conifers.

Two hours later, the weather was making a turn for the worse. A light snow was falling, and it was increasingly gray in all directions. Robert liked the feeling, though. It was that feeling you get when you know you are in wild country, far removed from today's reality. A bit of potential adventure with the weather, but that just made it all the more exciting. He couldn't think of a better place to be.

It was after two hours of patiently sitting that he heard a noise. He swung to the sound and saw a view full of antlers but could make out no body to accompany them. The bull had likely been pushed by hunters but was not looking overly alarmed, instead content to plod along at a steady pace.

The impact of a bullet into his vitals from Robert's M77 Ruger .30-06 was the first hint the bull had that he was not alone. The bull hesitated, started walking a bit toward Robert, and then fell to the ground. Robert had made a perfect shot in a sitting position from about 75 yards away.

Robert took a few minutes to admire a trophy the likes of which he had never even imagined, and then got a quick reality check by another good gust of wind. It was time to get out of there. He did a quick field-dress job and decided it would probably be best to retrieve the bull in the morning.

The next morning, they found Robert's elk despite the blanket of snow that had threatened to cover him up. A few trips later, Robert's big bull was reduced to possession, and maybe a bit of admiration.

Several angles are needed on this crazy bull just to see all the abnormal points.

Robert Hughes (left) and his father, Doc, pose for a memory neither of them will ever forget. Robert's bull is one of the most unique and non-typical bulls to ever come from southern Idaho.

Roger R. Davis
388-6/8 B&C Non-typical
Shoshone County, 1978
Owned by Aly M. Bruner

Idaho Non-typical Rank: 13   *Length of Abnormal Points: 15-0/8*   *Points (R,L): 7,7*
Inside Spread: 45-0/8   *Widest Spread: 51-4/8*
Main Beams (R,L): 50-5/8, 48-1/8   *Bases (R, L): 8-6/8, 8-1/8*

"You don't succeed without your heart, mind, and soul in it. Stalking, watching, spotting- all seasons." ~ Roger Davis

Not many people take hunting more seriously than Roger Davis; it wouldn't be fair to call it an obsession, but perhaps more aptly a way of life. And if you had ever seen his trophy room a few years back, you'd understand why. Roger has the second-largest non-typical Idaho elk taken with a bow, the state record typical mule deer taken with a muzzleloader, a Boone & Crockett whitetail, and a trophy room that would make rich men whimper. Only Roger isn't a rich man – he just hunted hard and hunted smart. Roger is one of those rare hunters who has the utmost respect for the game, the hunt, the heritage, and the lifestyle.

Before his body was worn too thin, he followed game in spring, summer, fall, and winter. Roger hunted every available season, with every available weapon. He left no tools unused, which leaves no surprise that he was trying treestands for elk hunting clear back in the 1970s.

He was in a treestand on September 27th, 1978 - the day that this monster bull came by. For most people today, putting a treestand up is little more than picking a spot with a slightly educated guess and hoping for the best, but not Roger. He put it right where it should go with knowledge that it would likely be successful.

The day Roger killed his biggest of many big bulls, he had ridden a horse to just short of his stand. He tied the horse up over the hill so that it couldn't scent the elk and spook or whinny, grabbed his Oneida Eagle bow, and set up. He took his position on his stand, which looked over a frequently used crossing. Did I mention that he also has the patience of a mountain lion?

He was at roughly 5200' elevation, plus however far he was up the tree. He had been in the stand a while when he saw his prize coming down the trail from 100 yards away. When the bull got to 20 yards, Roger let the arrow fly, and it struck solidly behind the shoulder.

An hour later, Roger left his treestand and recovered his winter's meat. When I asked Roger how he got his elk out, he replied, "I didn't have his hide tanned!"

His horse would earn its keep that day, packing out an animal in quarters that would have given it a run, pound for pound. For Roger, it was just another day's success on another fine and well-earned trophy. For us, it is a piece of history. Men of Roger's intuition and knowledge are a dying breed.

Roger Davis' trophy room from years ago. Roger has probably taken more world-class bull elk in a general season than anyone. Time in the field makes all the difference. Many of these great bulls were taken only a few miles from his house. A couple more of these bulls might be big enough for the records book, if ever measured. Roger's biggest bull can be seen at The Shooting Gallery in Challis, Idaho.

Daniel R. McClure
386-2/8 B&C Non-typical
Idaho County, 2005

Idaho Non-typical Rank: 14   *Length of Abnormal Points: 16-0/8*   *Points (R,L): 8,9*
Inside Spread: 35-6/8   *Widest Spread: 42-5/8*
Main Beams (R,L): 47-4/8, 47-7/8   *Bases (R, L): 9-6/8, 10-6/8*

As usual, we were up at 4:30 a.m. for coffee and to talk about the day's hunt. My brother Mike and I decided to go down to the knob where he and another brother Bob had seen a bull with some cows the evening before. The previous weekend, Mike had taken a bull down in the same area that we were heading to for today's hunt. After packing our daypacks we headed out, as it would take us about an hour and a half to get to where we wanted to be by daylight.

Getting closer to our destination, we stopped at the top of the switchbacks and listened. Sure enough, right down where they are supposed to be we could hear a bull all fired up. Other bulls were responding as well. Mike and I looked at each other. I knew he was smiling as big as I was, even though I couldn't see because we still had a half-hour before daylight. Bulls were bugling from both drainages, and the party was on. We slipped on down the trail, stopping and listening often. Those bulls were really getting after it!

I picked a spot and set up as Mike started out with some cow calling. We got a response almost immediately, with the bull giving out a big bugle. I decided to close the gap since the bull didn't seem to want to come to me. I felt sure I knew where he was going with his cows, because we've played this game in years past.

We moved around the knob to where the herd was in the saddle. At that point, I stopped and gave Mike the signal that I would set up just ahead. He gave me a few minutes and started cow calling. The bull answered right back, followed by two other bulls answering as well. Cows started appearing, and then the bull bugled. Mike threw a few more cow calls at him, hoping to steer him our way. It worked.

Past the cows I saw him coming, not seeing his antlers at first. He stopped, bugled again, and then came straight for me. At 40 yards, I could finally see what a heavy-horned mature bull he was. He quartered up toward me and stopped a measly 18 yards away. The bad news was I had no shot. Mike called to try to reposition him for me, and the bull responded by groaning. Every time he would call, all of the other bulls would, too. It was like they were in a bugling competition.

Then the bull must have decided he'd had enough. He turned and angled back the same way he came in. Just as he started to clear two small pine trees, I drew back and gave a chirp on my cow call. He stopped dead in his tracks and looked back right at me as I released the arrow.

I'm not sure what happened, but it wasn't good. The carbon arrow I was shooting just sort of "exploded" out of my bow. When it left my bow, it was to a different noise, and the last six inches of feather and nock was only six feet out in front of me. I had no idea where the rest of the arrow ended up. Of course this upset the elk, and he promptly gathered his cows and started into the thick north.

I walked back to where Mike could see and waved him over to me. We talked about what happened, and spent the next two hours making sure I didn't hit him.

The bull only took his cows a couple hundred yards into the thick stuff but it was like a fortress. To add insult to injury, he continued to bugle. We have gone into this thick stuff before chasing elk, but have never had any luck because of the thickness and the downfall - just too noisy.

We stopped for a bite to eat and just sat and listened for a while. The drainage was still full of talking elk. It's just one of those days that you dream about but are few and far between; but it's days like that that make us true elk junkies.

After we were totally convinced that my arrow did no damage, we made our next plan. We headed back up to the knob and dove down into the drainage where we had heard some bulls earlier. In no time, we were in elk again. One bull, on our hillside, was very active so we set up. It took him no time at all to close the gap, but he was just too nervous to come out into the opening the last 30 yards.

After some cow calling, Mike finally brought him out. A nice 6x6 stepped out 30 yards above me, headed in Mike's direction. As he gave me a broadside shot, I drew my bow. He caught my movement and turned straight away from me looking back over his shoulder at me. Two seconds later, he was headed right back from where he came. What a beautiful animal!

There were still bulls below us and across the creek that were screaming. No matter which way we wanted to go, it seemed as if elk would be there. Dropping down another 100 yards, we started to get a good look at the hillside across the creek. We found a spot and watched as elk started to appear. There was a bull screaming over there and another groaner up the creek. Then some other bulls bugled. Then Mike said, "There he is!"

I looked and saw a bull running across the hillside heading down the drainage. He was a heavy-horned bull with what looked like extra points. It was too far to see exactly what he was, even with my binoculars, but we knew one thing for sure; he was a monster!

He was both screaming and heading out at a fast pace, down the canyon a half-mile away and getting further every second. Mike bugled and I cow called, hoping to draw him back. Mike then spotted a bull across from us that was headed straight down the ridge to the creek bottom toward us. I dropped down the steep hillside to get set up as fast as I could.

After about fifteen minutes, I could hear the bull bugling, moving our way at a fast pace. Mike cow called above me about 60 yards or so. The bull was just out of sight below me, then around me, then by me, heading toward Mike. I tried to sneak up and get a look at him, but he was just out of view the entire time. The bull went past Mike, screaming.

Then another bull came in from the same direction that the first bull came from! I scrambled back down. The second bull came in just as fast as the first, and was getting around me like the other one had. I finally spotted him at 25 yards. Quickly, I pulled back, put my pin on him, and touched it off.

The elk took off, and when he got out of sight behind a big boulder, he let out a bugle! It all happened so fast; I must have hit one of the small trees because I heard a crack sound after I shot.

I nocked another arrow and waited, knowing he was headed straight for Mike and we would soon be busted. It seemed like forever and there was only deafening silence, except for other bulls in the canyon still fired up. We waited, but nothing happened. The bull should have exploded by now and made his way into the next drainage. What's going on?

I slowly made my way up to find my arrow. When I got to where I thought it should be, there was blood, and a lot of it! The broadhead took out a rib going into him, which was the cracking sound I had heard. I stood there for about ten minutes just listening. All was quiet.

Very slowly I made my way up toward Mike on the blood trail. I had never seen a blood trail like this one; he was pumping out a lot of blood with each step. Every one or two steps, I stopped and listened. I could hear Mike cow-calling, but couldn't see him.

I went another ten yards and Mike was really into a series of cow calling that was different. I looked up and finally spotted him, and he had the video camera in hand, frantically giving me the "hold up" sign. He then pointed just out ahead of me. I looked to where he was pointing and the bull stood up only ten yards away. He took a couple of steps and went back down. I froze.

We always make it a habit of waiting after a shot to give the animal time, and I was just making my way up to Mike to wait. Meanwhile, Mike was filming a big bull coming up the hill toward him, not knowing that this was the bull I had just shot. I still didn't know that this was the big bull that we had seen earlier across the canyon. As I walked around the tree that his head was behind, I couldn't believe my eyes. I just started shaking. The bull was an extremely heavy 7x8, with four "devil points" off his browtines.

With the bull to take care of, the work really began. I enjoy hunting with my family each year, and feel thankful to have a family that has grown together hunting and spending time doing the things that we love in the outdoors. I am truly blessed.

Richard L. Hansen
385-5/8 B&C Non-typical
Adams County, 1977

Idaho Non-typical Rank: 15   *Length of Abnormal Points:* 21-5/8   *Points (R,L):* 8,9
Inside Spread: 32-0/8   *Widest Spread:* 41-2/8
Main Beams (R,L): 47-7/8, 46-1/8   *Bases (R, L):* 9-5/8, 9-0/8

Richard Hansen moved to the New Meadows area in 1977 and wasted no time in starting to look for good elk hunting spots. The first year, he had little luck, finding not a single elk the entire season.

In 1977, only a season removed from being a draw-only elk hunt, Adams County was far from capacity for elk. Finding them could be downright tough, as a matter of fact. Richard was hard at it again, and this time found paydirt. He had spotted a giant of a bull only a few miles from town. A few attempts to reduce the bull to possession during bow season had been all but futile, but the short five-day rifle season was coming up, and he planned on giving it his all during that span.

Opening morning found him and Earl Myers at a different spot, apparently giving the big bull a fighting chance. After a short, unsuccessful hunt, they hopped into the pickup. Richard had decided he could no longer take it. He had to go after his big bull again. They sped down the road and made good time in getting back into the area he hoped his prized bull might be in.

He and Earl pulled off to the side of the road and eased to a stop. It wasn't exactly what they were hoping for on an opening day. Rain was pouring down hard, and suddenly neither man was chomping at the bit to part ways with the comfortable confines of the cab of the truck. That rain looked a lot nicer on the windshield than it did running down the back of their necks.

Eventually, they managed to get the doors open, however, splitting up to cover a favorite spot at about 1 p.m. Richard had walked only a few yards when he heard sloshing in a nearby creek. A quick check revealed it was just somebody's beef cow – or make it a bull.

He started off again, with the old Ford still in plain view a hundred yards distant, when he heard sloshing in the creek again. He looked over, with a predetermined view in mind, and felt an instant surge of adrenaline when he saw the source of the sound this time was a big bull elk! The bull had already parted ways with the creek and was quartering toward him. The bull had been covering some ground, that much was apparent, but he showed no signs of slowing down. He had obviously been spooked by another hunter, likely from quite a ways off.

Richard could see nothing but white-tipped, turned up browtines. He wasn't exactly long on time, so he raised his 7mm and pulled down on the front of the bull's chest and fired, connecting solidly. The bull hesitated but kept on. One more shot to the base of the neck and it was over.

Knowing they weren't going to get the bull into the truck by themselves, and not being too far from town, they went back and recruited help, in the form of six men.

Once loaded and on the way back, the pickup ran out of gas. As such, Richard had to leave his big bull in the back of the truck with Earl while he caught a ride to town. When he returned a half-hour later, he says the traffic was backed up a good quarter-mile with people rubbernecking to get a look at that big bull.

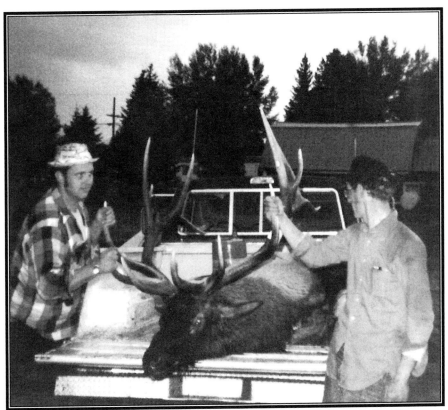

Earl Myers (left) and Richard Hansen show off Richard's huge bull. The rump of the elk is against the cab, and they weren't even close to being able to close the tailgate on Richard's full-size pickup. The body is so big, it actually makes the antlers look small. The next photo with Richard holding the rack should help put it back in perspective.

Look at the mass on that bull! Richard Hansen struggles to hold up well over thirty pounds of elk antler.

James A. Carpenter
385-1/8 B&C Non-typical
Latah County, 1985

Idaho Non-typical Rank: 16 *Length of Abnormal Points: 24-5/8* *Points (R,L): 9,8*
Inside Spread: 40-4/8 *Widest Spread: 51 2/8*
Main Beams (R,L): 50-5/8, 48-6/8 *Bases (R, L): 7-5/8, 7-4/8*

Somewhere along the line, hunting became unfair. Sixteen-year olds aren't supposed to kill 385-inch elk, especially for their first trophy. They're supposed to start with cows, then spikes, then raghorns. Then, at the culmination of their hunting career after 40 years of pain and suffering, they are supposed to be rewarded for all their efforts with 385-inch elk. But, as Clint Eastwood said in *Unforgiven*, "Deserve's got nothin' to do with it." No one informed James Carpenter of that rule, either.

The morning of October 2nd, 1985, James, along with his dad Ira or "Ike", his brother Glenn, and cousins Chuck Hatchel and Larry Smith, headed up on Highway 6 for a family elk hunt. It was a spot they had been scouting and had seen elk in.

They split up before dawn, with James and Chuck heading a similar direction. Chuck gave a bugle and was quickly answered. James motioned that he would go down into the draw while Chuck stayed on the ridge. They moved in on him together, but after a few hundred yards, they still couldn't see anything.

They met back up and discussed what to do. Chuck then went into the draw to bugle, with an agreement that if they heard the bull bugle, they would both charge him; they would run for ten full seconds and then stop.

When the bull obliged them, James ran for the allotted time and stopped. He looked up and was stunned to see the top of a big elk rack swaying back and forth as the bull moved crossways to him at 60 yards. The bull cut that distance in half, and then stopped.

James' view was very interesting. There was a fallen log in between them, and James' best shot was in a gap right in between the log and the ground! All he could see was the neck when he fired his .308 Winchester.

At the sound, the bull reared up and flipped over backward into the brush. The rack became hung up in the brush, even though the ground was very steep. The ineffective but intense flailing as the bull attempted to regain his footing had the bull throwing dirt over 50 feet. The bull kept scrambling, with his head sideways and on his side, kicking and kicking.

"I got him!" Chuck yelled. "I'll finish him!"

"No! No! Don't break the horns!"

"I won't," Chuck replied, and then shot the bull in the back of the neck.

Extra shots were needed to finally put the resilient bull to rest, and then they set out to get him back to the truck. That would require seven tough loads and quite a few sore backs.

Perhaps the most valiant effort of the day was that of James' young brother Glenn. He had to pack the liver and heart in the back of a big Filson coat. The bottom-heavy load whacked him in the back of the knees with every step. "I count that as a trip," James says proudly of his little brother's efforts.

A proud James Carpenter and an even prouder dad, Ike, take a minute to preserve some history. James was only sixteen when he brought down this bull.

The Carpenter clan takes a well-deserved break from packing. On the right is young Glenn Carpenter, with his heavy load in the back of that Filson coat.

Tim Papineau
385-1/8 B&C Non-typical
Clearwater County, 1996

Idaho Non-typical Rank: 16 *Length of Abnormal Points: 23-4/8* *Points (R,L): 7,7*
Inside Spread: 36-1/8 *Widest Spread: 44-0/8*
Main Beams (R,L): 48-7/8, 50-0/8 *Bases (R, L): 8-6/8, 8-0/8*

Tim Papineau had been chasing a herd of elk in the Elk River area throughout most of the archery season but could never get the break he was hoping for. In amongst the herd was a nice 6x7 bull that he would have loved to have arrowed, but thus far it hadn't been in the cards.

On opening afternoon of the rifle season, he found them again, but let them be. He decided the next morning might present a better opportunity, and more time, to move in on them.

The next morning, Tim and his son Chris headed in with high hopes. They covered the first two miles on an ATV, and then parked to walk the rest of the way, so as not to spook them.

They had gone all of 100 yards, and were making their way through thick, 30-foot saplings, when they jumped a herd of elk. They heard a bull grunt, but it was much too thick to hope for a shot. Shortly thereafter, the elk vanished.

Father and son continued on for half a mile when, at about 7:30 a.m., Tim looked down and nearly dropped his jaw on the ground. There in the creek bottom stood a monstrous bull that Tim had never seen before! It would easily dwarf the 6x7 he was after.

Tim quickly tried to get Chris to see it, but Chris didn't have a good view. Tim was torn, but knew if a shot wasn't fired quick, the bull would be gone; it was already starting to walk away. Tim quickly pulled up his rifle and took a 200-yard, steep downhill shot. Tricky downhill ballistics got the best of him, however, and the shot sailed high over the bull's back.

It was then that Tim caught his big break. Unbeknown to him, there was another group of hunters moving in on the bull, and were a mere 70 yards away from him! With the timber so thick, they never saw him. While the hunters were no threat to Tim, they had captured most of the bull's attention. As such, the bull was pinned, and instead of bailing, he froze.

That gave Tim all the time and experience he would need on the matter. He shot again, this second chance being more than sufficient. The bull took off on impact, with Tim and Chris following close behind.

As they got close, they split up, looking for sign. They could hear the bull moving through the brush ahead of them. It was then that Tim looked up and saw his quarry walking up toward an old logging road. Tim fired his aught-six once more, and miraculously anchored the bull right on the road!

Upon talking to the other hunters, Tim learned how truly lucky he was. Twice that day, the other party had had this great bull in their scopes, but just couldn't get a shot off in time. Oh, well. I'm sure Tim and Chris think it was for the best.

John Spratling
385 B&C Non-typical
Cassia County, 2001

Idaho Non-typical Rank: 18   *Length of Abnormal Points: 10-5/8*   *Points (R,L): 7,9*
Inside Spread: 47-5/8   *Widest Spread: 54-7/8*
Main Beams (R,L): 55-0/8, 56-4/8   *Bases (R, L): 8-7/8, 9-2/8*

Farming and hunting are often at opposing ends of the heartstrings, so for John Spratling, balancing hunting with his farming obligations was a juggling act. He had a landowner tag for unit 56 and had pushed it just about as hard as he could, but hadn't even seen an elk.

John was down to his last day. The season still had a couple more days, but this would be the last for him, as they were to take off for Disneyland in the morning. On that final and fateful day, he quit farming at 4:30 p.m. and headed up for a last-ditch effort and quick evening hunt. He didn't expect his luck to change, but that didn't stop him from trying anyway.

As was usual, he didn't see anything on this trek either. He decided to call it quits and head back to the truck. He made it back before it was even dark. He was putting his gear away when he decided he might as well make use of the last of the daylight, even if there wasn't any chance of seeing anything. He left most of his gear at the truck and headed back out to kill the last hour or so. He had nothing else to do.

To say that John wasn't expecting success would be an understatement. He had so little confidence in his last-minute stroll that he didn't even have a bullet in the chamber.

He was pushing a gully with tall sagebrush when jumped an elk not even 500 yards from his pickup! When he saw it, he knew instantly it was no ordinary elk. It was huge! The bull was motoring about 400 yards away when John took the first shot from his .30-06. His first shot hit in front of the bull. For his second shot, he led the bull by a good margin and managed to connect, albeit a bit far back. It didn't even seem to slow him down as he drifted out of sight.

John's adrenaline was up by now, and he followed with a brand new hope. He was still about half in shock that he had just had such an incredible opportunity, when he thought the hunt was over. The bull was slowing now, and John became more careful.

He had just walked out around some trees when he saw the heavy-horned bull 100 yards away. One shot behind the shoulder ended the uncertainty. As he walked up to his prize, he couldn't help but laugh inside. It wasn't the textbook way to get a big bull, but he wasn't about to argue the point.

John Spratling holds one of the biggest bulls to ever come from south-central Idaho.

Idaho's Greatest Typical Elk

BOONE AND CROCKETT CLUB®
OFFICIAL SCORING SYSTEM FOR NORTH AMERICAN BIG GAME TROPHIES

Records of North American Big Game
250 Station Drive
Missoula, MT 59801
(406) 542-1888

TYPICAL AMERICAN ELK (WAPITI)

MINIMUM SCORES
AWARDS 360
ALL-TIME 375

Detail of Point Measurement

Abnormal Points	
Right Antler	Left Antler

	SUBTOTALS	
	TOTAL TO E	

SEE OTHER SIDE FOR INSTRUCTIONS

		COLUMN 1	COLUMN 2	COLUMN 3	COLUMN 4
A. No. Points on Right Antler	No. Points on Left Antler	Spread Credit	Right Antler	Left Antler	Difference
B. Tip to Tip Spread	C. Greatest Spread				
D. Inside Spread of Main Beams	SPREAD CREDIT MAY EQUAL BUT NOT EXCEED LONGER MAIN BEAM				
E. Total of Lengths of Abnormal Points					
F. Length of Main Beam					
G-1. Length of First Point					
G-2. Length of Second Point					
G-3. Length of Third Point					
G-4. Length of Fourth Point					
G-5. Length of Fifth Point					
G-6. Length of Sixth Point, If Present					
G-7. Length of Seventh Point, If Present					
H-1. Circumference at Smallest Place Between First and Second Points					
H-2. Circumference at Smallest Place Between Second and Third Points					
H-3. Circumference at Smallest Place Between Third and Fourth Points					
H-4. Circumference at Smallest Place Between Fourth and Fifth Points					
	TOTALS				

ADD	Column 1		Exact Locality Where Killed:
	Column 2		Date Killed: Hunter:
	Column 3		Trophy Owner: Telephone #:
	Subtotal		Trophy Owner's Address:
SUBTRACT Column 4			Trophy Owner's E-mail: Guide's Name:
FINAL SCORE			Remarks: (Mention Any Abnormalities or Unique Qualities)
			OM I.D. Number

COPYRIGHT © 2006 BY BOONE AND CROCKETT CLUB®

Idaho's Greatest All-Time Typical Elk
(Boone and Crockett Scoring System)

Rank	Score	Year	Location	Hunter/Owner	Points R L	Main Beam R L	Widest Spread	Inside Spread	Bases R L
1	412-5/8	1954	Adams County	Elmer Bacus/Elmer Bacus	9,8	51-6/8, 51-1/8	47-4/8	42-5/8	10-0/8, 9-1/8
2	400-4/8	1965	Owyhee County	Cecil R. Coonts/ID Dept. Fish & Game	7,7	59-1/8, 60-1/8	49-0/8	42-6/8	9-3/8, 10-0/8
3	395-0/8	1964	Lemhi County	Fred W. Thomson/Randy Clark	7,7	56-2/8, 56-2/8	53-4/8	48-7/8	8-7/8, 9-0/8
4	394-4/8	1977	Idaho County	L.M. White/L.M. White	6,6	53-4/8, 53-2/8	54-0/8	46-4/8	8-7/8, 8-7/8
5	393-5/8	1955	Owyhee County	Picked Up/Joe Adams	7,7	56-2/8, 52-4/8	49-7/8	42-5/8	9-1/8, 9-4/8
6	393-4/8	2000	Blaine County	Darren K. Spiers/Darren K. Spiers	6,6	57-0/8, 56-0/8	48-2/8	46-6/8	9-7/8, 9-2/8
7	393-2/8	1954	Winchester	Doyle Shriver/Doyle Shriver	6,6	58-6/8, 52-1/8	49-0/8	45-2/8	9-6/8, 9-4/8
8	390-6/8	1963	Caribou County	Ken Homer/Ken Homer	7,7	59-6/8, 58-0/8	46-2/8	42-0/8	8-7/8, 9-0/8
9	389-3/8	1915	Salmon River	Unknown/Garth Anderson	6,6	56-5/8, 60-5/8	57-0/8	43-7/8	8-3/8, 8-2/8
10	389-2/8	1949	Nez Perce County	Picked Up/ID Dept. Fish & Game	6,7	49-4/8, 51-1/8	48-5/8	42-6/8	12-2/8, 12-3/8
11	388-0/8	1961	Clark County	Don W. Marshall & E. Jay Stacy/Same	7,6	57-1/8, 55-1/8	59-0/8	55-0/8	8-6/8, 8-1/8
12	387-6/8	1963	Fremont County	Charles A. Preston/Charles A. Preston	6,6	50-2/8, 51-7/8	45-6/8	43-2/8	9-5/8, 10-2/8
13	387-5/8	1994	Washington County	Rick H. Moser/Michael R. Damery	6,6	50-7/8, 51-6/8	44-4/8	41-5/8	8-3/8, 8-5/8
14	386-4/8	1957	Nez Perce County	Hilbert H. Schnettler & James Hanna/ID Dept. Fish & Game	7,7	49-2/8, 50-3/8	46-4/8	39-6/8	8-6/8, 9-0/8
15	386-2/8	1992	Benewah County	Lee C. Mowreader/Lee C. Mowreader	6,7	59-6/8, 60-4/8	51-7/8	47-4/8	9-7/8, 9-6/8
16	386-0/8	1957	Valley County	Kenny Poe/Poe Family	6,6	53-7/8, 54-4/8	57-7/8	51-0/8	9-6/8, 9-6/8
17	385-7/8	1976	Shoshone County	Jerry Nearing/Jerry Nearing	6,6	49-1/8, 51-7/8	49-3/8	44-3/8	7-7/8, 7-7/8
18	385-5/8	1971	Kootenai County	Arth Day/Arth Day	6,6	53-2/8, 53-0/8	47-4/8	40-3/8	8-4/8, 8-1/8
19	385-3/8	1988	Clark County	Dave Leonardson/Dave Leonardson	6,6	51-1/8, 49-7/8	48-0/8	44-1/8	8-7/8, 8-3/8
20	384-4/8	1967	Bonneville County	David W. Anderson/David W. Anderson	7,7	57-0/8, 56-4/8	45-0/8	43-4/8	9-5/8, 9-3/8
20	384-4/8	1972	Bonneville County	Keith W. Hadley/Keith W. Hadley	7,7	53-2/8, 53-7/8	46-7/8	43-0/8	8-5/8, 8-2/8
22	383-2/8	1956	Nez Perce County	Thenton L. Todd/Thenton L. Todd	7,7	52-2/8, 52-0/8	55-2/8	41-6/8	9-4/8, 9-2/8
23	382-5/8	1968	Kootenai County	Terry Cozad/Terry Cozad	7,7	52-3/8, 52-3/8	45-2/8	36-5/8	9-2/8, 9-0/8
23	382-5/8	1997	Butte County	Paul E. Harrell/Kirk Drussel	6,6	52-3/8, 52-0/8	43-5/8	38-1/8	8-6/8, 9-2/8
25	382-2/8	1963	Clark County	John A. Larick, Jr./John A. Larick, Jr.	7,7	54-2/8, 56-6/8	49-0/8	44-2/8	9-0/8, 8-4/8
26	381-7/8	1998	Idaho County	Charles E. Carver/Charles E. Carver	7,7	57-1/8, 56-6/8	43-6/8	40-7/8	9-7/8, 10-0/8

27	381-5/8	1997	Fremont County	Curt L. Stegelmeier/ Curt L. Stegelmeier	6,6	56-1/8, 54-0/8	54-5/8	49-7/8	8-6/8, 8-3/8
28	381-0/8	1966	Bonneville County	E. LaRene Smith/ E. LaRene Smith	7,8	48-0/8, 54-4/8	47-0/8	40-4/8	8-5/8, 8-7/8
29	380-5/8	1976	Custer County	Mark Williams/ Cabela's	6,8	62-4/8, 65-3/8	54-3/8	49-0/8	8-5/8, 8-5/8
30	380-0/8	2001	Blaine County	Howard W. Holmes/ Howard W. Holmes	6,6	53-1/8, 54-0/8	47-6/8	43-6/8	7-4/8, 7-3/8
31	379-6/8	1976	Adams County	William V. Baker/ William V. Baker	9,8	52-0/8, 51-6/8	47-5/8	36-2/8	10-0/8, 10-0/8
32	379-5/8	1961	Valley County	Joe Gisler/ Joe Gisler	7,7	53-7/8, 48-2/8	56-0/8	55-0/8	8-2/8, 8-4/8
33	379-0/8	1963	Big Creek	Picked Up/ George Dovel	6,6	50-4/8, 51-1/8	44-3/8	40-6/8	9-0/8, 8-6/8
34	378-4/8	1963	Shoshone County	E.L. Bradford, L. Harvey, & K. Hall/ Edward L. Bradford	6,6	54-3/8, 55-3/8	48-7/8	45-2/8	8-6/8, 8-6/8
35	377-4/8	1973	Idaho	Unknown/ Dale Rasmus	6,6	57-4/8, 55-1/8	46-7/8	37-4/8	9-5/8, 9-3/8
36	376-7/8	1980	Shoshone County	Roger Johnson/ Roger Johnson	6,6	56-6/8, 54-3/8	50-0/8	33-1/8	7-7/8, 7-5/8
37	376-6/8	1966	Adams County	Jack D. Sheppard/ Jack D. Sheppard	6,7	47-2/8, 50-3/8	N/A	39-2/8	8-6/8, 8-6/8
37	376-6/8	1996	Fremont County	Phil S. Foreseen/ Phil S. Foreseen	7,7	51-2/8, 51-6/8	47-1/8	40-0/8	8-1/8, 8-1/8
39	376-5/8	1966	Teton County	Edwin E. Schiess/ Tim Schiess	7,7	48-0/8, 50-1/8	50-2/8	39-3/8	8-5/8, 8-7/8
40	376-3/8	1985	Valley County	Ron Gastelecutto/ Ron Gastelecutto	7,6	55-6/8, 55-0/8	47-1/8	30-2/8	8-6/8, 8-4/8
41	376-1/8	2002	Bear Lake County	Gary J. Christensen/ Gary J. Christensen	6,6	51-0/8, 51-2/8	50-1/8	42-1/8	9-0/8, 8-4/8
42	376-0/8	1951	Clark County	Bud Gifford/ Darrel D. Riste	6,6	49-6/8, 51-0/8	44-0/8	39-2/8	9-0/8, 8-5/8
43	375-6/8	1983	Shoshone County	Ralph H. Brandvold, Jr./R.H. Brandvold, Jr.	7,7	52-1/8, 50-4/8	42-2/8	37-2/8	8-4/8, 7-7/8
44	375-2/8	1967	Bonner County	Barry D. Nelson/ Barry D. Nelson	7,6	56-2/8, 55-6/8	50-5/8	43-2/8	9-7/8, 9-2/8
45	375-0/8	1960	Fremont County	Eva Calonge/ Eva Calonge	6,6	52-6/8, 52-5/8	54-2/8	47-4/8	8-6/8, 9-0/8
45	375-0/8	2005	Owyhee County	Don J. Burch/ Don J. Burch	8,7	57-4/8, 56-0/8	41-5/8	33-4/8	9-2/8, 9-1/8
47	374-4/8	1959	Fremont County	Winston J. Solberg/ Winston J. Solberg	7,8	55-1/8, 57-4/8	49-0/8	45-0/8	7-7/8, 8-1/8
48	374-3/8	2003	Caribou County	Greg Agpawa/ Greg Agpawa	7,7	43-4/8, 52-6/8	49-4/8	44-1/8	7-3/8, 7-2/8
49	372-6/8	1929	Idaho	Ben Howland/ Rick E. States	7,6	55-3/8, 55-2/8	49-6/8	37-3/8	8-2/8, 8-4/8
50	372-2/8	1955	Bonner County	George Agar/ George Agar	6,6	51-6/8, 52-5/8	51-4/8	47-2/8	8-3/8, 8-4/8
51	371-3/8	1977	Custer County	David D. Lee/ David D. Lee	6,6	56-2/8, 56-2/8	56-5/8	52-1/8	7-4/8, 8-2/8
52	370	1961	Benewah County	Aaron C. Robinson/ Aaron C. Robinson	7,6	54-4/8, 54-3/8	44-0/8	36-2/8	9-1/8, 8-4/8
53	369-4/8	1986	Bonner County	Steve Noort/ Steve Noort	7,7	53-2/8, 51-2/8	41-7/8	39-4/8	7-6/8, 7-6/8
54	368-6/8	1964	Idaho County	Don Ruark/ Cindy Worth	6,8	50-1/8, 52-4/8	45-6/8	43-3/8	9-5/8, 9-1/8
55	368	1956	Caribou County	Junior Bitton & Rex Bassett/Unknown	8,8	57-3/8, 57-4/8	46-4/8	43-2/8	8-0/8, 8-3/8
56	367-5/8	1960	Fremont County	Alma Nelson & Grant Nelson/ Alma Nelson	7,7	53-3/8, 52-5/8	57-1/8	46-5/8	8-0/8, 7-5/8
57	367-2/8	1982	Lemhi County	Ben Fanholz/ Ben Fanholz	6,6	55-4/8, 57-7/8	50-5/8	46-0/8	8-0/8, 7-4/8

58	366-6/8	1962	Lemhi County	Larry K. Seymour/ Larry K. Seymour	6,6	52-2/8, 52-3/8	48-4/8	38-6/8	8-1/8, 8-3/8
59	366-5/8	1962	Shoshone County	D.A. Johnson/ D.A. Johnson	7,7	53-0/8, 53-2/8	50-4/8	45-3/8	7-5/8, 7-2/8
60	366-2/8	1995	Idaho County	Picked Up/ Bob & Gary McClure	6,7	53-2/8, 52-1/8	45-4/8	35-6/8	8-7/8, 9-0/8
61	366-1/8	1991	Waverly Mountains	Wayne Lewis/ Wayne Minkel	6,7	57-3/8, 57-4/8	54-3/8	49-1/8	8-6/8, 9-2/8
62	365-4/8	1970	Clearwater County	James Brian/ James Brian	7,7	51-4/8, 48-1/8	46-4/8	41-6/8	9-1/8, 9-1/8
63	364-3/8	1990	Kootenai County	Curtis Yanzick/ Curtis Yanzick	8,7	57-2/8, 51-6/8	41-3/8	37-3/8	9-3/8, 8-1/8
64	364-1/8	1998	Benewah County	Wallace Darkow/ Wallace Darkow	8,6	48-6/8, 50-7/8	46-1/8	40-2/8	8-5/8, 8-5/8
65	363-1/8	1995	Bannock County	Keith D. Harrow/ Keith D. Harrow	6,6	53-0/8, 55-1/8	50-4/8	43-7/8	9-5/8, 10-4/8
66	362-6/8	2005	Elmore County	Cary G. Cada/ Cary G. Cada	6,6	57-0/8, 56-2/8	49-7/8	39-4/8	9-5/8, 9-5/8
67	362-1/8	1994	Teton County	Robert Hansen/ Robert Hansen	6,6	55-2/8, 57-3/8	45-4/8	43-3/8	8-2/8, 8-5/8
68	361-6/8	1960	Lemhi County	Grant Hamilton/ Grant Hamilton	6,6	53-2/8, 52-1/8	49-2/8	45-6/8	8-4/8, 8-4/8
69	361-5/8	2002	Washington County	Perk Rose/ Perk Rose	8,7	52-1/8, 51-4/8	42-4/8	39-3/8	9-1/8, 8-7/8
70	361	1956	Fremont County	Wilbur Chitwood/ Wilbur Chitwood	6,7	49-4/8, 50-3/8	51-4/8	41-1/8	9-3/8, 9-6/8
70	361	1963	Idaho County	Robert L. Dixon/ Robert L. Dixon	7,7	50-2/8, 50-4/8	43-3/8	38-4/8	8-4/8, 9-4/8
70	361	1963	Salmon River	F.H. Sappingfield/ F.H. Sappingfield	7,6	53-4/8, 53-5/8	46-4/8	42-3/8	8-1/8, 8-0/8
73	360-7/8	1983	Lemhi County	Tony Latham/ Tony Latham	7,6	54-7/8, 56-1/8	46-2/8	41-7/8	7-0/8, 7-0/8
74	360-2/8	1957	Coeur d' Alene	Everett Bosanko/ Everett Bosanko	6,6	56-0/8, 55-7/8	46-0/8	41-4/8	8-6/8, 8-3/8
74	360-2/8	1996	Clark County	Tim Thomas/ Tim Thomas	8,6	54-5/8, 55-0/8	50-5/8	46-4/8	9-1/8, 8-4/8

Elmer Bacus
412-5/8 B&C Typical
Adams County, 1954
Idaho State Record Typical Elk

Idaho Typical Rank: 1
Inside Spread: 42-5/8
Main Beams (R,L): 51-6/8, 51-1/8

Points (R,L): 9,8
Widest Spread: 47-4/8
Bases (R, L): 10-0/8, 9-1/8

"So, Elmer, when you first looked out there and saw that bull, with that huge set of antlers, what were you thinking?" the author asked.
"Well," Elmer replied, *"we were hunting for meat, and he looked really big... and like a lot of meat!"*

Those words really epitomize the difference between how hunters viewed their prey in the good old days vs. today. Elmer had just taken the biggest bull elk in the history of the state of Idaho, yet he still thinks about how many steaks he got out of it. In fact, had it not been for a young hunter in the party insisting they take the antlers, they would have been reconsumed by the soil, as Elmer had already decided to leave them lay.

There are a great number of aspects of Elmer's story that mirror the changes and history of hunting in Idaho. Elmer's bull is yet another prime example of how sportsmen have always been the leaders and pioneers in wildlife conservation. To understand it all, one must really have a concept of history.

Historically speaking, elk numbers in Idaho were really never very high. By the turn of the 20th century, as pioneers, miners, and settlers came in, unregulated market and subsistence hunting had efficiently taken care of most of what was left. Concerned sportsmen and legislators slowly began making progress though. One example of such success is what helped lead to the possibility of the existence of Elmer's bull.

Around 1914, local pressure persuaded the state game warden into lobbying the U.S. Government for elk. The thought was to use these for "seed" in translocation and repopulation efforts.

State Senator Earl Wayland Bowman, from Council, was witness to the desecration of wild game in the Adams County area and had the foresight to try to do something to change its direction. Yellowstone National Park was looking to unload a burgeoning elk population, and an opportunity was being presented by the Park for whoever wanted them to come and get them. With this knowledge in hand, Bowman soon created a two-headed agenda. The first part was to create a safe haven for wildlife numbers to restock, and the second was reintroduction of extirpated species into this protected environment.

In 1914-1915, Bowman pushed for legislation to create the Black Lake Game Preserve. In February of 1915, two critical events happened in conjunction with one another. First, the Governor signed Earl Wayland Bowman's bill into effect, creating the Black Lake Game Preserve – a 67,000-acre set-aside. This was, in part, to create a sanctuary for the second event.

Following the establishment of the preserve, fifty head of elk (fifteen bulls and thirty-five cows) from Yellowstone National Park were shipped via rail from Yellowstone to an area north of Council and west of New Meadows. They were then basically herded and directed into some of the more rugged country to the north that encompassed part of the Preserve.

From the February 19th, 1915 edition of the Adams County Leader:

"Elk Coming"

"The governor has signed Senator Bowman's bill creating the Black Lake Game Preserve in this and Idaho counties. The U.S. Government has given Idaho 50 head of Yellowstone Park elk for the preserve. Our state game warden has already sent a man after them and they will be unloaded in Council the first of next week and taken to the preserve. There are about thirty-five cows and fifteen bulls which will soon replenish the species in Idaho if the animals are properly protected, and every citizen should take a pride in seeing that they are protected."

The February 26th edition of the Leader stated:

"Elk Arrive"

The 50 elk for the Black Lake Preserve arrived Tuesday evening in two cars attached to the passenger train, and nearly the whole town was down at the depot to see them. They were taken to New Meadows to unload and two of them escaped and took to the hills at that point. From there they are to be driven to the preserve via Little Salmon and the headwaters of Deep Creek.

From the May 14, 1915 Leader:

> *"J.W. Davis, deputy game warden, was in Meadows Valley checking on the new elk band. They are doing fine."*

Following that reintroduction, hunting in the Black Lake Game Preserve was banned. In 1935, deer hunting was again opened, but it would be thirty-five years from the point of reintroduction, in the fall of 1950, before hunters would be able to legally harvest an elk in the area. But by then, the preserve accomplished what it had attempted – even by 1946, the estimated elk population in the Payette National Forest was 3000 animals.

As a result of that historic reintroduction and further dispersion of more native resident elk herds, an unparalleled amount of mature bull elk were roaming west-central Idaho in the 1950s. Mammoth-sized bulls were reported being taken in that inaugural season.

From the October 6, 1950 edition of the Leader:

> *On opening day of the first open season, a large number of local men hunted this prime location. This was also opening day of deer season, and either sex was legal game for both species. For some time after it was light enough to shoot that morning, it sounded like there was a war going on in that vicinity. In addition to bucks, does and cow elk, eighteen bull elk were killed. A number of these bulls had trophy-sized antlers. One monster bull had ten points on one side and eleven on the other.*

By the fall of 1954, that portion of Idaho was only in its fifth season of hunting on this newfound abundant elk population. Logging roads had not yet significantly permeated these areas, so survivability had been good.

Thirty-one year old Elmer Bacus, along with Everett Harrington, Chet Jones, Charles Sale, Walt Draper, Darrell Abraham, and Ilo Estes, headed up into elk country for the 1954 opener. They camped at a spring, and would be hunting both deer and elk.

They had been there for two days and had seen elk in a particular spot of sub-alpine fir on the second day. Elmer remembers that there were 15-20 cows and two or three small bulls in the bunch.

The next morning, they sent the two kids, Ilo and Darrell, to a particular tree. The plan was to push the timber in a big circle and send the elk in front of the boys. Elmer says that the boys never made it to the tree. Whether they had become temporarily misplaced or not is probably open to interpretation.

The men in the party hadn't even gotten to their chosen drive location when they spotted a gigantic bull elk all by himself in the bottom of a canyon. The bull was about 100 yards away and standing broadside. True to the old tradition, all Elmer could see was a huge mound of hamburger.

At 8:30 a.m., Elmer sent a round from his Springfield .30-40 Krag into the midsection of the giant elk. The bull didn't even flinch! He quickly followed with another shot to the same location, with an identical same result. He was getting ready for a third shot at the seemingly indestructible brute when it slowly just tipped over backward and died.

The men quickly took care of the fieldwork and resumed their drive to the boys. They eventually scattered a bunch of elk, but since the boys never made it to the tree, it was all in vain. With that morning's hunt over, Elmer returned to his big unprocessed supply of winter meat, quartered it, and hung it in a tree.

Two days later, they came to get the meat as they were breaking camp. They loaded the quarters on the horses and were leaving when Walt Draper and Charles Sale asked about the antlers. Elmer had no intention of packing those enormous brush catchers out of the hills. Luckily, Walt and Charles were eventually able to persuade the group into taking the antlers with them. The men, one by one, took turns packing the massive tangle of bone out of the canyon.

Elmer remembers several things in particular about his big elk. First, the body on the bull was simply enormous - well over 1000 lbs. Secondly, the meat was as tough as leather. And third, the Fish and Game's estimate of age was thirty years old. This is obviously an excessive estimate, but the point being taken that the bull was very old.

Elmer Bacus' bull is an incredibly rare specimen. It has an 8x8 typical frame, "gross scores" 436-6/8, and stands head and shoulders above any other typical elk ever taken in the history of the state of Idaho. He is truly a tribute to successful wildlife management initiated by sportsmen, and is also a record likely to remain standing for some time to come.

Cecil R. Coonts
400-4/8 B&C Typical
Owyhee County, 1965

Idaho Typical Rank: 2
Inside Spread: 42-6/8
Main Beams (R,L): 59-1/8, 60-1/8

Points (R,L): 7,7
Widest Spread: 49-0/8
Bases (R, L): 9-3/8, 10-0/8

In 1965, the Idaho Department of Fish & Game opened up the Owyhee County country for general season elk hunting. It had opened as a controlled hunt unit in 1951, but had received only light pressure until then. As you might expect, it generated ample interest.

Cecil Coonts and his brother Paul, along with a few other friends, headed to the South Mountain area for the opener. Paul had seen a large-antlered elk in the vicinity the last couple of years while deer hunting, and going after him seemed as likely a plan as any.

The day of the opener it was bitterly cold and windy, and getting out of camp proved a real test of will. They did eventually leave that morning, albeit a bit late.

The hunters split up and Cecil headed high, toward the top of South Mountain. The higher he got, the colder and rougher it became, and Cecil found himself holed up in a patch of timber in an attempt to stay out of the biting wind.

As Cecil sat and hoped for a break in the weather, he had a great stroke of luck. From down below, another party of hunters had jumped a herd of elk. They all headed toward the timber, but a large bull, in classic elk style, peeled away from the main flow of the herd and headed right toward Cecil.

He fired a shot from his .30-06 and knocked the giant bull down, and added a follow-up shot to the neck, quickly dropping the bull for good. Paul was actually watching the events unfold, and saw a hunter shooting at the bull, but was so far away he had no idea who it was.

After the field-dressing, they were able to get a pickup to within 100 yards of the kill site. Even with that, they had to quarter the big bull in order to get him loaded and back to camp.

Cecil was about fifty at the time he took his historic bull. He has passed on now, and Paul was nice enough to share the story of one of his brother's best days in the Idaho mountains. Paul says Cecil was quite a sportsman, and loved to hunt and fish as much as he could spare the time. He also says that Cecil was one happy hunter that day. I'll bet he was, Paul. Wish we could have been there.

Cecil Coonts (left) and an unidentified man display one of the biggest elk racks in Idaho history.

Cecil Coonts' typical bull elk, the second largest in Idaho history, is undeniably a breathtaking animal. He is one of only two typicals in Idaho to ever score over 400 B&C. He also has very prototypical antlers for an Idaho bull – comparatively weak fronts and strong backs.

Fred W. Thomson
395-0/8 B&C Typical
Salmon National Forest (Lemhi County), 1964

Idaho Typical Rank: 3
Inside Spread: 48-7/8
Main Beams (R,L): 56-2/8, 56-2/8

Points (R,L): 7,7
Widest Spread: 53-4/8
Bases (R, L): 8-7/8, 9-0/8

Fred Thomson is no longer around to tell us the story of how he bagged his bull he worked so hard for. Bits and pieces gathered from people in the course of writing this book helped to piece together a brief glimpse.

Evidently, Fred was a real go-getter, hiking in for many miles to the area he chose to hunt, which lay on the North Fork of Camas Creek, near the Middle Fork of the Salmon River. He supposedly packed the bull out over the course of several days, by himself. It was late November, and so the meat kept all right while Fred made his trips.

Fred had been from the Idaho Falls area, but had moved later on to Missoula, Montana. Fred's big elk head hung in the Elks' Lodge there for quite some time before eventually being sold.

L.M. White
394-4/8 B&C Typical
Idaho County, 1977

Idaho Typical Rank: 4
Inside Spread: 46-4/8
Main Beams (R,L): 53-4/8, 53-2/8

Points (R,L): 6,6
Widest Spread: 54-0/8
Bases (R, L): 8-7/8, 8-7/8

Not a lot is known about the day Luther M. White took Idaho's fourth-largest typical ever. The bull was taken with a .300 Weatherby-mag. on a September afternoon in 1977. He is believed to have been on a guided hunt with pack mules in the Chamberlain Basin area of the Frank Church Wilderness.

Mr. White's bull, Idaho's biggest 6x6, appears to have no weaknesses. With a great inside spread and every tine reaching for the sky, it's easy to see how he ranks so high.

Picked Up (Joe Adams)
393-5/8 B&C Typical
Owyhee County, Prior to 1955

Idaho Typical Rank: 5
Inside Spread: 42-5/8
Main Beams (R,L): 56-2/8, 52-4/8

Points (R,L): 7,7
Widest Spread: 49-7/8
Bases (R, L): 9-1/8, 9-4/8

Joe Adams bought this big set of antlers in 1989. It had hung for many years in a lodge near Pine, Idaho. Joe says that the owner told him he had found it in a creek bottom after a bad winter.

When this rack was entered into B&C, it was put into the records books as being from Elmore County, since that was where Joe bought it. However, upon talking to Joe, it was learned that the owner said the rack had actually been found in the Owyhees.

Joe bought this rack at the same time he bought another huge rack (page 314). He later sold them to a collector in San Francisco, and neither have been seen since.

Darren K. Spiers
393-4/8 B&C Typical
Blaine County, 2000

Idaho Typical Rank: 6
Inside Spread: 46-6/8
Main Beams (R,L): 57-0/8, 56-0/8

Points (R,L): 6,6
Widest Spread: 48-2/8
Bases (R, L): 9-7/8, 9-2/8

After too long a wait, opening morning was finally here. It was 5 a.m. and all I could think about was the bull we had spotted earlier in the year. My summer had been spent scouting, talking to people, and studying maps in hopes of increasing the possibility of finding a good bull. Our preseason work paid off when my brother Shane and I were fortunate enough to find the true bull of a lifetime. Now we just had to make it happen.

At 5:45 a.m. on opening morning, we left camp. We headed right for the area we had last seen the huge bull. All of the typical opening day thoughts of huge elk raced through my mind as we set up and waited for the first hints of daylight.

It didn't take long for the action to start. Even before the sun came up, the elk were on the move. We started hearing bugles coming from all directions. Then, suddenly, two bulls started fighting in the middle of the meadow. It was amazing; the elk were everywhere!

We anxiously glassed all around us, hoping to spot the big bull. Suddenly, one bugle stood out from the rest. Judging from the deep growl and our reaction, it had to be the huge bull we had seen earlier in the year during our scouting trips.

Shane began calling, hoping that this would lure the bruiser out into the open. We had several bulls answer us from every direction. Right about then, we started to see elk moving into our view. First one cow, then two, then three cows; the line kept coming.

The bull finally appeared at the tail end, bringing up the rear. He was enormous – a perfect six-point with tines jutting far out into the sky.

They were moving out at a good pace, quartering away from us. I got ready for a shot, but the big bull never exposed his vitals to me. I was forced to helplessly watch them disappear like a mirage over the horizon.

After they had gone out of sight, we took off after them. I went one way and Shane went out across the desert to find a vantage point to see if he could see which direction they headed. A short time later, Shane came back and reported that he had seen the general direction they were going.

After half a mile of stalking, I was quickly starting to lose hope. To be so close to a bull so big, and come up empty, was tough. I figured that was the last time I would ever see that bull.

Not completely giving up, though, we pressed on and topped another ridge. Much to our surprise, there he was! He was separated from the herd, and was holed up in the lava rocks.

When he caught sight of us, he was startled and jumped to his feet only thirty yards away. I shouldered my .338 and quickly fired two rounds. The first hit through his lungs, and the other went through his left shoulder and into his heart. He only made it forty yards before dropping anchor.

I just stood there in shock. We really didn't have any idea how big this bull was until we walked up to him. He was even bigger than we had judged. Words could never describe my feelings at that moment.

I would like to give special thanks to Toby Ashley, Lance Vaughn, and Shane Miller for all their help they provided on this hunt. I couldn't have done it without them.

Darren Spiers gives the thumbs up after downing the sixth-largest typical in Idaho history.

Doyle Shriver
393-2/8 B&C Typical
Winchester, ID 1954

Idaho Typical Rank: 7
Inside Spread: 45-2/8
Main Beams (R,L): 58-6/8, 52-1/8

Points (R,L): 6,6
Widest Spread: 49-0/8
Bases (R, L): 9-6/8, 9-4/8

Doyle is no longer here to tell us the story of the magnificent encounter he had with this fantastic elk. The loss of an important history due to the passing of the hunters who took these great animals is, without a doubt, the major reason behind the series of books chronicling Idaho's greatest big game. To be able to know what happened that day, and how Doyle felt about it and might have described it would be simply priceless to all subsequent generations.

Through some digging, small fleeting pieces of that day were found, but only a few. Doyle was in the middle of the hunt when he glimpsed movement in the timber. He identified it as an elk and pulled the trigger on his .32. When he shot, he had no idea of the size of the bull he was about to become acquainted with. As he approached, he found this great bull thrashing in the brush, unable to free himself. While Doyle was much distracted by the size of the antlers, he was able to bring himself back to the issue at hand, which was to finish off his prize before it either escaped or had any prolonged suffering.

Doyle Shriver's tremendous bull, taken on the Deer Creek near Winchester area in 1954, is the seventh largest typical elk ever known to have roamed Idaho soil. Congratulations, Doyle; we wish we could have been there with you.

This quartering view shows the outstanding tine lengths, symmetry, and balance on this great bull.

Doyle Shriver's bull today, on a pedestal mount by Shiermeier Taxidermy.

Ken Homer
390-6/8 B&C Typical
Caribou County, 1963

Idaho Typical Rank: 8
Inside Spread: 42-0/8
Main Beams (R,L): 59-6/8, 58-0/8

Points (R,L): 7,7
Widest Spread: 46-2/8
Bases (R, L): 8-7/8, 9-0/8

"After all these years, I can still picture myself breaking out of the timber and seeing that big bull." ~ Ken Homer

If there is one common thread I have noticed in the course of writing this book, it is sentiment such as the comment above made by Ken Homer. Many of the greatest generation to hunt elk in Idaho are aging now. For many, it has been decades since the day they had their special encounter with their big bull. But almost unanimously, it seems as though it is etched in their mind like it just happened yesterday.

In 1963, Ken Homer was living in Montpelier and working for the railroad. He loved to venture out to new areas in Idaho's beautiful unknown, and did so on every available opportunity.

Ken's nephew, Phil, had told him about a great-looking elk spot he had found near the Wyoming line while fishing some beaver ponds. It was steep – really steep – and brushy, but seemed to hold a great multitude of elk. The lower elevations had quite a bit of mahogany, but the upper half was primarily aspen and conifers. There were plenty of springs and wallows up high – perfect for staying cool and keeping the flies off. The spot sounded perfect, so they made a plan.

In early October of 1963, 35-year-old Ken Homer, along with his brother Eddie, nephew Phil, and Darrel Hansen, headed on horses into the Brush Creek country northeast of Soda Springs. There they set up a 12x16 wall tent and began their quest for their winter's meat.

It was beautiful weather, but hot. Because of the heat, they had a somewhat self-imposed limit of taking no more than one elk per day between the group. The first day, Darrel took a nice cow. On day two, Phil followed with a spike bull. On the third day, they focused on the top of the drainage. Eddie killed a cow that morning, which left Ken as the final tag holder.

Ken left the scene of Eddie's kill, intent on going to get the horses for the packout. As he picked his path through the timber, he heard a series of crashing sounds. He took off on a dead run, breaking out of the timber just in time to see a large lone bull as it was about to disappear around a hogback ridge.

Just then, the bull made a fatal error, much to Ken's delight; he stopped. Ken made no hesitation and sent a .308 round into the big bull's boiler room at 150 yards. One additional shot followed and the bull was down for the last time.

Ken mad his way to the fallen monarch, stunned by both its size and beauty. He had taken elk before, mostly in the Selway, but never anything like this. After a few moments of humble appreciation, Ken finished the necessary fieldwork and then continued on down to get the horses, nearly four miles away.

They brought out Eddie's cow and Ken's bull on two horses each on an eight-mile round trip. They had no saw, and therefore left the antlers on the hill that night.

After they retired to bed, Ken spent half the night wrestling with whether or not to go back after that great set of antlers. He had covered over sixteen miles of rough terrain that day, and his body was reminding him of it every minute. Did he really have it in him to do another eight tomorrow? Ultimately, and fortunately for all of us, the answer was yes, and he made one last trip to the top of the drainage.

Unknown
389-3/8 B&C Typical
Salmon River, 1915

Idaho Typical Rank: 9
Inside Spread: 43-7/8
Main Beams (R,L): 56-5/8, 60-5/8

Points (R,L): 6,6
Widest Spread: 57-0/8
Bases (R, L): 8-3/8, 8-2/8

This great bull is one of the oldest on record in Idaho. As such, it's not surprising that there is little history to accompany it. Garth Anderson was nice enough to give us all the details of what he knew about the rack his dad acquired in 1965.

My dad was an elevator field serviceman in Boise through the '60s. In 1965, his elevator maintenance route included the Boise Elks Lodge. The elevator machinery was in the basement of the lodge. On one of his routine visits there, Dad saw a very large, old elk mount that was lying upside down on a pile of bricks in the basement.

He eventually inquired about the bull to an elderly gentleman that was the building maintenance foreman. The man explained that it had been taken in 1915 on the Salmon River by an unknown sheepherder. He further explained that it had been used as the Elks' mascot for about twenty years.

The rack, though very large, was not very symmetrical. In the 1930s, someone came up with a much more symmetrical and "attractive" mount. So, the big elk head had been taken to the basement and put upside down on the pile of bricks, where it had lain for the past thirty years.

Dad asked if the head might be for sale, and the elderly foreman replied that he would find out. Soon after, the old gentleman called Dad at home and said that the Lodge would be glad to get rid of it, and that they wanted $20 for it.

Dad bought the head and brought it home in the back of our 1951 Chevrolet pickup. The mount filled the bed of the pickup, with the antlers sticking above and outside the pickup bed. On the way home, he was followed by many sportsmen trying to get a better look.

The mount itself was badly deteriorated and the hair was falling out. We removed the antlers and they have been mounted on the current board ever since.

Dad took the rack to the Boise office of Idaho Department of Fish & Game to have it officially scored. The fellow who scored it asked Dad where he got it. Dad explained, and the man was thunderstruck. He had been a member of the Lodge for many years, but had never been to the basement, and had never known about the head.

This breathtaking bull has been on display at Sportsman's Warehouse in Idaho Falls since 2003. Garth Anderson is shown modeling the antlers.

Picked Up by Michael Throckmorton
389-2/8 B&C Typical
Nez Perce County, 1949

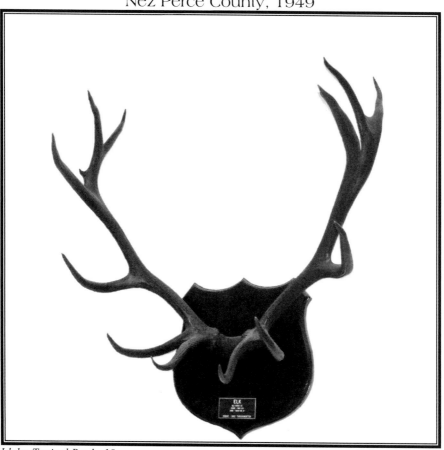

Idaho Typical Rank: 10
Inside Spread: 42-6/8
Main Beams (R,L): 49-4/8, 51-1/8

Points (R,L): 6,7
Widest Spread: 48-5/8
Bases (R, L): 12-2/8, 12-3/8

Michael Throckmorton was in the area of the confluence of the Snake and Salmon Rivers in December of 1949 when he encountered a sight to behold. It was the skull of a giant bull elk.

How it died is anyone's guess, including Michael's. It could've been a poorly placed bullet, a mountain lion, or any other number of causes. Regardless of how it died, Michael thought enough of it to pack the head out of that rugged country.

He held onto it for a number of years, until he finally decided to donate it to the Idaho Department of Fish & Game. It has, for many years now, been on display at their Boise office in the big conference room.

One interesting note on this massive bull – it has the largest base measurements of any bull ever recorded in Idaho. The right antler measures 12-2/8; the left measures 12-3/8. Not that the bull is spindly by any means, but the inflated base measurements really have more to do with the close natural proximity of the G-1s and G-2s rather than being extremely massive.

Don W. Marshall and E. Jay Stacy
388-0/8 B&C Typical
Clark County, 1961

Idaho Typical Rank: 11
Inside Spread: 55-0/8
Main Beams (R,L): 57-1/8, 55-1/8

Points (R,L): 7,6
Widest Spread: 59-0/8
Bases (R, L): 8-6/8, 8-1/8

In late October of 1961, Don Marshall, Jay Stacy, and Walt Thomas all headed for the Medicine Lodge Creek country in Clark County. It was a proven spot and all the men were excited to be in good country.

Their chosen elk spot for the day was mostly open country sage, with pockets of timber and aspens. It was a great mix of feeding and hiding cover. From first light on, they saw a lot of fresh sign. No snow blanketed the ground, but elk tracks literally had the ground chewed up in all directions.

All three men slowly progressed up the canyon. It was still early morning when a whopper of a bull broke out of the timber and ran down the canyon toward a mixed patch of aspens and fir trees.

Jay and Don instantly began contouring around the hill and angling toward the bull's hiding spot. Don stayed on the sidehill while Jay went around further, hoping to position the bull between them. The bull, not liking the situation he was about to get into, made a run for it. Don reacted quickly, aiming and firing instantly. The bullet found its mark, but the big bull found the strength to keep going. Jay followed with one shot and the widest typical elk in the history of Idaho fell to the ground.

The next part of the story is one that I wish we could all see on video. The men had two homemade Tote Gotes. They tied them together, loaded the bull whole, and headed down the canyon. Don notes that control of the contraption was sometimes in question. Their makeshift elk cart picked up some pretty good speed and knocked over more than one piece of sizable sagebrush along the way.

Sadly, this great bull was stolen from Don in the 1970s. Don had no pictures, and thus nothing whatsoever of a keepsake of their great hunt. If you have any information on the whereabouts of this set of antlers, please drop us a line. And to whoever stole them, please do the right thing and give them back.

Charles A. Preston
387-6/8 B&C Typical
Fremont County, 1963

Idaho Typical Rank: 12
Inside Spread: 43-2/8
Main Beams (R,L): 50-2/8, 51-7/8

Points (R,L): 6,6
Widest Spread: 45-6/8
Bases (R, L): 9-5/8, 10-2/8

Recipe: One Large Boone & Crockett Elk

Ingredients: 1 milk tube from local dairy
1 whittled cottonwood whistle
1 impromptu elderly and nearly deaf hunting partner
1 .308 round and a friendly follow-up

Stir.

Chuck Preston was lucky enough to draw a special elk permit for unit 60 in the fall of 1963. As the season opened, Chuck headed toward Bishop Mountain to set up camp. He was alone, but had coincidentally camped near another group of hunters.

Opening day was fairly mundane. Chuck had no luck and made it back to camp slightly wearier than when he had left. At camp, he learned that two of the three men in the other party had tagged out.

With only Chuck and one other man remaining, it seemed only logical that they might team up, and that's how Chuck Preston got to know Shorty Hoopes. Shorty was a man Chuck estimated to be about sixty years old, and it didn't take much conversation to realize that Shorty knew the area well, and knew how to hunt elk. It also didn't take long for Chuck to realize that Shorty was extremely hard of hearing.

As dawn broke on the second morning, Chuck and Shorty headed up the hill. It was a typical nice and sunny October day. After about a mile, Chuck stopped to try a bugle from his self-made elk call. Now remember, this was 1963. There were no high-tech, name-brand bugles on the market. Chuck had made his own, fashioned from whittling a cottonwood whistle and inserting it into one end of a milk tube from a local dairy. The entire contraption was about 12" long.

Chuck excitedly gave a bugle, which really was more of a shrill whistle, and was pleasantly surprised to receive not one, not two, nor even three replies, but four separate responses!

He tried desperately to get Shorty's attention, but the old-timer kept on going. Chuck even ran up to him and tapped him on the shoulder, but Shorty didn't understand what was going on, and so he just kept a-goin'.

Chuck had to stop and focus on business. He could hear one of the bulls coming in fast through a lodgepole pine thicket. The bull bugled and grunted as it closed the distance, and began to circle to Chuck's left. He was half mad, but still half wary, and circled while trying to get the wind in his favor.

At this point, the bull was only fifty yards away, and making plenty of noise, but it was too dense for the combatants to see each other. The bull then retreated, only to come back and perform the same ritual. This time, Chuck could make out elk hair through his riflescope. He waited patiently until the bull finally turned his head and swung that big rack into view.

The minute Chuck saw antlers, he pulled the trigger on his .308. The bull dropped, and then got up again just as quickly. He wheeled around and, in a flash, vanished into the doghair lodgepole.

Chuck was headed into the dense thicket when he heard a racket. He knew it would be quicker to back out and go around, so he eased back and headed for the other side. As he approached, he discovered that the bull had pushed his way clear through and was gone.

Chuck diligently followed the blood trail, but it was slow going. There was no snow, and the vegetation was thick enough to hide much of the sign. Chuck was confident in the shot, but hoping the difficult tracking wouldn't be the end to his chance at this big bull.

He had gone but a short distance when he suddenly heard the blast of a rifle, maybe fifty yards away, at most. He made his way carefully to the sound, only to see Shorty standing there over Chuck's bull.

Shorty relayed the story as Chuck listened. The bull had come right in front of him, staggering like he was punch drunk and ready to fall over. Shorty did the humane thing and put a bullet into the elk's massive neck, dropping it right where it stood.

As luck would have it, Shorty's buddies came by on horses as they worked on the giant bull. They were on their way to retrieve their elk from the previous day.

Once they were apprised of the situation, they hustled and packed out their elk, kindly coming back and hauling out Chuck's bull later in the day.

Shorty wasn't to be left out, though. He took a nice fat calf before the end of the hunt. It likely tasted a whole lot better than that big ol' bull, too. As Chuck said, when he described it, "Never seen anything like it; he was bigger than a horse!" Shorty would probably bet it tasted like one, too.

Rick H. Moser
387-5/8 B&C Typical
Washington County, 1994
Owned by Michael Damery

Courtesy of Michael Damery

Idaho Typical Rank: 13
Inside Spread: 41-5/8
Main Beams (R,L): 50-7/8, 51-6/8

Points (R,L): 6,6
Widest Spread: 44-4/8
Bases (R, L): 8-3/8, 8-5/8

Rick Moser loves to hunt big mule deer, but admits when it comes to elk, he's not picky. "They're all big", he says. "As long as it helps to fill the freezer, an elk's an elk."

In 1994, Rick once again faithfully put in for the Unit 31 controlled hunt bull elk tag. He had been lucky twice before, drawing the tag and filling it the first time with a spike, and the second time with a small six-point. To Rick's amazement, he had just drawn his third tag. By now, he knew the unit well, and would put that knowledge, and his horses, to good use.

Rick saw quite a few elk as the season wore on, but hadn't yet encountered the right situation to fill his tag. He wasn't trophy hunting, so any bull was fair game in Rick's eyes.

He headed out again on the 2nd of November, close to the season's end. He was alone, except for his horse, and had covered about five miles already that day. The rhythmic plodding of the horse's hooves and the view were more than enough to make it a day worth spending outdoors.

It was tough ground, and even tougher going. Much of his hunt unit is fairly open, but it's also in the rocky breaks country leading into the southern end of the Hells Canyon country. A good description might be that it's short on cover and long on steep.

He was just topping a rise when he saw a herd of what must have been 40 elk bedded out in the open country only 50 yards away. He quickly bailed off his horse, grabbed his rifle, and fired a round – and all just about that fast.

At that point, his horse took the opportunity to split like a bolt of lightning (a story in itself), but Rick kept his focus. His first shot had been a solid lung hit, but the bull had still managed to leave the scene. Rick followed, now on foot, and managed to jump the bull again. Two additional shots from Rick's .308 and his tag was once again successfully filled.

Rick was in awe of the antlers, which stretched further than any he'd ever seen. It was for sure more than he had hoped for, or even imagined. He managed to get the fieldwork done in spite of the distracting view, and then set out to recover his missing horse.

The next day, all stock once again accounted for, Rick and his son Quentin came in with two horses and quartered the bull. Once loaded, they headed back down.

As they made their way back to the truck, Rick's thoughts drifted back on his hunt. This bull wasn't like the other two. No, he wasn't a spike by any means, but nevertheless, he'd just have to do.

Hilbert H. Schnettler & James Hanna
386-4/8 B&C Typical
Nez Perce County, 1957

Idaho Typical Rank: 14
Inside Spread: 39-6/8
Main Beams (R,L): 49-2/8, 50-3/8

Points (R,L): 7,7
Widest Spread: 46-4/8
Bases (R, L): 8-6/8, 9-0/8

Late November of 1957 found Hilbert Schnettler and his brother-in-law Jim Hanna on a late season elk hunt in the Craig Mountains. They were in the breaks of Captain John Creek and were faced with snow past knee deep. Those conditions on a north slope are tough enough, but couple it with terrain steeper than the proverbial "cow's face" and it quickly became a real adventure.

Early in the morning, they picked up a lone elk track up top. They had followed it about 300 yards into the timber when a big bull spooked. Jim figures the bull had gone into the timber to get out of the wind and snow.

The massive elk made a run for it and was a good distance away across the draw when Hilbert and Jim both fired rounds from their aught-sixes. At least one struck the bull and slowed him down. Both men fired again and the bull was quickly down for good, buried in the snow.

Luckily for Hil and Jim, the bull stayed anchored long enough for them to get across the draw and tie him to a tree. Had the bull begun to slide on such a slick, precipitous slope, Jim says the bull would have made one hell of a splash in the still distant Snake River!

The two happy hunters marveled at the big set of antlers, dressed their prize, and then went back to town and borrowed a horse. It was nearly three miles to the elk, so trips in and out added time and effort at an exponential rate. They returned with a horse and took out half the elk, returning the same day for all the rest.

Jim and Hil were decidedly opposed on whether or not to pack out those huge antlers. Luckily, Hilbert won out and the rack was preserved. While the elk was tagged at nearly eight o'clock in the morning, it was an excruciating eighteen hours later (at 2 a.m.) when they finally arrived home with the last of the meat.

For many years, this trophy was listed with no information other than it was taken by H.H. Schnettler. It was one that the author thought had little chance of having its story told. Through much digging and a little luck, we were very fortunate to locate Jim Hanna, who was able to relate the story. He also had the priceless photo below.

The antlers were given to Doug Lisle. Doug, in turn, donated them to the Idaho Department of Fish & Game, who now display them at their office in Lewiston.

Hilbert Schnettler holds the prized antlers taken by him and his hunting partner Jim Hanna. This was one of Idaho's largest bulls for many years.

Lee C. Mowreader
386-2/8 B&C Typical
Benewah County, 1992

Idaho Typical Rank: 15
Inside Spread: 47-4/8
Main Beams (R,L): 59-6/8, 60-4/8

Points (R,L): 6,7
Widest Spread: 51-7/8
Bases (R, L): 9-7/8, 9-6/8

The romance of elk hunting would be a twenty-mile pack train, complete with wall tents, where the hunter kills a large bull on the last day of a wonderful wilderness hunt with breathtaking scenery. For the vast majority of hunters, however, the reality is more likely to be a day hunt based out of a pickup, and stuck pushing thick timber and brush. Such was the case of Lee Mowreader and the great bull he harvested in 1992, at the age of 62.

Lee spent many years of his life locating roads for the U.S. Forest Service, as an engineering tech. So, despite the fact that he was 62, he was in great shape and could still hunt with great vigor. He loved to chase elk any chance he could.

The morning of that fateful day, October 17th, Lee and his son-in-law Floyd McPherson got into their little Mazda pickup and drove around, looking for a place to hunt. They chose a likely spot, near the Palouse Divide, and started the hunt at about 9 a.m.

A skiff of snow welcomed them as they began to work their way into the timber. Lee and Floyd split up, and Lee started walking a logging road. He had been on the hunt a total of about twenty minutes when he heard a twig break.

He looked over and properly identified the body of an elk in the timber. Normally, one would wait to determine the sex of the animal, but Lee was only looking for meat, and in this particular area, any elk was legal. As such, Lee shouldered his .30-40 Krag and fired, striking the elk in the lungs.

At the shot, Lee's target took off on a dead run. Lee then saw a flash of antler, but really didn't have time to evaluate it. He fired again and the bull fell, crashing into a tree only 100 feet from his initial sighting.

As Lee walked to his prize, he quickly discovered he had taken a bull that would exceed anything he had ever even imagined. So large, in fact, that he couldn't even budge it. The bull was so big, and there was so much downed timber, that Lee had to go get a chainsaw just to create an area to work in.

Floyd watched the bull until Lee returned, and then they set out to finish the job at hand. They were eventually able to cut the bull in half and drag the halves out, as Lee carved a path with the saw (at least until the chainsaw quit working).

Finally, hunters, elk, and chainsaw all arrived at the pickup. They loaded the Mazda and headed back to St. Maries with big smiles, and with what would soon become the largest elk ever recorded from Benewah County. Lee remarks that it was quite a sight to see, with that big ol' bull filling up that little pickup.

Lee Mowreader looks like small potatoes compared to this monster bull. So does his pickup, for that matter.

Kenny Poe
386-0/8 B&C Typical
Valley County, 1957

Idaho Typical Rank: 16
Inside Spread: 51-0/8
Main Beams (R,L): 53-7/8, 55-4/8

Points (R,L): 6,6
Widest Spread: 57-7/8
Bases (R, L): 9-6/8, 9-6/8

This great bull is Idaho's second-widest typical, with a 57-7/8 greatest spread. The bull was easy enough to find, being on display at the IDF&G Headquarters lobby in Boise, but the story proved difficult. With considerable effort, we were able to gather most of the story together.

The original listing showed that the bull was taken by Denny Young and owned by Kenny Poe. We eventually were able to locate a Dennie Young (different spelling) and sure enough, it was him. After talking with Dennie, it quickly became apparent that Dennie hadn't killed the bull at all - Kenny had. Dennie said that Kenny had never been one to want to attract attention to himself or to brag, so he had entered it under Dennie's name, not understanding that the records book also listed the owner. Dennie had always been a bit perplexed over Kenny's decision, but figured it wasn't a big deal. When I mentioned it to another friend of Kenny's, Gene Missman, Gene just laughed. "Sounds just like Kenny," he said. "He never did want to take credit for anything. Too modest."

Kenny had been in World War II, on a Half-Track Weasel amphibious unit, and then returned to Boise, where he had worked fixing and installing furnaces at the Hotel Boise. In his spare time, he loved to hunt and manage softball for teams in the valley.

Kenny ran into this amazing bull in the Corduroy Meadows area near Bear Valley in 1957. He downed it, just like 90% of the rest of the hunters in that era, with a .30-06.

The area the bull was taken in was densely thick with doghair lodgepole and downfall, a matter complicated by having horses come in to pack it out. This proved to be a real test. Compounding the difficulty of the situation was an oncoming storm that really beat them up. Kenny had to leave the antlers behind, and even then, they barely got out of there, being much worse for wear by the time they finally got back to camp.

Kenny was able to go back to the location about two years later and retrieve the prized antlers. After that, they lay around somewhat haphazardly in Kenny's yard for some time. Gene Missman came by one day and almost ran over them. At that point, he said, "I'm going to have these put up somewhere where they won't get broke. Come and get them when you want."

For the following 10-12 years, they hung at Gene's business in Boise – Missman Electric. Eventually, Kenny did stop by and get them, as he had decided he wanted them mounted. He hauled them over to Gene Worthham for the taxidermy work. After waiting in vain for a considerable time for a good bull cape, the rack eventually got mounted onto a big cow elk cape instead.

Kenny died of leukemia in 1972, and unfortunately took the exact specifics of the story with him. The legacy of his special day in 1957, however, lives on.

Kenny Poe's wide bull now greets visitors at IDF&G's Headquarters in Boise.

Jerry Nearing
385-7/8 B&C Typical
Shoshone County, 1976

Idaho Typical Rank: 17
Inside Spread: 44-3/8
Main Beams (R,L): 49-1/8, 51-7/8

Points (R,L): 6,6
Widest Spread: 49-3/8
Bases (R, L): 7-7/8, 7-7/8

When Jerry Nearing pulled the trigger on one of northern Idaho's biggest bulls, he had no idea the animal was a little-known hay thief. The bull had spent quite a bit of time not too far distant, eating hay that had been left out for cattle at an old abandoned homestead.

Jerry left camp early that morning and made his way into a drainage he hunted fairly regularly. He had been hunting for about two hours when he suddenly made out an elk rack slipping through the brush with fine precision. He knelt down and waited as it steadily moved closer.

The bull approached head on, continually feeding, with nary a clue his most deadly predator lay in ambush. The bull continued to bob his antlers gently while he fed only thirty yards away. Jerry felt the current position might be his only chance, so he placed a .270 bullet into the front of the massive chest of his quarry.

The bull dropped as fast as gravity would accept him, and then regained his feet nearly as quick. He took off, mortally wounded, until Jerry ended it quickly with an additional shot.

While Jerry was quartering his prize, a man approached him. "That's the one we were lookin' for," the man said solemnly.

The man went on to tell Jerry the story. His friend worked for the Forest Service, and had heard about the bull from a rancher while working in the area. It was the same rancher who had been inadvertently feeding the bull.

Jerry, being first and foremost a meat hunter, nearly gave the antlers to the man right there on the spot. Antlers were no big deal to him. Something in the back of his mind just couldn't quite commit to the idea, though, and he stopped just short of making the offer. Of course, you can hardly blame him.

Arth Day
385-5/8 B&C Typical
Kootenai County, 1971

Idaho Typical Rank: 18
Inside Spread: 40-3/8
Main Beams (R,L): 53-2/8, 53-0/8

Points (R,L): 6,6
Widest Spread: 47-4/8
Bases (R, L): 8-4/8, 8-1/8

Arth "Art" Day and his friend, Bob Hollingsworth, shared many good hunts over the years. They bagged a lot of elk and have a ton of memories, but none of their hunts will ever be quite as memorable as the one in fall of 1971.

They were camped at the mouth of Mac Creek, next to a man that had both a mule and a burro. They had exchanged pleasantries but weren't hunting together in the same party.

The first morning out, Art had packed a rifle with a scope, but in true north Idaho fashion, the fog proved too much for the glass. Art couldn't have shot an elk if he'd had one butted up to the end of the barrel.

The next day, he opted for his M-1 Garand .30-06 with an 8-shot clip. The open sights on this rifle surely would not fog up on him. They were up at 7a.m., and headed up the hill in a heavy fog. Art was nearly two miles in when the fog finally started to lift.

He was packing a self-made bamboo whistle, and was anxious to give it a try. He had no more than blown it when he got a strong response from a bull in the timber. The bull was about 400 yards away, across the canyon, and on the edge of a little sugarloaf.

Art wasted no time in cutting the distance and, as he closed in on where the bull had been, he blew his whistle again. Again the bull bugled back, and again the bull was one ridge further over. This time, however, Art could see the bull walking, only 300 yards away. Art exclaimed under his breath, *"Holy mackerel!"*

What a magnificent rack he had on him! Art watched in amazement as the defiant bull stretched his neck out fully and let loose with a towering bugle.

Art didn't let the magnificent distraction unsettle him, though. He quickly got into a prone position, placed the bead on the heart of his target, and pulled the trigger. At the shot, the bull turned and came down the hill. Art shot again, turning the bull back uphill toward the direction of the first shot. A third shot nailed the bull square in the beam, low on its right antler, temporarily stunning him before he proceeded up the hill at a slowed pace.

Art raced down the hill and up the other side, hoping that at least one of the shots had found a good home. He found blood and was intently following the trail when a blue grouse flushed underneath him. It nearly sent Art's already racing heart right through the front of his shirt!

The bull was now headed back toward the sugarloaf it had been on when Art had first seen him. *At least he was headed in a good direction*, Art thought to himself.

It was then that Art came upon the bull. It was just lying there in its death throes. In sentiments only a reverent hunter can understand, Art's anticipation changed quickly to sadness. He described the experience: "It was one of the saddest moments of my life. Here was this magnificent animal that was dying, and there was a tremendous sadness on my part. I had killed him, and there was nothing to be said."

Art cleaned the bull and then headed the 2-1/2 miles back to camp. That night he recounted his adventure to both Bob and the other man that was sharing their campsite. A plan was formed for the next day, and luckily, they would have the use of the mule and burro.

The next morning they were back at the kill site early. Art debated as to whether he wanted to bring the antlers out or not. It wasn't in his nature to do so, and this would just add to the load. Bob made the decision for him. "You gotta bring these out!"

They set about quartering the bull to load on the stock. Art packed the antlers, while the elk was split evenly between the two pack animals. The mule was bigger, but the burro withstood the weight and the packing much better than the mule.

The man told Art, "Just take the halter off the burro and let him follow you. He won't give you any trouble."

Art did as told, and the burro followed him like a puppy. A couple of times, when the burro got tired, he would just sit down and rest for a bit and then get up and go on his own. The mule, on the other hand, fell twice and really struggled with all the weight. That was one of Art's favorite memories of the hunt, watching that little burro outpack that mule. Art figured the bull weighed well over 1000 lbs.

Bob Hollingsworth, Art Day, and Ken Fitch, with Art's historic elk – one of the largest ever taken in Idaho. Note the bullet hole on the bull's right antler.

Dave Leonardson
385-3/8 LHS Typical
Clark County, 1988
Idaho State Record Typical (Muzzleloader)

Idaho Typical Rank: 19
Inside Spread: 44-1/8
Main Beams (R,L): 51-1/8, 49-7/8

Points (R,L): 6,6
Widest Spread: 48-0/8
Bases (R, L): 8-7/8, 8-3/8

*H*e was one of those rare specimens that takes your breath away and you feel like pinching yourself to see if you aren't dreaming. It was 1987, and I had some wonderful close encounters archery hunting this unique bull on the Montana side of the Divide. One of those times, he and a very nice 7-point bull sparred in a grassy meadow when their two harems came together at a watering hole. The bugling was loud and frequent as I moved in on the two herd bulls. It was a perfect set up. The cows and calves had fed off after watering, leaving the two bulls to display their dominance. The distracted bulls didn't notice me moving in quickly with the fading light. The larger 6-point bull was clearly superior, and the smaller 7-point finally made a quick retreat, coming within 30 yards of my position as he crossed a small stream.

  Being a trophy hunter, I didn't think twice about taking a shot, even though the 7-point would have been my best archery elk. Just 60 yards away was a monster bull. I had seen him several times at a distance, but this was my first close encounter. He had everything you dream of. Another hunter had seen him earlier that year and told me he would score 400 points. I closed the distance to 45 yards, and pulled to full draw. It was then my heart sank. I had lost the precious daylight needed to see my pins on the sight. It would have been unethical to just let the arrow go and hope to get lucky, so I had to let him go.

    The fall of 1988 was dry and unseasonably hot. It was the year of the huge Yellowstone fires. I spend most of my elk hunting time in the Centennial Mountains, and throughout that fall, beginning with archery season, you could see the smoke billowing in big columns from the Yellowstone fires not more than 30 miles away.

    October 29th was the opening day of the Idaho general season muzzleloader elk season. My wife, Tarri, had been wanting to go for a horse ride in the mountains. She is kind of a "fair weather" outdoorsperson, and the fall weather was perfect for some quality time as husband and wife. To top it off, the Montana rifle elk season was also open. Since the area we would be hunting was Idaho on the south side of the Continental Divide and Montana on the North, and because I had purchased a non-resident Montana elk tag, I threw an extra scabbard on my saddle and carried both my .300 Weatherby rife and .54-caliber Thompson Center Renegade muzzleloader.

    We started riding our Missouri Foxtrotting horses about 30 minutes before daybreak, giving us just enough time to ride toward the head of the divide. There were some sagebrush openings between timber patches that traditionally had served as feeding grounds to large numbers of elk. I wanted to be in position to glass this prime elk habitat just as the morning broke – that magical hour of first light.

    As we rode through the timber and were nearing the openings, Tarri said, "Did you hear that elk bugle?"

    My first thought was to question her because it was late in the year for bulls to be bugling without encouragement. Before I could answer her, she said, "There it was again! Did you hear it?"

    No, I hadn't heard either one. My hearing was shot from too many years of shooting rifles, pistols, shotguns, and muzzleloaders without hearing protection.

    Just before we broke out of the timber, I finally did hear a bugle. It wasn't just any bugle; it was the distinct bugle of a very large bull elk that I had pursued for the last two years. We made our way to a vantage point where we could look toward the sound of the bugle. I was glassing him at about 250 yards when Tarri first saw him with the naked eye. "Whoa; look at those horns," she said in an excited whisper.

    Tarri stayed with the horses while I tried to get ahead of the feeding elk herd. Slipping the old Renegade from the leather scabbard I moved rapidly, staying in an old wash for protection. I knew the elk herd was moving to a bedding area that was cool and protective from the approaching hot October sun.

    Coming off a bench bluff, I could see that some of the elk had already made it to the thick timber. The big bull was within 70 yards of the thick foliage and feeding in that direction. He was broadside, but further than I like to shoot the open-sighted smoke pole. The only rangefinder I had was in my head, and I silently guessed him to be 130 yards away. Focusing on the bull, I continued to move slowly forward when his head was down. I didn't notice the cow and calf until they blasted out below me and ran right up to the bull.

He jumped forward and came to full attention. I knew I only had a second or two and he would be gone. I hammered back and heard the click of the set trigger and fired before he could run. When the smoke cleared, the bull had joined the herd of cows and calves and together they disappeared into the thick forest. The only thing remaining was the cloud of dust made from their hooves coming in contact with the sun-baked soil.

After reloading and collecting myself, I went down to the spot where the bull had stood. I couldn't find any hair or blood. I walked the distance at 120 paces – a long shot by traditional muzzleloader standards. I had killed many other elk with this combination of blackpowder and round patch and ball. Most, however, had been shot within 75 yards.

I followed the elk trail for about 70 yards. The forest began to open up enough that I could see a few cows and calves gathered. Rising above an subalpine fir tree, I could see this huge elk rack. While the tree blocked my sight of the bull, it was clear that he was swaying from side to side. It was then that I realized that the bull had been hit by the 220-grain roundball.

I backed off and dropped down the mountain. Belly-crawling for ten minutes, I looked up over a knob that should place me close to where the bull had been standing. To my relief the bull was down and my shot had been true, actually taking part of the main artery just above the heart.

David W. Anderson
384-4/8 B&C Typical
Bonneville County, 1967

Idaho Typical Rank: 20
Inside Spread: 43-4/8
Main Beams (R,L): 57-0/8, 56-4/8

Points (R,L): 7,7
Widest Spread: 45-0/8
Bases (R, L): 9-5/8, 9-3/8

David Anderson was packing his Winchester Model 70 .30-06 on a November day when he downed this giant bull, one of the largest ever taken in eastern Idaho. A 150-yard shot on this big bull left David a pile of work to do. He had to quarter the bull to get it out, packing it on his back to his Jeep.

Keith W. Hadley
384-4/8 B&C Typical
Bonneville County, 1972

Idaho Typical Rank: 20
Inside Spread: 43-0/8
Main Beams (R,L): 53-2/8, 53-7/8

Points (R,L): 7,7
Widest Spread: 46-7/8
Bases (R, L): 8-5/8, 8-2/8

Keith Hadley had been camped out in the Deadman Creek area for the 1972 elk season, where he and his old hunting partner, Lyman Cushman, were chasing the elk around in a skiff of snow. One evening early into the hunt, Keith had taken a crack at a whopper of a bull, but missed.

The next morning, Keith and Lyman headed back in on horseback to the same area Keith had missed the big bull in the night before. While they knew the chances of that big bull still being there were slim, they had to try. They were expecting nothing, but hoping that maybe that big bull might not have run clear into Wyoming.

Luck was with them. Keith found the big bull not more than a few hundred yards from where he had been the night before. This time, Keith took his time and made his rare second chance count. Two shots at 200 yards with his .30-06 did the trick, and Keith suddenly had more meat than he knew what to do with.

Thenton L. Todd
383-2/8 B&C Typical
Nez Perce County, 1956

Idaho Typical Rank: 22
Inside Spread: 41-6/8
Main Beams (R,L): 52-2/8, 52-0/8

Points (R,L): 7,7
Widest Spread: 55-2/8
Bases (R, L): 9-4/8, 9-2/8

Thenton Todd hadn't been able to join his dad E.J., brother Curtis, or their friend (a man named Robinson) for the first few days of the hunt. The hunting party, minus Thenton, had been up in the Waha area of west-central Idaho in pursuit of elk.

The area they were in is a country characterized by extremely rugged landscape. It's not one for the faint of heart, especially when considering what it would take to get an elk out of some of the steep canyons that make up the Snake and Salmon River breaks.

Eventually, Thenton was able to break away from commitments, and headed up to join the crew. He made his way up the high mountain road, excited to be a part of the hunt. At one point, he decided to stop and stretch his legs. He wasn't too far from the Zaza area, south of Waha. It was about 4:30 p.m. when he wandered over toward a meadow, his Remington model 721 .30-06 in hand just in case.

Just like most of us, when he took his rifle, he thought it was unnecessary, but like they say, "You just never know when you might run into something."

Thenton had only walked a few hundred yards when, in no time at all, he was face to face with the biggest elk of his life! The unexpecting hunter was stunned. It was only 200 yards away, and Thenton quickly dispatched it with his .30-06. He promptly field-dressed and tagged the animal, then left it for the next day.

As he arrived in camp and told his story, his partners were more than just a little bit unimpressed with Thenton's easy elk. The next morning, they returned, loaded it up, and Thenton headed back with what would be just about the easiest record book elk you could ever ask for.

Terry Cozad
382-5/8 B&C Typical
Kootenai County, 1968

Idaho Typical Rank: 23
Inside Spread: 36-5/8
Main Beams (R,L): 52-3/8, 52-3/8

Points (R,L): 7,7
Widest Spread: 45-2/8
Bases (R, L): 9-2/8, 9-0/8

Terry Cozad lives up in Alaska now, but can still easily recall, with fond memories, his many elk hunts in Idaho's northern mountains. He has taken dozens of bulls over the years, but none as large as the one pictured above.

One day during the 1968 season, Terry decided to venture into a new area about twenty miles from Coeur d'Alene. It was as typical as the rest of north Idaho – plenty of brush, particularly huckleberry in this locale. It was spitting snow, and conditions had Terry excited.

He had been on the hunt less than half an hour and was making his way through the timber when he saw something he will never forget; a great bull elk with a wide spread was alone and feeding in the timber. Terry could literally see the antlers on both sides of a tree as the bull fed, unaware he was being watched.

For five full minutes Terry watched, all the while only 75 yards away. With every bite and subtle change to a new bunch of grass, Terry watched the massive antlers and long tines bob and weave slightly and rhythmically. In the meantime, Terry was forced to endure the intensity of the situation, as the tree continued to block any access to the vitals and any hope of a shot.

Finally, his patience paid off and the bull's vitals cleared into open space. Terry fired his .300 Win.-mag. and made good on the only shot he would ever need.

Paul E. Harrell
382-5/8 B&C Typical
Butte County, 1997

Kirk Drussel holds the results of his and Paul Harrell's 1997 elk hunt.

Idaho Typical Rank: 23
Inside Spread: 38-1/8
Main Beams (R,L): 52-3/8, 52-0/8

Points (R,L): 6,6
Widest Spread: 43-5/8
Bases (R, L): 8-6/8, 9-2/8

In Paul Harrell's era in the lava beds and sagebrush desert of south-central Idaho, there weren't many elk - plenty of deer and antelope, but few elk. As such, he had never had the good fortune of pulling the trigger on one.

As Paul got older and the elk populations increased, controlled hunt permits in the Arco area began to appear in the big game regulations. Kirk Drussel, Paul's grandson-in-law, talked Paul into applying for one of these special permits and in 1997, at the age of 83, Paul drew one.

At this point in his life, Paul didn't get around real well. With some effort and some luck, he was able to obtain a special permit that would allow him to shoot from a vehicle.

The hunt began in mid-September, and Kirk did all he could to get Paul into elk. His efforts paid off in a big way. They were out in the desert between Little Lost River and the INEEL when they encountered a sight worthy of the early explorers. There before them, 250 yards away, was a herd of 150 elk including several big bulls. As they looked on, they could hardly believe it! They spied the biggest bull, and Paul exclaimed, "Look at that! He's as big as a saddle horse!"

Paul leveled his .270 on the giant bull and hit it right behind the shoulder. A second shot, after a brief chase, was placed in the neck and finished the job.

At 83 years old, and with Kirk's help, Paul had taken his first elk. Not only that, but he had done it at 250 yards with open sights!

Paul Harrell, with a little help from Kirk Drussel, proved that it's never too late to bag your first elk. This big bull was a fine way to start, and finish!

John A. Larick, Jr.
382-2/8 B&C Typical
Clark County, 1963

Idaho Typical Rank: 25
Inside Spread: 44-2/8
Main Beams (R,L): 54-2/8, 56-6/8

Points (R,L): 7,7
Widest Spread: 49-0/8
Bases (R, L): 9-0/8, 8-4/8

In 1963, John Larick, Jr., was just an uncomplicated 17-year-old kid from the tiny community of Kilgore. There aren't a lot of things to do in Kilgore so, like most rural kids, he hunted whenever the chance was presented.

That fall, John, along with his dad (John Larick, Sr.), Jim Seipert, Chuck Bowen, and Pat Bowen, headed up to elk camp near the Montana border. They were many miles northeast of Dubois. It was the start of the season, weather was good, and hopes and excitement high.

They set up camp and were ready to hunt on opening morning. John, Jr., and his friend Jim saddled their horses and split off from the group. They hunted a while before stopping to build a warming fire and have some coffee. Jim recalls that they had made no particular effort to be quiet in the process.

They had barely remounted and started moving when ten cow elk came running out of a little draw. John quickly dismounted and waited for them to come out of a small aspen patch. Any elk was legal, and John wasn't picky.

All of the sudden, at about 10 a.m., John heard a crash and a squeal. He looked over and there stood the biggest elk he had ever seen! The bull was coming out of a wallow and was only twenty yards away!

John had no time to think, shooting the bull in the neck as quickly as he could find a target with his grandpa's .30-06 Enfield. To this day, John almost feels like the shot was half in self-defense. The bull was passing right by him, nose close to the ground, when John reached out and shot the bull behind the left ear, dropping the giant right in front of him.

Young John and Jim then had quite a time in their attempt to remove the bull from his final resting place. It was so big that they had to use the horses and ropes just to maneuver him.

Eventually, the bull was all loaded up, and proud young John Larick, Jr., rode backward on one horse while Jim "drove." John held the rack upright for nearly two miles down an old forest service trail to camp where, at least for that season, he would be the camp hero, and the only hunter to fill his elk tag.

Charles E. Carver
381-7/8 B&C Typical
Idaho County, 1998

Idaho Typical Rank: 26
Inside Spread: 40-7/8
Main Beams (R,L): 57-1/8, 56-6/8

Points (R,L): 7,7
Widest Spread: 43-6/8
Bases (R, L): 9-7/8, 10-0/8

It started with some information my old roommate, Mike Fitzgerald gave me. We both grew up in Orofino, and both went to University of Idaho in Moscow. He is an avid antler hunter, and over the years has amassed some impressive horns, and covered as much country as Lewis and Clark in the process. He actually has the sheds from the bull I killed, nicknaming him "Whale Tail" due to the impressive beam length (the sheds are 6x6, my bull was 7x7 when I got him, so the "whale tail" sprouted another tine).

After a lot of prying, Mike finally told me the rough location of where he found those nice sheds. We spent three years hunting the bull, including the first year which was just getting to know the area. That first year I went into the area, I hunted alone for a whole week (in hindsight that was dumb – it's dangerous country.) On top of that, I forgot my heavy hunting coat, which wasn't discovered until I was already stuck there. I covered thousands of vertical feet every day. My legs were stiff, and over several days I became accustomed to living like a coyote and being in pain. My meals were instant oatmeal in the morning, and kipper snacks, peanut butter crackers, dried fruit, instant noodles, and jerky the rest of the time. It wasn't a luxurious outfitter-style event, and the weather was rainy/snowy nearly every day of that first year's hunt

I hunted with a Winchester 7mm-mag. Nothing fancy, but very effective and capable of a long-range shot if needed. It's a gun my dad gave me about ten years prior, and I still have it to this day (except I prefer archery these days).

I scoped five bulls that were all huge, and guessed they'd need to be on the ground, with tape in hand, to decide for sure which was the best. There were another half dozen or so pilot bulls, and over 30 cows. Whale tail was among them, he still seemed to be a 6x6, but it's possible I couldn't determine the smaller 7th points on each beam. He was too far away, though, and my hunt was ending. I had to enjoy watching him instead. It was a great hunt, and I'd been a full week in the roughest country possible, and hadn't seen another human – quite amazing. I am still amazed at the lack of mule deer I saw. It was disappointing to not see many mule deer or any nice bucks. I did find 1 set of mule deer sheds and some older elk sheds, which I left propped up against trees.

The next season I could go after the bull, my brother Rick Carver agreed to go, too. We followed the same basic agenda as I'd done year before, but I slightly modified the base camp location, remembering how I'd scattered the herd the year before. We had camp set at about 2 p.m. and then set off on a scouting trip. I had the same gun and he had binoculars (no hunting for him – he was a human pack mule to help out!) That first evening, we spotted a couple of nice bulls and managed to bugle one within 200 yards. My brother told me to shoot. I said, "Hell, no! He's a baby, and we've still got all week."

We both estimate he scored around 300. He had a very unique kicker off the back side of his left antler near the base, which jutted about a foot out over his upper shoulder. Most people would love to have that bull on their wall, but we let him walk off!

As darkness approached, we began to slowly work back down the mountain to where camp was located. At one point, we could see five cows and a huge bull about 800 yards below us, but it was nearly dark. I couldn't tell which one of the five bulls it was from the prior year, but I was sure it was one of them. It turns out it was Whale Tail, but I wouldn't know that until later. He'd grown up! We could see the big bull rear his head back and bugle, but it was barely audible to us. I decided we'd be as sneaky as possible back to base camp and set after him the next morning.

We were both so excited our hearts pounded, and it was all we could do to fight the urge to sprint across the mountain to get close enough for a shot. We walked for over an hour in the dark before reaching base camp, but were certain we hadn't spooked anything.

Well before light the next morning, we were gone on our quest. We hoped to time daybreak with our arrival to the general area the bull had been in the previous evening. We were crossing a ravine with running water when I thought I heard a bugle. The noise of the water was confusing my ears, but my instincts were on full alert. I whispered to my brother that I thought we were very close to elk. After the fact, I realized we were 200 yards away from the monster but didn't know it. Good thing we went into super-stalk mode right then. It was also fortunate that the wind was in our favor.

We very slowly stalked, scanning around everywhere for elk or movement each couple of steps. After half an hour, I caught movement in my peripheral vision to the left, and nearly fainted when I saw a HUGE bull only 40-50 yards away, quartering away from me! He had no idea we were there. I dropped to the ground and signaled for my brother to do likewise.

I am usually calm, but this time I had the jitters as I prepared the gun to fire. I eased up, placed the cross hairs, and shot. The bull didn't even flinch. I knew I couldn't have missed at that range, but doubted myself and rapidly shot two more times. Finally, I forced myself to relax. The bull went down in his resting place a few minutes later. He never ran or anything; he just stood where I first saw him until he lay down and died.

My brother volunteered to work across the ravine to where the bull was while I maintained position to keep him in sight, just in case. This all went down within minutes, and I don't even recall being judgmental about the antlers or anything. I just knew it was a big bull and that I needed to take the shot. My brother confirmed it when he reached the animal and yelled out, "He's a monster; I think you'll be happy with this one!"

We had him down before one hour after first light. The sun wasn't even shining down on us yet. It was and still is amazing to me when I think back on it. Of course, the work just began at that point as we worked to bone the meat and make the numerous trips back to base camp. On one of our trips, I noticed a large aspen tree that had been mauled by an elk. Later, we compared the bark remains. It was Whale Tail who'd done it, and it was fresh from the night before. Bark still floated on some areas of the creek in that ravine! He still has that bark on his antler to this day, as he rests on my wall.

We relocated camp, fishing and lazing around until we were picked up. In the meantime, we stored the meat in a small, cold nearby creek, since we still had a week to wait. It turned out to be a lazy week once the hunt was over, and I was so nervous about leaving the antlers that I didn't dare go on any hikes! We did end up seeing other people that week, but they were too late, thank goodness!

We dined on fish and elk steak for the rest of that week, which was a genuine luxury compared to how I'd lived in the area on the previous trip. It was the hunt of a lifetime, and he's the trophy of a lifetime, with good memories to go along.

Courtesy of Charles Carver

Curt L. Stegelmeier
381-5/8 B&C Typical
Fremont County, 1997

Idaho Typical Rank: 27
Inside Spread: 49-7/8
Main Beams (R,L): 56-1/8, 54-0/8

Points (R,L): 6,6
Widest Spread: 54-5/8
Bases (R, L): 8-6/8, 8-3/8

For a typical Idaho kid growing up on a ranch, school and work often get in the way of more important things, like hunting. It was no different for Curt Stegelmeier and his older brother, Chad. They had drawn late season bull tags, but found themselves spending most of the season going to school during the day and feeding cows at night. With only a few days left in the season, they finally managed to finagle a few days off.

The Saturday before the end of season, they headed out and, before long, Chad had taken a nice six-point bull. The boys spent that morning getting the bull out, and then headed back to the ranch with bull in tow.

After taking care of business and having a quick lunch, the boys headed back out. There was already more than two feet of snow on the ground, so the boys were doing all of their traveling on snowmobiles. They covered quite a bit of country that day, and saw what looked like a big bull, but there was really no chance to get on him.

The next morning, Curtis, Chad, and the boys' father Roy all went out to the area again. They were able to locate the tracks of a few elk, but had to return to the ranch, as Roy had to be at work. Before he left, though, he told the boys where he thought they should go for their afternoon hunt.

The boys headed back out into the cold and snow at about 3:30 p.m. Half an hour later, they parked their sleds and started up the hill on a compacted snowmobile track that not only was easier than walking in more than two feet of snow, but also allowed them to be much quieter.

They had only gone a few hundred yards when they started hearing some sounds up ahead. Further inspection revealed it was three bull elk all milling around a tree. The boys continued to watch the three bulls, which included a small six-point, a raghorn bull, and the big bull they had seen the day before.

Chad spoke softly to his little brother. "Take your time, and shoot the biggest one."

Curt lined up the open sights, steadied his aim, and then fired his 6mm. Within moments, his first elk had just been anchored to the ground. They were both more than just a little excited when they were able to finally see the wide-racked giant up close.

They left the bull to go and recruit some more help, in the form of Chad's friend, Brett Reynolds. It took all three of the boys, and all three of their snowmobiles, to drag the bull out to a more manageable location.

Curt notes that when using three snowmobiles all tied together to drag out a giant bull elk, make sure his antlers don't hang up on any trees. It has a tendency to stop the sleds cold and send all three boys flying over the top of the hoods!

A cold and tired but nonetheless excited Curt Stegelmeier, holding up the antlers of one of eastern Idaho's biggest bulls.

E. LaRene Smith
381-0/8 B&C Typical
Bonneville County, 1966

Idaho Typical Rank: 28
Inside Spread: 40-4/8
Main Beams (R,L): 48-0/8, 54-4/8

Points (R,L): 7,8
Widest Spread: 47-0/8
Bases (R, L): 8-5/8, 8-7/8

As I climbed up the ridge, I told myself I had to be calm, quiet and careful. I was coming into the area from whence came that early morning bugle I'd heard while standing on the mountain where we were camped. Slowly, I skylined myself to take in the panorama of the big ridge looming across from me.

Then I heard it – that same old hoarse, croaking bugle I'd heard this morning. Emerging over the far ridge came four cow elk being pushed along by a nice six-pointer. He was anxious to keep them moving. I was sure he wasn't the big guy I'd been hearing, but this one would do just fine for my first elk hunt. He got them running down the mountain, straight below and closer to me.

Just then, a huge bull appeared through the pines, topping over at the same place the younger bull had just come with his cows. The big guy stopped and threw out a roaring challenge to the escaping group below him.

I realized I had no choice. The big old king was my new target. I let the smaller bull go down into the ravine and disappear. My .300 Savage was a strong gun, but my estimation of the distance seemed an awful stretch. There was a shallow hollow and a steep but short climb to the top of the small ridge that lay between me and the open mountainside. I needed to be on that ridge if I was to have any chance at a clean shot. "No time to think; just charge down into that dip and get to the next ridge," I told myself as I did just that.

When I topped out on the ridge it gave me a great view. The big bull had stopped for some reason. Something had caught his attention and he was looking up toward the peak where we had our camp.

Now he was closer to me, but he was standing at a quartering angle with his hindquarter toward me. This made my heart/lung target very narrow. Man, I didn't want to shoot him in the rear end. I leaned against a small tree to steady me. Oh, how I love my open sights. It always seemed like I could put my shots where I was aiming as long as I held steady. I was gasping for air, what with that mad dash to get to this ridge and all the excitement of the hunt. I'd just have to stop breathing long enough to get my sights right on and then squeeze off the shot.

I lined up my sights, but I was shaking. *It's now or never, now hold steady*, I told myself. I swallowed, smoothed out my aim, and squeezed the trigger. His hind legs dropped. "Oh, no! I've hit him in the rear end," I thought to myself.

I took another fast shot. He was up; he was down; and then he lay still.

I ran down from the little ridge into the gully and all the way up to the bare mountainside where I'd last seen him, hoping he hadn't jumped up again. He hadn't.

What a huge, beautiful beast! My first elk! I nudged him with my gun. I kicked him with my foot. No response, so I got out my trusty hunting knife I'd used to cut the jugular of many a mule deer. The 4" blade just got through that tough hide and partway through the neck meat but not even close to his jugular.

My husband, Vern, who'd heard my shooting, was just coming around the mountain. He had a larger knife, so together we proceeded to gut him out. Next thing you know, my husband was doing all the work while I was stroking those beautiful antlers, and counting and recounting points. Eight on one side; seven and a bump on the other. What a trophy! My gamble to go for the big bull had paid off.

LaRene Smith, up close and personal with one of Idaho's finest bulls.

It turned out my first shot entered just behind the rib cage high and traveled up through the lung and into the heart. The second shot did something that may have never happened before, or ever happen again. It drilled a hole right through the main beam about two-thirds of the way back, then continued on and drilled another hole clear through the other main beam in a similar (albeit larger) fashion.

BEST WOMAN'S SCORE for elk antlers in the world records of the Boone and Crockett Club should be this entry, bagged last fall in Madison County by Mrs. LaRene Smith. It scored preliminary measurements of 397-6/8 points and presently ranks third largest ever shot by either sex in Idaho. It should place eighth in the world record book's next edition.

This article came out in the Blackfoot newspaper a few months after the hunt. The score and location were inaccurate, but the significance of the hunt remained. No, Larene didn't look like your average elk hunter!

Mark Williams
380-5/8 B&C Typical
Custer County, 1976
Owned by Cabela's

Idaho Typical Rank: 29
Inside Spread: 49-0/8
Main Beams (R,L): 62-4/8, 65-3/8

Points (R,L): 6,8
Widest Spread: 54-3/8
Bases (R, L): 8-5/8, 8-5/8

This huge bull, taken by Mark Williams in Custer County in the mid-1970s, has the longest main beams ever recorded in the state of Idaho. What a bull! Unfortunately no information was available on the circumstances of the hunt. Perhaps someone will come forward so we can tell this story in a later book.

Howard W. Holmes
380-0/8 B&C Typical
Blaine County, 2001
Idaho State Record Typical (Archery)

Idaho Typical Rank: 30
Inside Spread: 43-6/8
Main Beams (R,L): 53-1/8, 54-0/8

Points (R,L): 6,6
Widest Spread: 47-6/8
Bases (R, L): 7-4/8, 7-3/8

In the early '70s, a good friend of mine, Dick Vail, invited me to go bowhunting. I immediately became hooked. I have always enjoyed watching animals and being in at close range, and have always liked the challenge.

In the early years, there were a lot of close encounters, but it was mostly just exercise. There were many great times, but also a huge learning curve. There wasn't as much information on bowhunting and calling elk like there is today. It was 1976 before I was in on a successful bowhunt. Dave Barnard took a nice bull that I had called in out of a clearcut. It would be another four years before I would tag one.

As the years went on, we had more exercise, and a little more success. One of my most memorable hunts was when I took my son, Christopher, out of school for a couple of days to hunt when he was fifteen. The first day of the hunt, he harvested a six-point bull. That would complement the Pope & Young bear he got that spring.

As the years wore on, I began to think more and more about trying to get a truly large bull. A friend, Gary Benson, said, "If you always shoot a little one, you will never shoot a big one."

At 3 a.m. on opening morning of the 2001 archery season, I turned off the alarm and got my aging body out of bed. An hour and a half later, I parked my truck and began the two-mile hike into my treestand. My buddy, Brian Hamel, and I had found the spot the previous year. It was an ideal spot, where a spring of water came out and ran a little ways before diving back into the ground.

I put fourteen hours in on the stand that day, and counted eighteen different mule deer does and fawns. It was entertaining, but grueling. I knew after that day that it would be difficult to do that on consecutive days, so I mixed it up a bit. The next day I took it a little easier and did some exploring.

On the third day, it was back up early and into the stand. I saw a fox come in to drink, had some fun with a hawk, and finally, a hummingbird came in and perched himself on my arrow. I thought, "Well! There you go; you just blessed my arrow!"

That night, as I walked out, I started to rethink not only the way I was hunting, but what it was I was after. I decided to do something different in the mornings, and then hunt the stand in the afternoons. I also decided that taking a Pope & Young trophy wasn't as big a priority as it was before. Being out and having fun is what I was here for.

The next day, I helped my buddies, Brian Hamel and Chris Poynter, remove their antelope blinds. That evening, we did a mule deer hunt down a closed road.

On September 3rd, I did some camp chores. That afternoon, I headed back into the stand. I arrived there at 5 p.m. It was another warm day, and I had the usual resident deer come by for a visit, along with a couple of small bucks.

About 8 p.m., high on the ridge, I spotted some elk coming out to feed. Soon, it was ten. As I scanned the edge of the brush with my binoculars, I spotted a huge bull elk! I even said to myself, "Now, that's a bull."

He began to herd his cows over to my side of the draw. I had to decide between whether or not they would be over here by dark, and to move after them, or to stay put. I decided to stick with the original plan.

Within minutes, I could hear limbs crashing. They were coming in to water! I grabbed my bow and made ready. As all ten cows and the huge bull came in, I was caught off guard. The bull never held back. He just came right on in with the cows.

I took a quick look at his rack, to make sure it was the same bull. It was, and he was majestic. I never looked back at his antlers, instead burning a hole with my eyes into the area I wanted to place the arrow. Unfortunately, I couldn't move, as his cows were looking all around, including at me!

I held perfectly still, moving only my eyes. Then, for whatever reason, all the cows drifted off. I took a look to make sure they were gone, then directed my attention to the bull. He hadn't lifted his head once. I brought the bow up and to full draw, and couldn't help but notice how easy it seemed to pull back. I held the forty-yard pin on him, and when everything looked right, I released the arrow.

The bull bolted and ran toward the cows. He then stopped under a large fir tree, trying to locate the danger. He was now at thirty yards and broadside. Ever so quietly, I knocked another arrow, came to full draw again, and placed another arrow behind the shoulder. He lunged forward and out of sight, and two seconds later, he was down. I began to go through a whole bunch of emotions, ranging from joy to relief to sorrow. It's just hard to explain until you have been there.

I got down from the stand, picked up what was left of my second arrow, and began to blood trail, even though I knew right where he was. As I approached, I was in awe. I also knew I had my work cut out for me.

The first arrow had penetrated from just in front of the right thigh and lodged in the left front shoulder. The second arrow had taken out his heart. Either would have done the job just fine.

After field-dressing, I jogged the two miles back to the truck to get help. I eventually recruited my hunting partner Jim Sherman, who was due into camp just that night, along with Chris Poynter, Brian Hamel, and Paul Ramm. Coincidentally, Brian and Paul had just taken a deer each that same evening.

We spent the whole night boning out the bull and packing him out. We had him to the locker by about 7 a.m. It was difficult to get any sleep that morning and for several days after.

Being over 60, I know my elk hunting days are numbered; I always knew they would be. Like the words of a country song, "Lord I want to go to heaven, I just don't want to go tonight." I won't ever want to quit elk hunting, but I know some day I will have to.

William V. Baker
379-6/8 B&C Typical
Adams County, 1976

Idaho Typical Rank: 31
Inside Spread: 36-2/8
Main Beams (R,L): 52-0/8, 51-6/8

Points (R,L): 9,8
Widest Spread: 47-5/8
Bases (R, L): 10-0/8, 10-0/8

William V. "Bill" Baker was hunting in the New Meadows area when he encountered this amazing bull on September 30th, 1976. A well-placed 100-yard shot from his .30-06 made sure the bull was anchored to the ground for good.

This bull is very unique in the way he is built. Very few bulls in recorded history have ever had an extra matched pair of normal-appearing points before the G-4 or "sword" point. B&C has a special rule on this for elk stating that if they are matched and normal they will be scored as such. That enables this bull to be scored as a typical rather than non-typical.

This bull received an Honorable Mention at Boone and Crockett Club's 16th Awards Program in 1977.

B&C Official Measurer Stuart Murrell poses with William V. Baker's exceptional 1976 bull taken in Adams County.

Joe Gisler
379-5/8 B&C Typical
Valley County, 1961

Idaho Typical Rank: 32
Inside Spread: 55-0/8
Main Beams (R,L): 53-7/8, 48-2/8

Points (R,L): 7,7
Widest Spread: 56-0/8
Bases (R, L): 8-2/8, 8-4/8

Every fall in the 1950s-60s, Joe Gisler and wife Jeane, along with Lamont Herbold, Lee Higley, and Gerald Hawkins, would load up and head for Bear Valley. They always had the same camp, about 40 miles west of Stanley in the mountains. The group had some old jeeps that could really get up into some rugged places, and they had a particular meadow they loved to stay in.

They primarily hunted an old burned area that had gone up in smoke in the 1930s. It had recovered substantially in the decades since, and offered plenty of browse for game. It was an area that they had hunted since 1953, so they knew it very well.

On the third day of the season, October 7th, Joe and Lee jumped into the Willys Jeep and headed up the mountain. They navigated the vehicle up an old bulldozer trail (a remnant of the fire) until they got to the top. Once there, Lee hunted back down while Joe stayed high on the mountain.

Joe was packing his .264 Win.-mag and was practicing something that day that was none too common for that era. He was after a big bull, and before long had passed up a couple of spikes and several cows.

Not an uncommon occurrence in Idaho, that early fall day was plenty warm. Warm enough for a nap, that was for sure. Joe had a particular tree he liked for just such an occasion, and visited that tree once again for a quick noontime snooze.

He had been awake for about half an hour and started heading for a saddle - one he knew had already been pushed by his hunting party. It was about 1 p.m. as he approached the saddle, and he heard a noise. He looked up in time to see a great big bull with a light-colored coat picking his way through the lodgepole. Evidently, Joe's party had pushed that bull right through that saddle!

At 75 yards, Joe aimed behind the bull's left shoulder and pulled the trigger on his .264. The bull instantly took off, making Joe think he had missed. The bull started to make his way down a gully, only to make a sharp u-turn and head back to within fifteen feet of where he had been standing when Joe shot! This time, Joe aimed carefully and shot the bull in the neck, dropping him.

Joe had no idea how big the bull was until he approached him. One thing that didn't take long to realize, though, was that it was way too big for one man to pack out! Luckily for him, they were able to drive the jeep right up to him.

Joe was thirty-one years old when he tagged this great trophy. Even though it happened over 45 years ago, he can remember one of his finest experiences in the mountains as if it were yesterday. If you ever get the chance to see his bull, it now hangs in the Elks Lodge in Rupert, and Joe would be more than happy to tell you all about it!

Joe Gisler, with his 1961 Valley County bull. Joe should've shot a smaller elk. With a monstrous 55-inch inside spread, this bull is too wide to hold his rifle.

Picked Up by George Dovel
379 B&C Typical
Big Creek, 1963

Idaho Typical Rank: 33
Inside Spread: 40-6/8
Main Beams (R,L): 50-4/8, 51-1/8

Points (R,L): 6,6
Widest Spread: 44-3/8
Bases (R, L): 9-0/8, 8-6/8

George Dovel was accustomed to spending much of the fall season in Idaho's rugged backcountry. Back then, he was working as a guide, spending his efforts attempting to put less experienced hunters in front of an elk.

Late in the fall of 1963, George took a week off to trap beaver and explore. His journey was to take him east of Big Creek, into the West Fork of Rush Creek drainage. A guide that was working with George dropped him off, with the intention of a rendezvous a week later. The weather was surprisingly moderate for that time of year – a welcome occurrence for a man alone in the backcountry.

George made his way down into the bottom of the drainage and quickly stumbled onto quite an unexpected discovery. There before him lay the carcass of a giant bull elk. The grand bull had lain there dead for at least a few weeks. All that remained of the remarkable creature were a few tattered pieces of hide; the rest had been ravaged by scavengers. But in spite of the condition of the rest of the bull, the rack, in all its splendor, lay there in perfect condition. There was no sure way to tell how this great bull met his fate, although George surmises it was likely a poorly placed bullet that took too long to do the job.

George knew he had quite a find on his hands, and went to great lengths to preserve them. Sadly, all the effort was, in the end, for naught. The rack was stolen from George many years ago. He was actually able to trace them down to the thief that took them, only to find they had been cut up into pieces for handles and buckles. Only the pictures, and now the story, remain of one of Idaho's great elk racks.

Edward L. Bradford, Larry Harvey, & Kenny Hall
378-4/8 B&C Typical
Shoshone County, 1963

Idaho Typical Rank: 34
Inside Spread: 45-2/8
Main Beams (R,L): 54-3/8, 55-3/8

Points (R,L): 6,6
Widest Spread: 48-7/8
Bases (R, L): 8-6/8, 8-6/8

In the fall of 1963, three of us sixteen-year-old schoolmates decided to go hunting. Larry Harvey and Kenny Hall and I jumped into an old 1936 Chevy sedan and went up into the hills on the south side of the greater Silver Valley, which was the South Fork of the Coeur d'Alene River. The drainage we hunted was Pine Creek, which included Pinehurst and upper Pine Creek villages. We hunted in the hills above them. The exact location where we downed the bull was Trapper Creek.

It was a cool, sunny, beautiful day and not a breath of wind. We parked the car up near the summit of the major ridge, and went down a spur ridge. We then divided up on separate finger ridges about 1/8-mile apart.

A short time after we split up, I heard a shot from Larry's direction. I listened for a long time to hear any signal shots or yells that he might have something down. Nothing. Later on, I met up with Kenny and we were chatting about Larry maybe having something down when Larry came hustling up to us very excited. He said he hadn't gone far when he suddenly came upon a huge bull. He only had an instant to fire, and had taken a neck shot that he thought had connected. Dad always told me to go for the lungs, as it's hard to make a kill on a big bull when going for the neck.

Anyway, now we knew we had a wounded elk in the area and we calculated a plan of attack. Kenny was the only one with a scope on his rifle, so we positioned him where he could observe a partially open hillside on the opposite side of the drainage. Larry and I split up quite a distance and headed down into the very steep canyon to find or flush the bull.

I had been gone only about ten minutes when I saw a small treetop shaking about two hundred yards below me close to the canyon bottom. I instinctively knew by the size of the tree that this must be the bull coming into contact with the tree.

The hillside was so steep that when you would jump down the hill it looked like a broad jump. We were all in tremendous shape at that age, so this was an effective way to cover terrain.

All of the sudden, the big bull came into view, only twenty feet away! I was shocked by the size of him. I got a huge case of bull fever, and had nowhere near the calm I wanted in this overwhelming excitement. I fumbled with the safety on my ol' .30-40 Krag, and that's all the time the bull needed to be off and moving like the blazes again.

The bull and I were both near the bottom of the canyon, and it appeared to me that he was going up the other side. I yelled as loud as I could, knowing that Kenny was positioned and ready for a possible open shot. In the dead air of the canyon, he heard me and was ready.

I continued as fast as I could on the trail of the bull, hoping I might be able to catch up for a shot. Well, that big bull still managed to get 400 yards ahead of me, even though he was wounded and going uphill.

The bull then made the mistake of coming out into an open area across the canyon from Kenny. We don't know how far it was across that canyon, but Kenny said later that after firing a few times, he put a healthy lead on the animal and finally scored a hit.

Kenny yelled and said he had hit the bull, and that it was coming back down into the canyon. It couldn't have been more than thirty seconds and here came that bull, like a freight train, headed right for me. I had but just a second to move out of the way and shoot as he went by me a few feet away! The bull collapsed and that was the end of it.

I yelled with great excitement into the canyon that we finally had him down. Three kids all erupted into war hoops and filled the canyon with our yells of joy.

It took us boys close to three days to backpack the meat to a ridge, go get a horse from Kenny's home, and eventually get it packed out. That is a whole story in itself! All in all, it was a wonderful adventure.

Young Ed Bradford, along with his dad, Robert, show off their two prized bulls, both taken in 1963 on separate hunts. This photo has been in Ed's wallet for four decades.

Ed also wrote a general essay on hunting back in the good ol' days. It is interesting, so I included it.

Our family hunted and fished all over the northwest, mostly in Idaho. We went fishing or hunting every weekend while I was growing up. Even when I was in the service, until I was 38, I spent my leaves back home in Idaho fishing and hunting.

We started out with canvas tents, eventually graduating to pickup campers when they were introduced. Our first hunting clothes were World War II surplus. There weren't a whole lot of Eddie Bauer and L.L. Bean stores around.

Catch and release and trophy hunting wasn't our style, and it really wasn't in vogue then in our setting. We hunted and fished for enjoyment, to be together as a family, and to put food on the table. The freezer was always full of elk steak, roasts, and burger. Deer were made up into jerky and summer sausage for sandwiches. There were smoked kokanee and king salmon, along with ducks, geese, and grouse. I rarely if ever had domestic meat on the table. All of this was our lifestyle. Our style of elk hunting was to stillhunt them. We hunted the Coeur d'Alene, Clearwater, and St. Joe drainages. The timber and brush, for the most part, offered shots only in the 30-50 yard range. Paying attention to habitat, feed sources, rubs, et cetera, would put you into an area where the elk were, and from then on it was very, very slow and quiet stillhunting. Quite a few of our kills were from less than 100 feet. No elk bugles or calls or spotting scopes were used.

Our first rifles were the WWI Springfield 30-06 and Spanish-American War .30-40 Krag. In later years, I used a .300 Weatherby, which was my favorite. Dad always handloaded all our ammo.

I never experienced anti-hunting on any scale as it is today. All boys (not many girls) were taught by their fathers, grandfathers, or uncles how to safely handle and maintain firearms. I attended firearms safety classes in '59 and '61. It was routine and just about every boy attended, even though some didn't hunt.

Today, there are fewer and fewer families with male head of households to pass on the heritage of harvesting wild game and in teaching the responsibilities, safety, and integrity encompassed within.

Unknown Hunter
377-4/8 B&C Typical
Idaho, Circa 1973

Idaho Typical Rank: 35
Inside Spread: 37-4/8
Main Beams (R,L): 57-4/8, 55-1/8

Points (R,L): 6,6
Widest Spread: 46-7/8
Bases (R, L): 9-5/8, 9-3/8

The Soulen Ranch, located on the breaks of the Snake River west of Cambridge, is one of those Idaho ranches that epitomizes the remote and self-sufficient nature of Idaho's early pioneers. It is the ideal of the far-removed. During the winter, the ranch is even more isolated, as the only way out is down the Snake River via Brownlee Reservoir or by snowmobile.

Harry Soulen had a hired hand wintering on the place as a live-in worker. After a period of time, Harry began noticing beef were coming up missing, as well as some possible poaching. Harry finally gave the man the boot and hired a new hand.

Dale Rasmus knew the new ranch hand, and was told that there might be some good hunting opportunities there. Dale made a few trips to the ranch to help with various projects in exchange for the privilege of being able to hunt there. This was quite a commitment, as Dale lived far out of state.

On one of Dale's visits to the ranch, he noticed a gorgeous set of elk antlers hanging on a horse barn. He inquired about their origin, but could only trace it to the point of discovering that it was already attached to the barn when Soulen bought the property. It was probably taken in the Washington County area by a local, and proudly displayed in that location for many years.

Dale asked Harry if he was interested in doing anything with them or maybe selling them. Harry's reply was typical for a western ranchman who was part of a generation not too concerned about antlers. "Go ahead and just take 'em. When you get tired of messing with them, just throw 'em away."

Luckily, Dale knew better, and has helped to preserve a small piece of Idaho's elk hunting heritage. This great bull, with the 23"-plus G-4s, truly stands out as one of Idaho's finest.

Roger Johnson
376-7/8 B&C Typical
Shoshone County, 1980

Idaho Typical Rank: 36
Inside Spread: 33-1/8
Main Beams (R,L): 56-6/8, 54-3/8

Points (R,L): 6,6
Widest Spread: 50-0/8
Bases (R, L): 7-7/8, 7-5/8

Before all the roads fully infiltrated the Coeur d' Alene River area, there were probably as many or more big bulls in that drainage as perhaps any place in Idaho. Tough to access areas, ravines choked with dense brush, and difficult weather to hunt them in all helped to provide a perfect refuge in which to grow big elk.

Roger Johnson and Steve Kennedy left town early one morning in the fall of 1980 with daydreams of elk running through their thoughts. They had a spot picked out where seeing another hunter was a rare occurrence.

They parked the truck and began hiking up a knifelike finger ridge at daybreak. When they began to level out a bit, they stopped so Roger could try bugling. This, of course, was before the boom of hunting accessories, so no advanced bugle system was available. Instead, Roger had brought a piece of corrugated natural gas line. If he blew it just right, he could get two different notes out of it – not bad for a piece of flexible tubing with no mouthpiece. He received an immediate response on his first attempt of the morning. It was so quick and easy that their first impression was, "Oh, great, more hunters."

They decided they had better investigate, however, and moved in carefully. It was then they heard a grunt and an exhale, and knew that this was no hunter!

They kept moving in quietly, careful with every step, and finally Roger shifted his concentration off the ground and looked up. His eyes instantly grew wide as he saw a giant bull coming in from only fifty yards out! He had no time to think, and in his haste to fire, he missed on his first attempt, nailing a tree behind the bull. Instead of getting out of Dodge, the sudden blast caused the bull to freeze, and Roger made good on a much appreciated second shot, dropping the bull with a shot to the neck.

The most outstanding features on Roger Johnson's giant bull are his third points. Most Idaho bulls are stunted here, but not this one. This bull's huge body may even outclass his great antlers. What a great photograph of a giant bull and one happy hunter. Even the hat is perfect.

Jack D. Sheppard
376-6/8 P&Y Typical
Adams County, 1966

Idaho Typical Rank: 37
Inside Spread: 39-2/8
Main Beams (R,L): 47-2/8, 50-3/8

Points (R,L): 6,7
Widest Spread: N/A
Bases (R, L): 8-6/8, 8-6/8

Not a lot of people were bowhunting back in 1966. It was a facet of hunting gaining steam, but in typical rural Idaho it was far from commonplace. Jack Sheppard had gotten into it, and the opportunity to hunt early and longer was a fair part of the reason.

With a borrowed Bear Polar recurve bow with no sights, Jack headed into elk country for opening day of the bow season. Blaine Morris was with him, and it was Blaine's brother Bruce from whom Jack had borrowed the bow.

They loaded the two horses and led them away from the trailhead that morning. Their plan was to get into the next big drainage and spend most of that day making their camp. Funny how plans can change when elk get in the way.

They topped the rise and looked over into their destination. It was gorgeous high country, full of beautiful views, expansive lodgepole thickets and, hopefully, some elk.

They began their descent and soon heard a bugle not too far away. They quickly tied the horses and started moving in on the serenading bull. Jack gave a little chirp here and there as they got closer.

They were getting close when a five-point abruptly appeared only ten yards away. "Here he is, Jack!"

At the same time, Jack witnessed a sight he will never forget. A big bull pushed up off his front legs and stood out of his bed. The rack swayed back and forth with each movement, accentuating a size that was already beyond description. It was huge! The bull was probably 45-50 yards off – a questionable shot, but Jack didn't have a lot of time to think. He released an arrow quickly and hit the bull in the spleen from the left side.

Elk suddenly exploded in every direction. There was no telling how many, but brush was being crashed through at a record rate.

Tracking elk can be a real challenge in even the best of situations, but this was a nightmare. Elk had gone everywhere, ripping up the ground, the brush, and the lodgepole as they went. After a concerted effort, they managed to separate the big bull's track out from the herd. Jack had plenty of time by now to realize just what kind of bull he had before him, and he wasn't about to let it slip away. They stayed on the track and then lost it again in thick huckleberry brush.

By now, they were almost five hours into tracking down the giant bull. They had begun to conduct a circle pattern in attempt to regain the track when they heard an unmistakable groan. Following the sound, Jack came upon the big bull as it lay, collapsed into an alder patch. The bull was on its side, breathing its last.

Jack hastily sent another arrow at the bull, which hit the brisket and bounced back out. No matter – the bull was dead.

They admired what lay before them for a few moments, speechless. Blaine then headed back and got the horses while Jack began the work on his bull. When Blaine returned, they set up camp close by and finished caping and quartering Jack's elk for the packout in the morning.

As Jack lay in bed that night and recounted his adventure, he knew he had taken a great bull – one he would likely never beat.

As much as he appreciated his good luck, the magnitude of what he had accomplished still remained unknown to him. Later, he would find out that his bull was, at that time, the largest elk ever taken with a bow. In 1969, it would be certified as the Pope and Young Club's World's Record Yellowstone Elk, a record that would stand until 1977. It has since fallen a few more rungs down the ladder, but when you consider elk management at the time, elk numbers of the era, and lack of special hunts or private land management, Jack's trophy certainly shines as one of rare and magnificent quality. He took his bull on public land in general season, with a primitive bow. This truly sets Jack's bull apart as one of the great trophies of any kind ever taken in Idaho – or in North America, for that matter.

Jack Sheppard, in the summer of 1968, getting ready to make the long haul to Boise to get his bull officially measured.

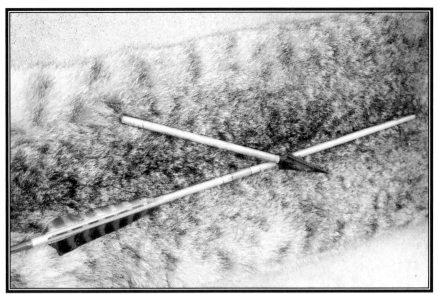

One of a kind – This is the arrow used to make the kill shot on Jack's former Pope & Young Club World's Record elk.

Jack Sheppard received the plaque above, recognizing both his accomplishment and his elk as the World's Record.

Phil S. Foreseen
376-6/8 B&C Typical
Fremont County, 1996

Idaho Typical Rank: 37
Inside Spread: 40-0/8
Main Beams (R,L): 51-2/8, 51-6/8

Points (R,L): 7,7
Widest Spread: 47-1/8
Bases (R, L): 8-1/8, 8-1/8

In the summer of 1996, Phil Foreseen received in the mail the notice we're all hoping for. It was a post card from IDF&G saying he was successful in drawing a controlled hunt elk tag. The area was for north of St. Anthony and, with enough weather, there was a good chance of intercepting elk migrating out of Yellowstone to wintering grounds in Idaho.

Phil, accompanied by son Craig, headed out into the high desert. It was November 24th, and conditions were already rough; they trudged along in nearly two feet of snow, and the roads were nearly blown in.

About 1-1/2 hours into the hunt, Craig spotted two huge bulls over a mile off. They watched as the heavy-racked bulls waded through the snow and made their way into an aspen patch at the bottom of a butte. Phil was confident the bulls couldn't leave the aspens without them seeing it, so they began to close the distance. In deep snow, this was a slow and painful experience, especially while trying to keep their nerves in check.

At 150 yards, the bedded bulls stood up. Phil and Craig were both in awe, as both bulls were true trophy-class animals. Phil couldn't tell which was bigger, so he simply chose the one that offered him the best opportunity for a clean shot. His .270 was his weapon of choice, and one shot to the neck ended Phil's hunt instantly.

The other bull ran to the edge of the aspens and then stopped, affording Phil and Craig one last look. He was an incredible bull, and father and son watched as he turned away and melted into the aspens.

They returned to town and made arrangements with Phil's sister to come back out with horses. At that point, the weather was all they could handle; a blizzard had moved in, and they were barely able to see their own boot tracks.

Once back at the scene, they hooked up the bull to both horses and dragged him out on the snow, much like an old-time horse logger would drag out an old pine log with a team of draft horses!

They were back by 6 p.m., with a full supply of meat and some antlers that would for sure be the topic of many conversations. Perhaps more importantly, however, Phil and Craig had shared in an adventure that neither will ever forget.

Ron Gastelecutto
376-3/8 B&C Typical
Valley County, 1985

Idaho Typical Rank: 40
Inside Spread: 30-2/8
Main Beams (R,L): 55-6/8, 55-0/8

Points (R,L): 7,6
Widest Spread: 47-1/8
Bases (R, L): 8-6/8, 8-4/8

It's better to be lucky than good sometimes. In the cold, clear, morning air, I could see the vapor rising from the noses of the elk. They were slowly working their way up the mountain and, if they continued on this same path, they would pass by me at twenty yards. With my gut and throat tightening, and my heart pounding, I waited. The minutes ticked by like hours. Finally they started to appear one by one, and I started to believe my luck was about to change.

It had seemed like this day would never get here, and it felt good to be out hunting on this crisp October day. I was a high school teacher and a football coach, and what had been a dismal football season was finally over. This gave me the opportunity to finally get out of town, pursue another passion, and clear my head. Injuries, team miscues, and unfortunate referee calls had plagued us all season long, stealing victory from us just when we thought we had turned the corner. The season could have been summed up with the old expression, "If it wasn't for bad luck, we wouldn't have any luck at all."

My Saturday started at 3:00 a.m. To be even more accurate, I should say that the previous day never ended. After our season's last Friday night game was put to rest, equipment checked in, and coaches meetings concluded, I numbly made it home around 2:00 am. This gave me about an hour to get my hunting gear together, load the truck, kiss my wife goodbye, and leave to pick up my hunting buddy. Monte was a good friend I met in college and was an assistant coach on a nearby rival high school team. We had been friends and hunted together for many years and could still tease and laugh at each other's mistakes.

It was the last weekend of the elk and deer season and we didn't have an opportunity to do any preseason scouting. To complicate our hunt further, we were going to hunt an area relatively new to both of us. We settled on this area because it was one of the few units still open for both deer and elk. If a logical person looked at our chances of success, they would conclude them to be slim or none.

During the early morning drive, we decided we would split up when we arrived, giving us a better chance to cover more area. The lack of sleep and the mental drain of the last 24 hours were catching up fast. When we arrived, we elected to flip a coin to decide who would hunt the top half of the mountain and who would hunt the lower half. I lost the coin flip and after some gentle ribbing and a smile on his face, Monte chose to stay low.

The sun was thirty minutes away from revealing a beautiful cloudless sky as I tackled the major elevation gain. The season's problems were fading fast as I deeply breathed in the cold, frosty mountain air.

After an uphill trek of about two miles, I reached a good vantage point from which I could glass the surrounding area and give my tired legs a rest. It didn't take long until I spotted a herd of elk midway down the canyon. There were fifteen cows and two bulls - a 5x5 and a huge 6x7!

As I sat there watching them and trying to figure out how to get into a better position, I noticed the elk seemed to be working their way up to a pocket of pine trees, possibly to bed down. I knew my best chance would be to catch them before they entered the timbered pocket, spread out, and bedded down. If nothing spooked them and they continued on their present path, it would lead them up a steep draw along a narrow trail that topped out on a ridge before entering the trees. I felt if I could be set up as they came out of the draw, I would be in a perfect position for a shot. The morning breeze was blowing up the canyon, creating the perfect conditions for the ambush; the only problem was, could I cover the 1000 yards quick enough without being heard?

I eased back behind the ridge of rocks and started running toward the head of the draw where I felt they would appear. As I settled in behind an outcropping of rocks, the minutes ticked by like hours.

Finally, the first lead cow came into view. One by one, they passed by me at twenty yards. Then the tines of a bull started to appear as he broke into view. I could tell it was the 5x5 I had glassed earlier. The questions began to race through my mind. *Should I take him, or wait for the bigger bull? What if the bigger bull broke off and isn't with the herd anymore? If I pass on this bull, will I get another chance? How lucky do I feel?* I decided to wait, as seven more cows came up the trail.

Then, as if by magic, the tine of another bull began to materialize; it was the 6x7 herd bull! He was in no big hurry, and the lead cow was now past me. It would only be a matter of seconds before she winded me and sounded the alarm. *Come on, just a couple more steps.* A couple more steps and he would be in view for a shot at 25 yards.

I settled the crosshairs on his neck and slowly squeezed the trigger on my .30-06. As soon as the rifle sounded, the bull dropped dead and the rest of the herd exploded, heading down the mountain. I quickly went over to admire the magnificent animal and gave thanks for the needed meat my young family would enjoy.

My attention then went to the size of the bull. It became immediately clear, not so much the antlers, but the size of the body. It was going to be a huge task packing this animal out.

No sooner had reality settled in than I heard a shot lower on the mountain in the direction the herd had headed. *Was that Monte? Did he get a shot?* My question was quickly answered by the hoots and hollers coming from the canyon below. After dressing out my bull, I headed in the direction I heard the shot, where I found Monte dressing out a beautiful 5x5 bull. I told him of the bull I just shot and, after some high fives and slaps on the back, we set about quartering the elk to pack out. Later that evening, during the fourth trip out with an elk quarter on our backs, we wondered if we had too much good luck.

Looking back today, the problems don't seem as bad, the load as heavy, or the distances to the truck as far. The only true memory is the adrenaline rush of harvesting such a magnificent animal. Thank God for selective memories.

Gary J. Christensen
376-1/8 B&C Typical
Bear Lake County, 2002

Idaho Typical Rank: 41
Inside Spread: 42-1/8
Main Beams (R,L): 51-0/8, 51-2/8

Points (R,L): 6,6
Widest Spread: 50-1/8
Bases (R, L): 9-0/8, 8-4/8

I was fifteen years old when my dad and I put in together for a trophy bull hunt in southeast Idaho. I didn't expect to draw because so many people put in for such few permits. When I received the letter from Fish & Game saying I'd been drawn, I was excited, to say the least.

We spent that archery season watching two giant bulls. We watched a friend come ever so close to getting one of them several times. I could only hope what we had learned about them that archery season would help on my upcoming hunt.

The night before the opener, my dad went out and watched them. He watched the bigger of the two bulls raking his antlers on the sagebrush no further than fifty yards off the road. The bull was a giant 6x6. He didn't spot the other bull, but they were always close together. It was cool to watch them. One day they would be fighting all day; the next day, they would bed down together. One day the six-point would have the cows; the next day the seven-point would have them.

That night was the longest night of my life. I dozed off at 2 a.m., and woke up just a few hours later to six inches of snow.

We loaded the four-wheelers and set out for where we had seen the bulls last. My uncle Shawn and Travis went with us that morning. We left the rigs, walked out to a knoll, and waited for first light.

A bugle broke the morning silence, and then it was like the brush came alive with elk. It was unbelievable; there were nearly 175 head of cows. Unfortunately, they were all headed the wrong way.

We hurried as fast as we could to cut them off. We eventually crested a ridge and, through the fog and snow, we spotted a cow. We looked for the rest of the herd, but the visibility was too poor. Then, like an apparition, a rack just materialized. I knew right away which bull it was – the big 7x7. Dad said, "Take him!"

I raised the rifle and, for reasons I still don't know, I said, "You take him."

Dad didn't know what to think. "You sure?"

I told him yes, and then watched through my scope as Dad's bullet hit him. The hit was solid, but the bull didn't go down. We had to follow, and after some insurance shots, the bull was down. We walked up to him, finally seeing one of these two big boys up close. He was enormous!

I didn't think that day could get any better. We took care of him, loaded him up, and everyone wanted to see this giant on the way home.

After taking care of Dad's elk, my uncles and I talked Dad into going out that evening. We got there late, only having about an hour of daylight left. We went to where the other bull was the night before, and saw a raghorn a mile away. We figured he wouldn't be far from the rest of the herd, so we headed that way.

As we made our way over there, we could hear screaming bugles the entire time. I was beyond excited. My uncles Shawn and Andy started cow calling, and I could hear the big bull coming up over the top.

He appeared only 75 yards away. I took a deep breath and tried to settle my nerves. I raise the 7mm and squeezed off a round. The bullet entered in front of his shoulder and exited by breaking the last rib. I followed with another shot as he faded off down the ridge. We followed him off the ridge, with me trying to keep up with my uncles. Keeping up with them was hard enough without the snow.

The big, wounded herd bull came into sight about 400 yards out. I was breathing way too hard, and was trying to take a shot off of my uncle's shoulder. We agreed I would shoot on three. One... two... hold our breath...three. I shot, and hit him right behind the shoulder. After another brief chase, we finally had him.

I ran down the hill and marveled at the size of him. He was the biggest I had ever seen. He was even bigger close-up than on the hoof.

We had to leave him overnight. It was already getting dark, and there was just no way to do anything else. That night, no one wanted to believe that my bull was at least as big as Dad's.

The next morning, several friends and relatives came and helped get him out. This hunt was, without a doubt, as good as it gets – two big bulls, taken by my Dad and me on the same day.

My bull scored 376-1/8 B&C, and Dad's scored 357-1/8. It was a hunt we will never forget.

Rick Christensen (left) and son Gary hold the results of one of Idaho's most successful elk hunts.

Bud Gifford
376-0/8 B&C Typical
Clark County, 1951

Idaho Typical Rank: 42
Inside Spread: 39-2/8
Main Beams (R,L): 49-6/8, 51-0/8

Points (R,L): 6,6
Widest Spread: 44-0/8
Bases (R, L): 9-0/8, 8-5/8

No history was able to be traced on the great bull taken by Bud Gifford. Darrell Riste bought the rack years ago from Bud but knew nothing of the details. Hopefully this book will help to bring someone forward who can help us relive Bud's tale.

Ralph H. Brandvold, Jr.
375-6/8 B&C Typical
Shoshone County, 1983

Idaho Typical Rank: 43
Inside Spread: 37-2/8
Main Beams (R,L): 52-1/8, 50-4/8

Points (R,L): 7,7
Widest Spread: 42-2/8
Bases (R, L): 8-4/8, 7-7/8

It has been often said that hunters are the world's biggest optimists. This is likely an accurate statement; hunters must be, for they almost always have at least that infinitesimal belief that what they seek could still be over the next ridge, even when it wasn't for the first twelve before it, or for the first week before that.

Ralph Brandvold surely fit the description of the eternal optimist. For ten hard-fought years, Ralph had diligently pursued his elusive quarry, with nothing to show for it but a few memories and a couple of pairs of worn-out boots.

The fall of his tenth hunting year, 29-year-old Ralph once again took to the mountains, this time with his father-in-law Rodney Wolfe, and brother-in-law Rod Wolfe. They piled into a pickup early in the morning of October 20th and weaved their way through the mountains to their chosen location. It was going to be just another normal day of hunting elk in north Idaho – raining light but steady, thick timber and brush, and topped with a layer of fog.

As daybreak approached on, the three men split up with plans to meet further up on a ridge. Ralph hunted toward their rendezvous location, and that afternoon began pushing a heavy brush patch. He had just begun to top out, when he looked up and saw antlers coming over a ridge and heading right toward him!

With only thirty yards of air separating the two, Ralph took the best shot he had with his .284. It nailed the bull, which instantly took off like a rocket, straight into a dreadfully thick and brushy area. Ralph was confident in the shot, but as every hunter is when his target runs off, he was still a bit apprehensive.

It was at this point that Ralph learned that his brother-in-law Rod had been only 100 yards away when he shot! Ralph quickly briefed Rod on the events, and the men were deciding on a course of action, when the bull suddenly appeared. He was running right underneath them. Both men quickly launched a barrage of ammunition at the wounded bull before he got out of sight.

Ralph took off on a sprint, then pulled up after only thirty yards and shot again. This shot did the trick, putting the bull right down with a solid hit behind the shoulder.

Ralph says as they walked up to the bull that they really didn't have a full appreciation for the size of the antlers simply because the body was so huge! In fact, both men together could not budge the bull; they had to "piece work" it for a while before it lightened up enough so that they could reposition it.

As they began to field-dress Ralph's trophy, it became obvious that darkness would set in sooner than they had hoped. With no way to get the big bull out that night, they went ahead and finished the field-dressing and headed back to their pickup with only their gear and the big rack. As Ralph lugged that big set of antlers back, he wondered more than once if they weren't still growing; they seemed to be getting heavier with ever step he took.

They set up camp at their vehicle that night, rather than go back to town. Tomorrow was going to be a brutal pack on brushy sidehills and transporting the elk on their backs through the brush. They sat around the campfire that night – a brief respite before the work would start again. It was only then, when Ralph had a few minutes to really relax and soak it all in, that he realized how truly big those antlers were and the rare good fortune that had been bestowed upon him.

Quartering angles of Ralph Brandvold's magnificent 7x7 show one of Nature's finest sculptures.

Rod Wolfe (left) and Ralph Brandvold, Jr. show off a couple of big north Idaho bulls.

Barry D. Nelson
375-2/8 B&C Typical
Bonner County, 1967

Idaho Typical Rank: 44
Inside Spread: 43-2/8
Main Beams (R,L): 56-2/8, 55-6/8

Points (R,L): 7,6
Widest Spread: 50-5/8
Bases (R, L): 9-7/8, 9-2/8

Thirty-six-year-old Barry "Buck" Nelson, along with Don and Buzz Watts and a friend of the Watts', left in the dark that morning from Sandpoint. They were headed for a spot near the Montana line. They knew of a herd of elk up the Clark Fork, up in what they called the High Drive country on the north side of Lake Pend O'Reille.

The men gained the necessary elevation and began a drive, intent on pushing the herd between them. The country was largely heavily timbered, but the area more specific to the hunt was fairly open and high, with scrubby-looking firs. Buck was packing a pre-'64 model 70 .30-06 with a 4x scope, a pretty standard setup for the time.

The drive worked just as they hoped, and soon Buck had a bull, cow, and calf within eyesight. They came out of the bottom and circled around toward Buck. The bull was only 75 yards above him when they stopped in the brush.

Buck knew his only chance was a good head/neck shot, and he wasn't about to let it slip by. He fired, and the bull whirled and ran back toward the cow and calf. He would later find the shot had clipped the bull's jugular vein.

Buck was fine through the first shot, but the excitement was now starting to get to him. He sprinted up about 15 feet, quickly shouldered his rifle, and shot again. The bull bolted out of sight, then Buck heard some heavy crashing, and then all was quiet.

Being a seasoned hunter, the excited hunter went to the last place he physically saw the bull, rather than follow the sound. Blood was thick on the ground. He followed the bloodtrail for 75 yards, where it led him to a sight he would never forget. Lying there before him was an elk with antlers so immense he could scarcely make sense of it.

Barry "Buck" Nelson has to stretch to reach the wide beams of this great bull. If this bull had grown its seventh point on the left antler to match the right, it likely would have been one of the top seven typicals in the state.

Eva Calonge
375-0/8 B&C Typical
Fremont County, 1960

Idaho Typical Rank: 45
Inside Spread: 47-4/8
Main Beams (R,L): 52-6/8, 52-5/8

Points (R,L): 6,6
Widest Spread: 54-2/8
Bases (R, L): 8-6/8, 9-0/8

Unlike today, when elk seem to be proliferating many areas of southern Idaho, many areas in the late '50s and early '60s were not exactly thick with elk. As such, many areas that now have general seasons were controlled hunt areas back then.

Fifty-one year old Eva Calonge was one of the lucky ones in the fall of 1960, drawing a tag for the Fremont County area. Her son, Harold Calonge, Jr., wasn't so lucky, but would tag along and help her on the hunt. He was excited to try a new bugle he had fashioned out of a piece of bamboo; his uncle, who hunted elk quite a bit in the Selway, had shown him how to put it together.

It was the 1st of October when Eva and Harold parked the truck and headed down an old logging road near Swan Lake. It was fairly non-descript country, with not much in the way of landmarks or relief in topography. It was a typical flat lodgepole habitat characteristic of the land that surrounds Yellowstone.

Harold had been in the area messing with his bugle and had seen elk recently in the area they were headed to. He had, on previous trips, gotten responses from bulls in the area. He hadn't had much chance to use the bugle that morning before thirty head of elk came running right at them, spooked by a hunter not with their party. Harold yelled to his mom, "Shoot!"

Eva, a seasoned elk hunter in her own right, had taken more than one elk with her husband, Harold Calonge, Sr. As such, she didn't hesitate. She simply pulled up and put a perfect shot between the ribs of the big old bull, slowing him instantly. A second shot followed, right behind the shoulder. It was only after the second shot that her nerves began to get the better of her. Perhaps by that time, Eva had gotten a proper look at the antlers. Instead of loading the next shell, she handed the rifle to Harold and said, "I need more bullets!"

Harold quickly handed her back the rifle. "Mom, you've got five!"

Eva hastily readied for a third shot but the bull, now wobbly-legged, collapsed before she could fire. They began to head toward the bull, and in the process actually had to "shoo" away five other bulls that had watched the action unfold, evidently not quite understanding that they could have been next.

It didn't take long for Eva and Harold to realize that wrestling this huge-bodied elk was going to be an exercise in futility. They instead retreated back to Ashton, where they recruited some able bodies to assist with the packout. Eva Calonge might not have been big in stature, but with her accomplishment that day, she easily towered over the men who would pack out her elk!

Eva Calonge, posing proudly with her big elk, looks as though she could easily fit right inside it.

Don J. Burch
375-0/8 B&C Typical
Owyhee County, 2005

Idaho Typical Rank: 45
Inside Spread: 33-4/8
Main Beams (R,L): 57-4/8, 56-0/8

Points (R,L): 8,7
Widest Spread: 41-5/8
Bases (R, L): 9-2/8, 9-1/8

Early morning, November 4th, 2005, I was working my way up a juniper and mahogany-covered ridge. I noticed some fresh tracks and droppings, as well as a large mahogany bush that had been destroyed by an elk.

I had taken only five steps after that when I jumped a lone bull. He went through a gully, and I saw him at 150 yards angling up a sidehill of thick cover. I next saw him at 500 yards, as he paused for a second before going over the top. I never got an accurate count on points, but I knew he was big and had long tines.

I knew of a thick juniper pocket about half a mile away, and thought he might stop there. An hour and a half later, I came in on that pocket with the wind in my favor. It was a small pocket, maybe 150 yards wide by 150 yards long.

I worked as slow as I could move toward a higher vantage point. I felt a slight wind change, and that was followed by the sound of hooves pounding and antlers hitting trees. There was a lot of open ground on any side of this pocket, so I made a dash to a rocky knob in the direction I thought the bull had gone. When I got there, I saw and heard nothing.

After five minutes of glassing in the distance, I glanced down and spotted a large bull standing under a juniper and looking right at me! His horns were long and narrow, so I thought this was the bull I was chasing, but was amazed that he covered so much country so quick without me seeing him.

An hour and a half later, I had this bull at 196 yards as he lay in a small shady opening between junipers looking away from me. He was a six-point, had narrow but long main beams, and looked similar to the one I had first jumped. I studied the bull for an hour before deciding I was going to pass, as I still had 20 days to hunt, and I was hoping to find his big brother.

I had five days until my next hunt, so I spent a majority of that time looking through every magazine I could find, trying to improve my field-judging. I wanted to be better prepared the next time we met.

On November 9th, I started on the same ridge I had jumped the big bull on five days earlier. This time, I stopped to glass that chewed up mahogany at a distance, and immediately saw yellow in my optics. Three bulls moved out of the junipers into an opening. Two of them were small, but the third was big, long, and narrow. He stopped broadside and looked at me. I could see as soon as he turned his head back that he was the big one I had jumped right off on the last hunt.

It was a long shot, but it was what I had in front of me – good thing I practice for these scenarios. The bull saw me, but remained calm, likely because of the distance between us. As my friends Gordon and Gill King watched, I settled into a rock pile, got a steady rest, and fired.

At the report of the bullet, the bull spun and tried to escape to the same gully he had used the first time. He made it about fifty yards, with each step bringing him a little closer to the ground than the last one. Then he was out of sight.

We picked our way through the cover and down to where we had last seen him. As we approached, we could see he had cashed in his chips. All of us were stunned at how big and beautiful he was. After three hours of hard work prepping him for a full body mount and field-dressing him, we were finally ready for the real fun, also known as the packout, to begin.

Don had just purchased a new camera before this trip, and didn't realize until it was too late that the photos didn't turn out like he hoped. Even though this one is blurry, it shows enough to help paint the scene, so it has been included. What a huge animal!

Ben Howland
372-6/8 B&C Typical
Idaho, 1929

Idaho Typical Rank: 49
Inside Spread: 37-3/8
Main Beams (R,L): 55-3/8, 55-2/8

Points (R,L): 7,6
Widest Spread: 49-6/8
Bases (R, L): 8-2/8, 8-4/8

The events behind one of Idaho's most historic elk hunts have passed away with time. The successful hunter, Ben Howland, has long since departed for better hunting grounds, taking the memories of this special encounter with him.

One of the only things left, however, just happens to be one of the best. Ben and whoever hunted with him that day had the foresight to bring a camera with them, something rarely done with something rarely even owned in that era. One of the oldest and finest hunting photos taken in Idaho's history, it shows the lucky hunter struggling to keep the massive beams and points out of the dirt.

It is presumed this bull was taken near McCall, since it was the only area close to where Ben lived that had a season at the time. It was neither likely nor practical in that era to travel more than about a tank of gas away in search of table fare.

The year 1929 was still toward the infancy of managed elk hunting in Idaho, and many areas of the state were off limits to hunting. Game preserves had only recently been created to protect the new populations of reintroduced elk transported from Yellowstone National Park.

Many bulls of this caliber likely serenaded lonely canyons in Idaho in 1929, but this is one of the few relics to survive from such a bygone era. Seventy-seven years later, this bull was finally officially recognized as one of the best and most historic ever taken in Idaho.

This awesome photo appeared in *Idaho's Greatest Mule Deer* as an example of the types of photos we are hoping to document and preserve. In the photo is Ben Howland, with his 372-5/8 B&C bull he took in 1929, before a scoring system even existed. How he got that on his back is a real head-scratcher; that has to be at least a 150-lb load. Ben nearly fits inside the length of the rack. This photo is one of the most historic elk hunting photos ever taken in Idaho.

George Agar
372-2/8 B&C Typical
Bonner County, 1955

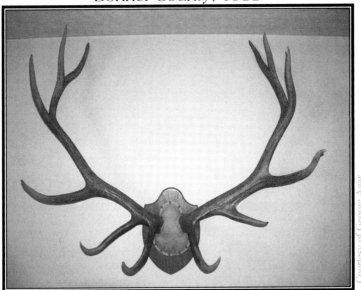

Idaho Typical Rank: 50
Inside Spread: 47-2/8
Main Beams (R,L): 51-6/8, 52-5/8

Points (R,L): 6,6
Widest Spread: 51-4/8
Bases (R, L): 8-3/8, 8-4/8

I have been waiting to write the account of slaying of my first elk until the 50th anniversary of the event. That year was 2005, and it arrived none too soon. My memory is slipping with the passage of time, but I'll give it my best shot.

There are many details that make this hunt interesting. It was my first big game hunt of any kind, and I was "greener than grass"; I hadn't the slightest idea of where to look for elk, let alone how to hunt them; the hunt almost didn't happen as I overslept due to a heavy date (football game) with Margaret and missed my meeting time with, Art Croy, at their home in Hope; the antlers, which I now prize so highly, were left in the woods for nine months after the kill. During that time, they could easily have been damaged or dragged off by animals and/or humans.

The year was 1955, and I was a freshman at the University of Idaho. I was rooming with my long-time high school friend, Art Croy. He was, in comparison with myself, an old pro at elk hunting, having taken a couple of cows during hunts to the Lochsa with his father, Paul Croy, who was an expert hunter.

It was the opening day of elk season, around October 10th. Art and I had come home from college for the express purpose of hunting elk on Saturday, but I figured there was no reason why I shouldn't combine "business with pleasure." So, it was off to the football game with my sweetie for the evening. I don't recall it being too late of an evening, but it was enough to cause me to sleep through my alarm.

I awoke with a start, realizing I had overslept. I was supposed to meet Art, his dad, and a friend of his dad's at their place for breakfast. Still hoping, I wolfed down some breakfast, threw my gear in the old 1938 Buick, and sped toward Hope.

I was too late! They had given up and left for the hunt. What to do? I decided to go up to Becker's Gulch and poke around on my own. Becker's Gulch was an abandoned homestead off the Spring Creek Road between Hope and Clark's Fork. There was an old log house, several beaver ponds, and some cleared ground. It was the cleared ground that was the reason Art had earlier introduced me to this idyllic spot; the old 'stump ranch' was a haven for ground squirrels we loved to hunt.

Upon arriving at the parking spot, I was amazed to see my hunting partners just getting out of their vehicle. Apparently they had waited quite a while, and so were just arriving.

I can't recall precisely, but Art must have selected this spot for the two of us to hunt that day; but, because I hadn't shown, his dad and friend had decided to hunt with him. My arrival allowed them to revert to the original plan, and the two older gents went elsewhere while Art took off up the trail with me in hot pursuit.

The trail up Becker's Gulch was an old mine access foot trail, a bit overgrown but still usable. It ended about a mile up the gulch at an old miner's cabin with the name "Becker" painted on a board. That is how locals knew it as Becker's cabin, eventually leading to official recognition as a geographical location on USFS maps.

Beyond the cabin, the terrain got much steeper. We were soon climbing rapidly on the west side to get to more suitable ground for hunting near the ridge tops. As mentioned earlier, I was a complete greenhorn at navigating in the woods on my own so was real glad to follow Art, who seemed to know what he was doing.

After about two hours of laborious hiking, Art suggested we split up and begin hunting. He asked me which way I wanted to go. While I had no knowledge on which to base a decision, I had thought I heard a faint noise off to our left, so opted to go in that direction. Things were about to get exciting.

I had not gone further than fifty yards when I spotted movement thirty yards ahead. There, rocking back and forth in the brush, was a set of elk antlers so big that they looked like a dead tree trunk and branches. Although I couldn't see the body of the elk, I knew in a couple of nanoseconds what they belonged to. I moved into position behind a small evergreen and waited with rifle at the ready.

Meanwhile, Art was still within viewing distance of me as I stood there with my rifle pointed at some unseen target. He was wondering what was with this greenhorn flatlander he had brought along on his hunt. Art didn't get to wonder long. The bull obligingly took two steps forward and presented his head in full view and *barrroooom* went the old rifle!

I may not have been much of a hunter, but I was a good shot. I hit him right between the eyes with the .30 Remington. He went down so fast, it was almost as if a giant club had knocked his feet out from under him. We wasted no time in racing to the spot, but that bull was going nowhere.

Art and I paused a bit to admire our prize. I needed the rest, as I was feeling a bit weak in the knees. I was a victim of PEEKS (Post Exciting Elk Kill Syndrome). For most people, this phenomenon would strike as they were lining up their shot and be referred to as buck fever. But, being Irish, which is a lower order of life form with slower reaction times, it didn't strike me until well after the incident was over.

I had scarcely recovered from my shaking when a hunter emerged from the woods and complimented us on the nice animal. He then announced that he was a game warden and would like to see my license and tags. These I had, so all was well, but he did advise me to get the tag on the animal before any more time elapsed.

With the excitement over, the work began. I had no experience and, while Art had been in on a couple of elk kills, it was his father who had done the gutting and butchering chores. With considerable effort, we did manage to remove the entrails.

We were wondering what to do next when shots rang out about 200 yards upslope. It seems there were more elk in the area, and the game warden that had visited us had killed another bull. About thirty minutes later, we could hear him using a hatchet in the process of dressing his bull. That gave us the idea of borrowing his axe to cut through the backbone of our elk to reduce it to movable sized pieces. This we did, and began to drag the bull.

During this episode, we were further amazed by yet another bull running downhill past us, about 200 feet to the side at breakneck speed, making as much noise as a herd of elephants in a bamboo forest. He apparently wandered into the area, caught our scent, and threw all caution to the wind in making a hasty escape.

Our plan was to drag the shortened rear half back to the car (three miles distant). We each grabbed onto a hamstring and started dragging. The ground was bare, so it didn't pull easy. In fact, the only way we could move it was downhill.

The good news was the ground was steep and getting steeper the further down we went. The bad news was that it was leading us straight down the fall line into the bottom of Becker's Gulch. Once there, there was no way we could move it further.

Plan B was quickly developed. We would leave it there, come back the next day with pack boards and a saw, split it up, and pack it out on foot. We beat feet to Art's place and announced our success with considerable pride and excitement.

It was decided that Art and his dad would take their packhorse and try to access the kill site via the Bee Top – Round Top trail and retrieve the front half. This would be a longer route, but one a horse could traverse. Art's dad's friend (Tom, I believe) and I would go back to the rear half, split it, skin it and pack it out.

The second half of our plan went pretty well. The first half had some good and bad news. The good news was that they were able to find the kill site in spite of coming in from a new direction. The bad news was, upon cutting into the brisket, a significant abscess was found. Because of the doubt created as to the usefulness of the meat, the front quarters were left there. Having no way to communicate the finding to the 'human pack string' working on the rear half, those quarters did arrive home. And, because the horse wasn't carrying a load, it was decided to take a shortcut down Becker's Gulch. That decision drove yet another - the decision to leave the antlers behind - a major disappointment for yours truly. However, I really didn't know how special this bull was at the time, because he was the only one I had ever seen.

I was out of time and had to return to school, but I hadn't forgotten the antlers. Two weeks later, I returned and tried to find them, without success. I was hampered by my lack of woods savvy (Art's guide skills weren't available that day). This difficulty was compounded by the area being covered with 1-½ feet of new snow. Whatever landmarks I was hoping to key in on were covered. The antlers would just have to "winter in."

My friend Art wasn't discouraged. He was already hatching a plan to hike into the site from another direction via the Porcupine Lake Road in the spring. This we did the next June. And, true to his reputation as a "guide of renown", he led me straight to the antlers, which had survived the winter without so much as a rodent tooth mark. Against all odds, there they were, and in great condition.

We quickly loaded them onto a WWII packboard and headed back. This went quite well except for the head-high snowbrush, which grabbed onto the antlers at every opportunity. The passage down the cirque head wall was even a bit fun. There was a bank of dense snow that was steep enough to enable one to ski down on our shoes. This we did, holding the antlers between us.

The antlers hung at my parents' place for the next decade, until we built our own home. Margaret says our house was designed around creating a space to display the antlers. I'm not denying that might have been a consideration. I haven't gotten tired of admiring them and they do create a bit of interest among visitors.

Well, there you have the tale of my first, nicest, and most memorable elk kill - a tale of an elk that should've gotten away. It came together in spite of long odds. I consider my acquiring this bull a feat only slightly less likely than me flying to the moon on gossamer wings. Almost makes me suspicious of providential intervention.

A young George Agar stands by his trophy elk antlers in June of 1956. George had to wait for eight excruciating months to return and retrieve the antlers. Check out the shiny new VW Bug toting those antlers!

David D. Lee
371-3/8 B&C Typical
Custer County, 1977

Idaho Typical Rank: 51
Inside Spread: 52-1/8
Main Beams (R,L): 56-2/8, 56-2/8

Points (R,L): 6,6
Widest Spread: 56-5/8
Bases (R, L): 7-4/8, 8-2/8

It was October of 1977, and I was hunting with my father, David O. Lee, in the Sawtooth Mountains in central Idaho. We separated early that morning to hunt different areas, and were supposed to regroup later that day.

It wasn't long after we separated that I cut fresh tracks. In no time, it seemed, I started to smell the musky scent of elk. The area was in heavy timber, and conditions were very dry. I was making a lot of noise!

Suddenly, and to my amazement considering the conditions, there I was standing among several cow elk. No matter how I tried, I couldn't put horns on any of them. I was able to sneak a little further and there he was, about 120 yards away. The cows were getting real nervous, so I had to act quickly. I was able to rest my Model 70 Winchester .270 on a rock and take aim. With the crack of the shot, the bull disappeared.

I could hear limbs and brush crashing where I last saw the bull, so I ran down to the source of the sound. When I got there, I could see I had hit him high in the spine area. He was traveling very well, despite having only the use his front legs. He was actually trying to hook me with his antlers!

I quickly dispatched him, and set out with the task of getting him packed out. This was no easy chore on packframes and a two-mile walk each way.

My father showed up after hearing the shots to see if I needed any help. The first thing he said was, "I'm sure glad we have good teeth, because were going to need them to eat this one."

As it was, he was very good eating, and the meat was not as tough as we first thought. Later, we learned his total dressed weight was in the 550-lb. range - a real monster!

David D. Lee holds a great bull taken by his dad, David O. Lee, in 1973 in the Sawtooth Valley near Horton Peak Lookout. The bull was busted sleeping under a fir tree. This 7x6 bull is nearly 50 inches wide.

Aaron C. Robinson
370 B&C Typical
Benewah County, 1961

Idaho Typical Rank: 52
Inside Spread: 36-2/8
Main Beams (R,L): 54-4/8, 54-3/8

Points (R,L): 7,6
Widest Spread: 44-0/8
Bases (R, L): 9-1/8, 8-4/8

By the fall of 1961, 45-year-old Aaron Robinson already had more elk under his belt than he would likely have been able to remember. He usually hunted in the mountains of his home country around St. Maries, and knew the country about as well as a man could.

Shortly before noon on that fateful November day, Aaron and two friends were driving down the road in about ten inches of snow near St. Joe. They were up on Bond Creek when they saw tracks in the road up ahead. When they got out to investigate, Aaron quickly recognized the tracks as the biggest set of elk tracks he had ever laid eyes on.

Aaron slung his 7mm onto his shoulder and headed up one side of the draw the tracks led into, while his friends took the other side. His companions were on the same side of the draw as the bull, and with any luck, they would herd that big ol' boy right into an opening for Aaron.

Their plan worked like a charm. Aaron hotfooted it up the draw, quartering higher as he went, as fast as he could make it up to a good vantage point. He chose a spot across the draw from a good opening and waited. As if on queue, Aaron's future trophy walked right out into the middle of the opening, having been flushed out by Aaron's companions, and stood there in the open, motionless.

Aaron took careful aim with his 7mm and hit the bull with two shots to the body from 250 yards. The bull retired on the spot.

The next day, four of Aaron's friends came and helped him drag out his bull. The scene resembled a team of horses, as all the men grabbed a hold of the rope and dragged the bull whole out of the canyon and down to the road. More than one of them suggested along the way that maybe those horns ought to be left where they lay, but Aaron knew a bull like this one was a rare beast. Luckily for all of us, Aaron carted those antlers out, and today we have the good fortune to be able to see one of the finest elk to ever have come from Idaho.

Aaron Robinson's heavy 1961 bull has a whopping 67-2/8 inches of mass measurements – a staggering figure. The beams look like the business end of a baseball bat all the way past the G-4s.

Steve Noort
369-4/8 P&Y Typical
Bonner County, 1986

Idaho Typical Rank: 53
Inside Spread: 39-4/8
Main Beams (R,L): 53-2/8, 51-2/8

Points (R,L): 7,7
Widest Spread: 41-7/8
Bases (R, L): 7-6/8, 7-6/8

Bowhunting for elk can be one of the most rewarding and exciting ways to chase them; it can also be among the most frustrating. To be so close so many times without result can leave a hunter with some mighty mixed emotions. Luckily, the thrill of the close encounter almost always outweighs the limitations of the weaponry.

Steve Noort had been after a big bull in his home county for five straight days. He had several glimpses of the object of his desire, but none of the scenarios worked out in his favor. It was his first season packing a bow, and he was learning the hard way, and fast.

On the fifth day, he headed back up again, hopefully not to get his ego bruised yet again by the smart old bull. It was rolling timbered hills, with plenty of willow and alder brush. There was also a good percentage of aspen and birch mixed into the conifers.

Steve worked into the area very gingerly, knowing the bull had a harem helping him watch for trouble. He took nearly two hours to work in on them, but he was getting close. So close, in fact, that Steve found himself right between the bull and his cows in a patch of aspens. It was the perfect scenario.

He got out his bugle, which consisted in large degree of plumbing material, and sounded a challenge. It pushed the bull's buttons, and in no time the angry bull came charging. Steve admits it was intimidating watching all those long antler tines come right at him and being driven by that worked up bull.

Steve had to sidestep the bull and duck behind an aspen as the bull charged on by, not quite aware of where his challenger was. When the bull was past, Steve drew. The bull stopped, walked around, and kept looking for his enemy. With no luck locating him, the bull turned and started coming back, offering a perfect 25-yard shot, which Steve took with full appreciation. The arrow entered the bull's lungs behind the right shoulder with perfect accuracy.

The mortally-wounded bull took off, gaining perhaps 100 yards before "fishhooking" and coming to rest only 60 yards from where Steve stood watching. In only his first season hunting elk with archery equipment, Steve Noort had managed to take one of the largest bulls ever in Idaho with a bow.

Steve Noort, with an all-time Idaho great. Steve wanted to point out that he had just changed out of his camo before the picture was taken.

It's not often you get to see a bull of this caliber lying whole in the back of a pickup truck. This is a great photo for reference when people talk about how big a set of elk antlers were sitting in the back of a pickup bed. Below, Steve's big bull easily dwarfs the meat cutter in the left portion of the photo. If that bull were standing on his tiptoes, he would have to be pushing ten feet.

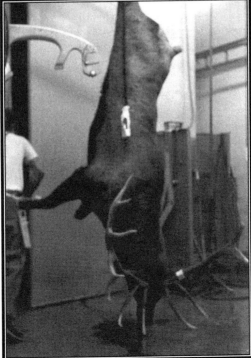

Don Ruark
368-6/8 B&C Typical
Idaho County, 1964

Idaho Typical Rank: 54
Inside Spread: 43-3/8
Main Beams (R,L): 50-1/8, 52-4/8

Points (R,L): 6,8
Widest Spread: 45-6/8
Bases (R, L): 9-5/8, 9-1/8

While Don Ruark loved to hunt, and loved his big set of elk antlers from 1964, he wasn't one to beat his own drum. In fact, he was so quiet about them that his daughter, Cindy Worth, didn't even know of their existence until one day she went into Rae Brothers Sporting Goods to get her fishing license. She looked up on the wall and was shocked to see her dad's name under a giant set of elk antlers. Inquiring, her question was affirmed. Her dad had indeed taken the big bull decades earlier. "The Blewett boys brought those horns out, because Don left them there," she was told.

Herb Blewett, Don's hunting partner and father of "the Blewett boys", had the following to say about the hunt, and of Don:

> *I remember that hunt like it was yesterday, even though in actuality it was 1964. It was a warm day, too warm to hunt.*
> *I saw that elk first, and when I spooked him, he went toward Don. It was a wonderful hunt and a wonderful shot – he got him right in the neck.*

The place was near old Melody Mine. It was on the north side about half a mile from Mountain House, near the old Elk City stagecoach road, headwaters of Clear Creek on Kay Creek.

We had to hurry to save the meat, which we did. We were so tired when we got back to the cabin; I think Don didn't want to leave those horns, but there was a lot of meat to pack out. But we both had families to feed and feeding them was important.

My boys (Jim and younger brother Bob) went back to get those horns, which I believe Don was happy about. They took turns carrying them, and what they remember most is that they hung up on nearly every bush they walked by.

If you look east to Lookout Butte, at the head of Clear Creek, you could see where that elk was shot at. Every time I would go back there, I would think of Don's big elk, and have never seen one that big since.

Thank you for having me relive this hunt. Don was a wonderful friend and a wonderful hunting partner. That was many years ago, but it feels like it was only yesterday.

Junior Bitton & Rex Bassett
368 B&C Typical
Caribou County, 1956

Idaho Typical Rank: 55
Inside Spread: 43-2/8
Main Beams (R,L): 57-3/8, 57-4/8

Points (R,L): 8,8
Widest Spread: 46-4/8
Bases (R, L): 8-0/8, 8-3/8

After a while of trying to find this story, I had about given up. On what would have been a last attempt, I finally located Kevin Bitton, the son of Junior Bitton. Kevin didn't know a lot about his dad, nor did he know much of what happened on the hunt. He did, however, think that he might actually have a photo or two of the elk I was inquiring about. Imagine my surprise when this photo arrived in the mailbox. Every time I look at it I shake my head. What an unbelievable photograph. They just don't get any better than this one.

Junior, on the left, and Rex Bassett, along with all of their hunting partners, had one heck of a day elk hunting that October of 1956. The hunt took place in Dry Valley in eastern Caribou County.

Finding a photo like this one, and helping to preserve it, is what this book is all about. The above photo is one of the best old-time elk hunting photos there is. Turn to page 373 to see one of their hunting party that might be even better.

Alma Nelson & Grant Nelson
367-5/8 B&C Typical
Fremont County, 1960

Idaho Typical Rank: 56
Inside Spread: 46-5/8
Main Beams (R,L): 53-3/8, 52-5/8

Points (R,L): 7,7
Widest Spread: 57-1/8
Bases (R, L): 8-0/8, 7-5/8

Thirty-one year-old Alma Nelson and his brother Grant headed up to their favorite elk hunting spot in fall of 1960 just as they had for many years previous. It was an autumn ritual they both looked forward to and planned for accordingly. They set up their five-foot wall tent and planned for the next morning's adventure.

A week later and many hard miles logged, they still were without elk. The morning of October 15th, they once again got up with a hunter's eternal optimism. They hunted high on the mountain that morning, without any luck. It was a beautiful and sunny late fall day, and there was plenty of hunting left to do, so they headed out for a new spot lower on down the mountain.

As they rolled on down the road in the lower country, they looked over from their moving vehicle and could hardly convince themselves of what they saw. It was a huge bull elk, and he was just standing out there 200 yards away grazing in the open sagebrush! The bull looked over, as if to acknowledge them, and then went back to feeding!

They couldn't get a shot from right there, so they went down the road a ways and got out of the truck and into position. Both brothers were shooting a .30-06, and both fired two rounds apiece toward the body of the big bull. Alma notes that on all four hits, the bull never even flinched one time, taking them all like they were nothing more than gusts of air.

After the shots, Alma and Grant realized that the big herd bull had seven cows with him. He took off after the fourth shot, leading the cows, which they both found fairly unusual.

At that point, they were both fairly confident they had missed, due to lack of any physical reaction by the bull. Being good ethical hunters, however, they went up to make sure.

A quick survey revealed blood on the ground, and a renewed enthusiasm quickly resulted. They started tracking the bull, and found him 75 yards away, lying there dead in a timber patch. Alma says, "The spread was so immense; someone could have easily walked by it, thinking it was nothing but brush."

The two brothers approached, and knew without a doubt they were not looking at brush. They had just bagged the biggest, widest bull they had ever seen. A quick check showed they had hit the bull all four times; he was just one tough ol' bull.

They were able to get the elk to a logging road by dragging him whole, and loaded him into the pickup in similar fashion. It was perhaps one of the easiest elk they had ever taken, but they weren't about to second-guess a free gift.

When interviewing Alma in late 2005, it was apparent that even at 76, he wasn't about to give up hunting. "Been hunting since I was old enough to walk. Killed a four-point bull this fall, and I'm not done yet!"

A quartering view of Alma & Grant Nelson's perfectly built 7x7 bull.

Alma Nelson (left) and Grant Nelson show off their 1960 prize, with their hunting rig as a perfect backdrop. Take a good look at the Nelsons' bull, Curt Stegelmeier's 381-5/8 typical, and Eva Calonge's 375 bull, all from Fremont County, and you can definitely see some specific genetic characteristics they share in regard to wide inside spreads and "bow-shaped" beams.

Ben Fanholz
367-2/8 P&Y Typical
Lemhi County, 1982

Idaho Typical Rank: 57
Inside Spread: 46-0/8
Main Beams (R,L): 55-4/8, 57-7/8

Points (R,L): 6,6
Widest Spread: 50-5/8
Bases (R, L): 8-0/8, 7-4/8

We left early on the morning of September 2nd, 1982, and had a long way to go to get to the series of meadows we planned to hunt. As we left the truck, the dawn was just breaking. It was clear and cool as we started up the mountain.

We had walked about half a mile when we heard the faint but shrill scream of a bugling elk reverberating through the canyon. We headed for the direction of that bugle. We hadn't gone far when I glanced up and saw a large tan object in a meadow high on the ridge. I took off my pack and dug out my binoculars for a closer look. My heart began racing as I saw it was a good bull. As I looked closer, I could see his massive antlers on the skyline, moving back and forth as he fed.

This was my hunting partner's first year of bowhunting, so we agreed that I would attempt the challenge of making a stalk on the big bull. I figured a stalk would be best, as I didn't have much experience at bugling bulls in at that time.

I checked the wind as I started up the ridge. When I was within 75 yards of the bull, I spotted a large tree that would work well to put in between the bull and me. After what seemed like hours, I finally made my way to the base of the tree. I carefully worked my way around it, and the bull presented me with an excellent opportunity for a shot. He stood broadside feeding, with his head hidden by a large dead log.

As I started my draw, the bull suddenly lifted his head and looked in my direction! I froze, thinking the bull had surely spotted me. Just as quick as he had raised his head, he dropped it and began to feed again. Once again, I drew my bow and judged him to be 35 yards. I released, and the arrow seemed to disappear into the bull.

As he bolted and ran off, I could see clearly the orange vanes sticking from his lower chest area. He then disappeared over the knob.

I stood up and could see his antlers as he stopped to look back. Then the large antlers whirled and disappeared! In a matter of seconds, I heard a large crashing sound.

I then motioned my partner up the ridge. After waiting twenty minutes, we walked over to where the bull had stood. There we found a good blood trail. We had tracked him only 75 yards when we found him piled up against a tree.

I was amazed at how large his antlers were. His last three tines were huge! I suspected he would score high in the book. The hard work ahead seemed so much easier with a bull of this magnitude on the ground. I was one happy hunter!

D.A. Johnson
366-5/8 P&Y Typical
Shoshone County, 1962

Idaho Typical Rank: 59
Inside Spread: 45-3/8
Main Beams (R,L): 53-0/8, 53-2/8

Points (R,L): 7,7
Widest Spread: 50-4/8
Bases (R, L): 7-5/8, 7-2/8

Duane A. "Bud" Johnson worked as the general sales manager for Interstate Typewriter Company in Coeur d'Alene. He was also an authorized Fred Bear Bow dealer. As such, Bud was somewhat on the cutting edge of archery in northern Idaho in the 1960s.

Early in the 1962 season Bud, along with brother-in-law Art Turner, John Ruthven, Chuck MacDonald, Everett Erickson, Tom Jones, Gordon Ormesher, Floyd Krause, Darrell Wells, a Mr. Jefferies, and others headed to the area near Graham Mountain. The men weren't all in the exact same party, but were loosely camped together.

Bud and Art were camped together, but split up for the day. It was early September when Bud walked out on Character Ridge. Before long he had called in a big ol' bull about a mile from camp. The only shot the bull gave him was front-on, and Bud took it, connecting solidly with his 52-lb. Bear Kodiak bow at 40 yards. The fatally-wounded bull traveled only fifty yards before expiring.

Bud had already made a trip back to camp, stashed the antlers in the tent, and was gone before Art made it back. Not knowing where Bud had gone, he waited there. In the meantime, Bud had recruited help from some of the other men in camp to help pack out his bull, meaning poor Art missed out on the whole miserable experience of packing out over 500 lbs of elk.

After the rest of the carcass was retrieved, they tied the antlers to the front of the jeep and headed to town. More than one passerby got whiplash watching that big set of antlers go by, headed for Coeur d' Alene.

News spread quickly on Bud's success. When it was all said, done, and official, D.A. "Bud" Johnson's 1962 archery elk became the new Pope & Young Club World's Record. Not only that, but the bull it toppled was taken by none other than Fred Bear himself.

Bud Johnson with the Royal rack from his new World's Record bow and arrow elk taken from the Coeur d'Alene National Forest.
Kyle Walker Photo

This photo appeared in the 1963 Idaho Fishing and Hunting Guide. Kyle Walker took the photo and wrote the following paragraphs, which show just how much the times have changed:

North Idaho boasts a wide variety of hunting and fishing and the resident or visitor of this area is richly blessed in these pleasures. Let us consider the matter of big game. Deer, elk and bear are rather plentiful in areas adjacent to Coeur d'Alene. The Coeur d'Alene National Forest, with headquarters in the city, contains some 800,000 acres of public domain. Here you will never find a NO TRESPASSING, a NO HUNTING, or a NO FISHING sign. In today's expanded population centers this in itself is a blessing.

In these forested acres there is an abundance of white tail deer, a lesser amount of Mule deer and a rather constant herd of elk. There are also a lot of black bear.

These elk, which were reintroduced to the area quite a few years ago, have made rapid strides and today are quite numerous, with many large trophy heads coming out of the region. As an example, Bud Johnson of Coeur d'Alene, calmly walked out of the opening day of the archery season – September 10, and by nine o'clock in the morning had downed a new world's record bull elk with bow and arrow. The head is one of beauty and symmetry – a royal head, which is the connotation given to an elk head having seven points to the antler. Bud's bull dressed out 525 pounds of meat when completely dressed and hanging in the locker. According to a local representative of the Boone and Crockett Club this head surpassed the previous record head taken with a bow and arrow by the well-known Fred Bear, who is not only a bowman of great repute but also manufactures some of the finest bow hunting equipment available. Incidentally Johnson's elk was also taken with a Fred Bear bow and arrow.

Like much of the hunting in the Coeur d'Alene forest, Bud Johnson drove to easy hiking distance of his happy hunting grounds. There is very little hunting done by pack horse in the Coeur d'Alene. A hunter here must have a strong back, however, as a considerable amount of his game will be taken some distance from the end of the road. It should be pointed out that there are more than 2000 miles of good forest service roads through this forest and the hunter is able to navigate into a great many places. It is also quite possible to locate game while driving along some of these roads but this is not the recommended manner of hunting here. It should be pointed out that in Idaho it is unlawful to shoot from or across a highway at any game so care should be exercised when driving and doing so called "road hunting." With a reasonable amount of perseverance a hunter stands a fair chance of connecting with either an elk or a deer in the Coeur d'Alenes. The seasons usually run simultaneously and are quite generous in length. Animals of either sex or any age may be taken in both deer and elk.

We recall that a few years ago a mammoth bull elk was taken from this forest, which dressed out far in excess of 600 pounds and would have stood more than a thousand pounds live weight.

Picked Up by Gary & Bob McClure
366-2/8 B&C Typical
Idaho County, 1995

Idaho Typical Rank: 60
Inside Spread: 35-6/8
Main Beams (R,L): 53-2/8, 52-1/8

Points (R,L): 6,7
Widest Spread: 45-4/8
Bases (R, L): 8-7/8, 9-0/8

Gary and Bob McClure headed up the Salmon River from Riggins on a steelhead fishing/shed antler hunting combo trip in March of 1995. They hiked up a drainage and were poking around in the flatter portion of the creek bottom in a brushy and timbered area. Piles of fresh sign dotted the drainage.

It wasn't long before they made an amazing find. A large bull elk skeleton lay there, apparently dead for quite some time. It seemed probable that it was a wounding loss from the previous hunting season, as it would likely have had more left on the carcass if it was a winterkill.

They hauled him partway out, but had to leave the huge rack overnight in order to get out of there and make it back to the jet boat by dusk. They came back the next day and finished packing the head, despite the unpleasant odor.

They later compared the antlers to a few different sheds they had found over the years. Sure enough, they soon realized they had picked up this bull's shed antlers the year before.

This bull doesn't necessarily seem to have any particular features that stand out over the rest, other than some good G-3s. What he does have, however, is one of the prettiest, most well-balanced racks an elk could grow.

Cindy Moffis models Bob and Gary McClure's giant elk from the Salmon River Country in spring of 1995.

Bob also found this giant shed antler in Idaho County. The mass on this ol' boy is just awesome. What a bull!

James Brian
365-4/8 B&C Typical
Clearwater County, 1970

Idaho Typical Rank: 62
Inside Spread: 41-6/8
Main Beams (R,L): 51-4/8, 48-1/8

Points (R,L): 7,7
Widest Spread: 46-4/8
Bases (R, L): 9-1/8, 9-1/8

Dale Brian and his friend Steve Bristol (affectionately known as "Hippie") were camped out for the elk season up in the Headquarters area. Dale's dad James headed up to join them for the weekend, expecting the boys to already have the elk tied to a tree for him. Instead, when he arrived, the boys were still laying in the tent! "There ain't no elk up here," they hollered from their comfortable confines.

After rousting them out of bed, James hauled them to the top of the mountain and dropped them off. He then drove back down to the bottom and started working his way toward them, pushing up the steep, brushy slopes. The hope was to get the elk moving between them.

Their game plan worked like magic, as Dale and Hippie pushed a cow, calf, and a bull by James. They jumped from a tangled slashy area of thick second-growth timber. James raised his .30-06 and hit the bull behind the shoulders from about 90 yards. After the length of a football field, the bull's escape came to an abrupt end.

James made those young men pay for sleeping in. Not only did he bag the big bull of the day, but they also got to pack the quarters out for him. They toted them down to an old road, at which point James shuttled them the pickup with a trail bike.

(Above) a front view of James Brian's tremendous Clearwater County bull from 1970. An abnormal point and unmatched G-6 keep this bull from showing how big he really is. (Below) James' son Dale took this big bull in the same area a few years later. This bull has incredibly strong fronts and an awesome overall appearance to him. This bull will score very close to 360 and could possibly make the records book as well, if officially measured.

Curtis Yanzick
364-3/8 P&Y Typical
Kootenai County, 1998

Idaho Typical Rank: 63
Inside Spread: 37-3/8
Main Beams (R,L): 57-2/8, 51-6/8

Points (R,L): 8,7
Widest Spread: 41-3/8
Bases (R, L): 9-3/8, 8-1/8

Curtis "Bumper" Yanzick is just like most of the breed of small-town Idahoans who live by and make their living from the mountains. He works in them during the day, and still can't seem to get enough of them in the evenings and weekends. Any chance to jump on a dirt bike, hike a new ridge top, or see a new bull is a day well spent.

On a September day in 1998, he slipped home from logging and headed up the hill to try a bugle before dark. It was no time before he saw a bull and eight cows, but they were too far off in fading light to make out any size.

The next morning, he hopped on his trail bike and rode it in about a mile before hiking in another mile or so. It was always a battle pushing his way through huckleberry, snowbrush, and choked hemlock timber, but that's where the elk were, and you can't kill 'em where they aren't.

He bugled off and on for about an hour, but received no complementary reply. He was just about to move on when he heard an unmistakable grunt. Bumper wasted no time in moving in. He bailed down the hill and circled partly around the bull, coming in from below. He knew he was getting close, so he stopped and sent out a probing bugle.

What happened next Bumper had no way to prepare for. The bull came charging in so fast, Bumper had no time to prepare. All of the sudden, the bull was just about on him. The only thing that would end up separating them was an 8-inch fir sapling. The bull was going to have to head on one side or the other (evidently thinking his rival was much further down the hill). If the bull broke to Bumper's side, he would likely steamroll right over him. Luckily, the bull chose the other side of the tree, and Bumper made his move. He could likely have reached out and touched the elk, had he wanted to, and made no effort to even aim his Martin bow, as he practically had the broadhead sitting against the bull's side at full draw.

He released the arrow, and the broadhead penetrated from a ways back, angling forward into the chest cavity. The bull turned tail instantly, and ran about 100 yards before stopping to let out a defiant bugle. Then he was gone.

Bumper waited awhile, partly to cool his own nerves in addition to the elk's. He then went down to where the bull last bugled. There on the ground lay the rear portion of the arrow, and he could see where the bull had actually bitten the arrow off and left it lay. He could find little blood in the tough tracking of heavy brush.

He decided to sit down, eat, and mull it over. As he sat there, he happened to look down. Right below him was a small spot of blood, right between his legs on the ground! With renewed hope, he got up and resumed the search. He soon found prints in the dirt, and then he saw the big sign of relief he was hoping for. An antler was sticking up out of the brush, only 75 yards from where he had been sitting!

He rushed up and pulled the antler out and was so blown away he thought he might fall over. In the hastiness of the encounter, he really had had no look at the antlers at all. The antlers he now held in his hands surpassed his wildest dreams.

He caped the bull out and then went back for help. He returned with Pat Flanagan and Tim Morgan, and they quartered him at about 11 p.m. The next morning, the three tired men packed the bull out with backpacks and then on motorcycles. As you can tell from the photos, it was one ugly packout, but for Bumper, it was well worth it.

A very happy Bumper Yanzick on the morning after the hunt.

This photo pretty much sums up how a body feels after packing out elk all day. Bumper struggled and stumbled more than once trying to keep those beam tips from carving a trench in the dirt.

Curtis "Bumper" Yanzick shows the fruits of what hard work, time in the field, and more than just a little savvy can produce. Bumper is a logging contractor, and lives among the elk both in and out of hunting season.

Wallace Darkow
364-1/8 B&C Typical
Benewah County, 1998

Idaho Typical Rank: 64
Inside Spread: 40-2/8
Main Beams (R,L): 48-6/8, 50-7/8

Points (R,L): 8,6
Widest Spread: 46-1/8
Bases (R, L): 8-5/8, 8-5/8

North Dakota isn't exactly noted for its elk hunting opportunities. As such, Wallace Darkow headed to Idaho for a new experience chasing a new animal. Wallace was lucky to have a friend in Tensed, namely Phil Sergeant, with whom he would have a place to stay and a hunting partner, too.

His first two years out, he had bagged two cows. By 1998, he was ready for something more.

As the planned their hunts, they were always looking for a new area. There was a spot they had always wanted to hunt, and finally they got up the nerve to ask the local rancher that owned the property. "Sure," he said. "I haven't seen any elk around, but go ahead."

The next day, they headed in early on ATVs. They parked them a ways back and walked in the remaining distance. They crossed a pasture, and set up for Phil to try a bugle while Wallace cow-called.

On their third attempt, much to their surprise, they got a response. For the next hour and a half, they worked him. The wind was blowing hard, which helped, and as they continued to move, the big bull kept working the cedars.

They were getting close. Finally, just before the bull came into view, he gave a blood-curdling bugle. As Wallace says, "He was mad as hell!"

The bull showed himself at 100 yards, but was head on and provided no good shot. Wallace waited, half in agony from the intensity of the situation. Finally, the bull shifted to a broadside position after he had cut the remaining distance in half.

The bull took off with the impact of the shot, only to collapse in a clearcut 200 yards away. The ol' Enfield had done the job.

Phil went to get help as Wallace worked on the bull. He had propped the bull up with a stick, which gave out as Wallace had knife in hand. The slip caused Wallace to cut himself fairly seriously above the knee. The bleeding quickly became fairly significant; Wallace had to quit, lay down, apply pressure, and wait for help.

When Phil returned, it was to a scene far different than what he had imagined. "We've got to get you to the E.R.!"

"Not 'til we get this elk off the mountain," was Wallace's reply.

Phil had brought two friends with him, so three and a half men lugged the big bull down the hill. They used a come-along to eventually load the bull whole into the pickup.

They then took Wallace to the emergency room. It was a good thing they didn't wait much longer; Wallace was beginning to go into a mild shock. But, Wallace had his priorities. Like many an elk hunter who has roamed Idaho's mountains, there are more important things out there than worrying about a little bit of blood loss!

"We should've brought a bigger truck."

Partly in the shade, and partly in the sun, Wallace Darkow is fully in elk. Wallace looks tiny compared to this old monarch.

Keith Harrow
363-1/8 B&C Typical
Bannock County, 1995

Idaho Typical Rank: 65
Inside Spread: 43-7/8
Main Beams (R,L): 53-0/8, 55-1/8

Points (R,L): 6,6
Widest Spread: 50-4/8
Bases (R, L): 9-5/8, 10-4/8

In 1985, I was able to draw a limited entry permit for an area that had been closed for several years. My son David spent many days scouting and was able to locate three big bulls. Prior to the hunt, the biggest bull broke his G-4 on one side, so we decided to go after bull #2.

Opening day found me, my two sons (Dave and Jeff), my friend Kelly Beckstrom, and his son Kyle hiking into the canyon we intended to hunt. We had barely arrived when a bull let out a short bugle. The bull we wanted was right in front of us! I dropped to the ground and put the crosshairs on him and let go of a bullet. It found its mark!

We were all very excited, having a monster bull down on a beautiful October morning in the Idaho mountains. It was an elk hunt that none of us there will ever forget.

Keith Harrow barely clears the top of his 1995 Idaho bull. This bull is very prototypical of Idaho genetics – strong backs, long main beams, and a hint of a "devil tine" or two off of his eyeguards.

Cary Cada
362-6/8 B&C Typical
Elmore County, 2005

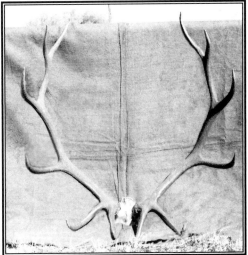

Idaho Typical Rank: 66
Inside Spread: 39-4/8
Main Beams (R,L): 57-0/8, 56-2/8

Points (R,L): 6,6
Widest Spread: 49-7/8
Bases (R, L): 9-5/8, 9-5/8

Wayne Cada must be getting just a little tired of watching his brother Cary have all the family hunting luck. You may remember from "Idaho's Greatest Mule Deer" that Wayne creased the skull of a giant 242-7/8 non-typical mule deer in 1975 shortly before Cary made the kill shot on one of the most impressive muleys ever taken in Idaho.

In 2005, Wayne was about to be witness to another incident that added Cary's name to a rare and select list. Cary had drawn a controlled hunt elk tag for an area in south-central Idaho. Wayne and George Earll decided to accompany Cary, even though they would have no tag or weapon.

That evening, the three men eased up onto a ridge and heard a bull serenading his cows in some timber across and up the draw from them. Over the course of the next 45 minutes, he proceeded to repeat the process a good 25 times.

Cary slipped down to get to a better vantage point and realized he had a good angle at an opening across the draw a little better than 200 yards away. He staked it out, hoping the bull might walk through it.

About then, he noticed a cow and calf coming toward him. He watched as they came to within 20 yards of him, and he snapped a few pictures of a great chance encounter. Unbeknown to him, while he was busy socializing with the local wildlife, a heck of a bull had just sallied through his selected opening. He realized his mistake only when he looked up the hill and saw Wayne motioning furiously with arms stretched wide, indicating big antlers. Wayne then motioned for Cary to beat feet down the draw and around – the direction the bull had gone. Wayne dared not yell the instructions as the cow and calf were still well within earshot.

Cary hustled down to look. Nothing! He had just started walking back when he happened to glance down the draw and caught the bull taking a drink out of the creek. Aspens obscured the view (and the shot) so Cary strained to better make out what he was seeing. He had positively identified it as a bull, but couldn't tell for sure how big. He decided to use Wayne's gestures as his yardstick, and let loose of a round from his .25-06.

The bull fled 30 yards to a knob and stopped. Cary sent another round into the vitals area behind the shoulder. The bull bolted again, and Cary let him have one more in the same spot as he went into the timber. Suddenly, all was quiet.

Cary sat and waited, all the while anticipating the sound of the bull hitting the ground. It never happened. Finally, he got up and slowly crept over to investigate. There was the mortally wounded bull, struggling to keep on his feet, too stubborn to go down. Cary aimed carefully for the spine and let a final round go into the bull's neck, dropping him instantly.

It wasn't until Cary approached that he really saw the antlers for the first time. He was in total awe. He was so intent on getting the job done that he hadn't really had the chance until that moment. He also inspected the bull for other bullet holes and found that all four shots had hit their chosen mark; the bull was just one tough warrior.

What a day – great view, big elk, and friends there to boot. Plus, two grunts to help him quarter up this big bull he had down. Things could have been worse.

Perk Rose
361-5/8 P&Y Typical
Washington County, 2002

Idaho Typical Rank: 69
Inside Spread: 39-3/8
Main Beams (R,L): 52-1/8, 51-4/8

Points (R,L): 8, 7
Widest Spread: 42-4/8
Bases (R, L): 9-1/8, 8-7/8

Not all hunts end the way we want them to. In fact, not nearly enough of them do. Perk Rose has taken many bulls over the years, but it was his biggest that gives him the most heartache. While Perk sometimes struggles to enjoy it, it shouldn't have to be that way. Sometimes there's no explanation; sometimes things just happen.

Things started with a bang. That mid-afternoon, his daughter had just given birth to his grandson. Perk, being a family man first and elk hunter a close second, was grounded enough to at least spend an hour with the youngster before jetting for home and an evening archery hunt.

He had a spot where he had been seeing six cows and calves for about ten straight nights, and he felt like a bull should be joining them at some point soon. He made it out to his chosen location with time to spare. Sure enough, the cows came out again; only this time, they had another seven cows and a giant bull with them! They were still half a mile off, but coming his way.

Perk backed off and then hoofed it down to a favorite ambush spot. Soon the elk came, marching past him in single file only 18 yards away. After about a 30-yard break, here came a mountain of an elk. Perk drew back, released an arrow, and sent the bull on his way. Perk was confident all the while, not knowing his broadhead had just barely clipped a miniscule piece of sagebrush. Perk got on his phone and told his son Paul, "Get home. I just killed an awfully big bull."

Perk was somewhat pinned and continued to watch the bull, which had gone a few yards and they lay down. The longer he watched, the more he began to rethink the events of the shot. *Why was he still alive?* Just at dusk, the bull stood up, walked eight feet, and lay back down – not a good sign. Perk was beginning to get a sick feeling in his stomach.

Light was beginning to get low. Perk would occasionally flicker a light that direction, and could still make out the reflecting eye of the bull in an upright posture. Finally, Perk moved. The bull promptly got up and, in a flash, was gone. Perk stayed on the mountain until 3:30 a.m. looking for sign of the wounded bull.

Early the next morning, Perk and his sons Paul and Tyler joined the search. They hunted from dawn until past dusk, covering several square miles between the three of them. They had exhausted every possible track, trail, and scenario.

The next morning, they were at it again, and looked until noon before returning home for a brief respite. They had no sooner pulled into their farm when a kid pulled up and asked them if they had heard about the big bull that had been found dead. Perk lunged up, got in his truck, and took off without saying hardly a word.

It turned out the bull had made it over two miles during that first night, and coincidentally had fallen and died inside an old, dilapidated round corral. Even going that distance, Perk had at one time been within about 300 yards of the elk during his search. Who ever would have looked there? A farmer had been swathing hay when he saw the magpies. Going to investigate, the discovery was made.

Perk was sick inside, knowing that one of his most special days and best opportunities had ended this way. He had just put too much into his love for hunting and elk to have this happen. He was a responsible archer, and went out of his way to make sure he would never be in a scenario like this one.

He punched his tag and was done for the year. He wouldn't be chasing another elk. He borrowed a backhoe and buried the bull near where he had fallen.

Perk is not a trophy hunter. Sure, if given the chance, he wouldn't mind having a nice set of antlers, but the primary enjoyment is the meat, and knowing this bull was wasted will never sit well with him. Perk doesn't need any critics; he is his own biggest critic, which is unfortunate. A man that puts that much into the enjoyment and respect of elk should be able to enjoy those antlers just a little more than he lets himself. He just hopes there's a lesson to be learned, particularly if someone else can hear about it.

Perk's son Paul (left) also took a nice archery bull later that same season.

Wilbur Chitwood
361 B&C Typical
Fremont County, 1956

Idaho Typical Rank: 70
Inside Spread: 41-1/8
Main Beams (R,L): 49-4/8, 50-3/8

Points (R,L): 6,7
Widest Spread: 51-4/8
Bases (R, L): 9-3/8, 9-6/8

At the tender age of 17, Wilbur Chitwood was scarcely older than the big bull that would soon be linked to him for eternity. One lucky shot and one chance encounter would be all that he needed to seal the deal.

The Chitwoods were camped on Swan Lake, north of Ashton. Wilbur's dad Ralph was there, as was his uncle Hollen and Hollen's son David. For the first two days, they had little luck finding elk.

On a crisp October morning that would mark the third day of the hunt, the Chitwoods all piled into their hunting rig and headed up the road toward Bishop Mountain. From there they all split up to cover separate territory.

Wilbur was packing an old .30-30 Winchester carbine – the same one his dad had started hunting with, which had been given to him by *his* dad in 1923. *Wouldn't it be something to take a bull with that old rifle*, Wilbur thought.

He walked along enjoying the morning, hunting some thick lodgepole and scattered yellow pine on rolling, slightly hilly country. He was only an hour into the hunt when he came upon a heck of a sight. In the middle of a meadow was a whopping big bull elk attacking an old downed tree, rubbing his antlers with vigor and scattering bark in all directions.

They made eye contact not much after Wilbur saw him, and the bull turned tail and took off. Not wanting to shoot his meat supply right in the rump, Wilbur kept trying to hit the bull in the neck or the head. His first shot was a clean miss. Shot number two put a bullet right through the main beam, knocking him senseless for a second or two. A third shot nailed a good chunk of his browtine. That shot turned the bull more broadside, and Wilbur knew he needed to make the next one count. One more squeeze of the trigger and he hit the bull's-eye (almost literally) and Wilbur's elk dropped like a sack of potatoes.

Wilbur's dad started yelling, "Is that you?"

Wilbur yelled back, "Yes!"

"Get 'im?"

"Yes!"

Wilbur's dad went back and got the 1952 pickup truck, which they were able to back right up to the monstrous carcass and load whole. Wilbur remembers it filling up the entire 8-foot bed. He also remembered the meat from the big ol' elk being similar in toughness to that old pickup bed he was laying in! The bull weighed 480 lbs. hanging weight.

Wilbur has continued to hunt elk through most of his life, but never quite came across anything else like this again. Better once than never, though.

Wilbur Chitwood and his 1956 trophy elk. Wilbur knocked this bull for a loop when he put a bullet right through its main beam. And you thought it hurt when you hit a baseball wrong.

Cousins David and Wilbur Chitwood, with Wilbur's first bull.

Robert L. Dixon
361 B&C Typical
Idaho County, 1963

Idaho Typical Rank: 70
Inside Spread: 38-4/8
Main Beams (R,L): 50-2/8, 50-4/8

Points (R,L): 7,7
Widest Spread: 43-3/8
Bases (R, L): 8-4/8, 9-4/8

My fraternity brother Phil Clock asked if I would join him and his brother Ralph on an elk hunt. I was eager to go and able to take a little time off work, so I said I would. At the appointed time, I was able to get a flight on a private plane to Lewiston. That plane lost an engine, but that's another story. Phil, Ralph, and Hugh Riley (a rep. for Fenwick fishing tackle) met me. Hugh had made most of the arrangements for the trip.

We proceeded to Riggins by car. At the time, Riggins consisted of a small store/café/post office near the edge of the Salmon River. We arrived early to meet our guide, Paul Filer, who would come down the Salmon, by boat, to pick us up.

After having some food, Filer arrived with a small riverboat with two Mercury outboards. We loaded our gear and started upriver, going astonishingly slow because of the rapid current caused by the steep fall of the river. After a while, we reached Filer's ranch and had some time to look around before dinner. I also sighted in my new Remington Woodsmaster .30-06 with a 3x10 scope. Phil had bought it for me, saying my .30-06 Springfield with open sights wasn't up to par. I had used that gun since I was fifteen.

The next day, we were up early for breakfast and off on horseback up some very steep trails to the wilderness area. My memory of the trails was a lot of places with the foot of the trunk of good-sized fir trees on our left and tops to our right. Over their tops we had impressive views of the country. After awhile, we heard an elk bugle down off to our right. Phil rode up to Filer, who was in the lead (no small feat on that narrow trail), and asked if we could stop for a few minutes to try our luck. "Son," as Filer had taken to calling us, "there is no point; he's too far down the hill, he will hear you coming, and we have to keep going to reach the areas where we are to camp."

Phil asked again, and Filer relented. As luck would have it, this was fairly heavily-wooded with some areas of gravel talus on the steep slope. Phil and I got off our horses and started leaping and sliding down the talus slope – we had just left the reins over their heads and on the ground as there was nowhere for them to go on that trail.

In several minutes, the very surprised bull was between us, about 50 feet from each of us. Filer was very surprised when we got back up to the trail to say we had a six-point bull down. It was a much longer trip back up that hill than it was going down!

Filer left the wrangler to dress the bull and pack it back to the ranch so we could keep moving. We reached camp about dark, as I recall, and helped Paul unpack the horses, set up camp, and prepare dinner. I don't recall when the wrangler got back, but I think it was the next day.

The next day was a fairly normal hunting trip day and I don't think any of us saw much. The following day we had a more organized hunt and Ralph got a five-point bull and Hugh Riley got a cow, I believe.

The following day, we were hunting individually and I took off following what I thought were fresh tracks of several elk. After awhile, I heard some bugling. I started to move slowly, staying downwind. Several cows and a bull were making some noise moving in the heavy brush, but I couldn't see them except for an occasional quick glimpse. Still taking care to stay downwind as they moved, I was able to get closer until, finally, after several hours I was surprised as I was sure I heard heavy breathing but couldn't see anything because of the heavy brush. Then it got quiet and I found myself looking into a very big eye through the thick brush! He was only fifteen feet away! It shook me up, but I shot him with my .30-06.

That's when pandemonium erupted! Elk cows began running in several directions and the big bull fell into the brush, making the first opening I had seen in the heavy brush. After sitting a minute or two to let my breath catch up, I started to dress the seven-point bull. Dressing it out, I was surprised that straddling the chest cavity, one or the other of my feet would be off the ground, he was that big – and I am over six feet tall! I also realized that by the time I had it dressed out, I would have a problem getting back to camp before dark.

It was then that my friend Ralph appeared out of nowhere. He had heard the shot and came over to investigate. He also had his video camera with him to record the event.

We finished cleaning the bull and hung it up the best we could and started back to camp by a more direct route than I had come, hoping to save time and get us back before dark. There was a lot of beetle-killed downed timber, so it was slow going, and we got back after dark. Paul Filer didn't seem worried about us as I recall, but when I told him I had gotten a big bull, and described where, I will never forget his comment. "Son, if you got a bull you will never find it where you say you were."

I didn't argue and just stayed quiet. Hugh Riley had brought a bottle of J&B to toast our trip and that was the best tasting scotch ever.

The next morning after breakfast, I took off with a small chainsaw to clear the bigger deadfalls and mark the trail for the wrangler with the packhorses. Fortunately, Filer was wrong and I found the spot again!

That night, after getting the bull back to camp, I had my second best shot of scotch. The following morning, we started back on the horses, and at the ranch, had a great dinner.

The following morning, as we loaded the boat for the much faster return to Riggins, I noticed the six-point bull we had taken first had several broken tips as well as considerable dried blood on his antlers. We assumed he had been fighting a lot and was probably very frustrated that my seven-point had the cows with him further up the mountain. Filer looked at the two sets of antlers we had, and commented, "Not bad for city kids."

Robert Dixon (right) holds the giant bull he bagged during his 1963 elk hunt in the Salmon River country. Ralph Clock is likely thinking about the work that lay ahead. This still frame was actually taken from a video.

F.H. Sappingfield
361 B&C Typical
Salmon River, 1963

Idaho Typical Rank: 70
Inside Spread: 42-3/8
Main Beams (R,L): 53-4/8, 53-5/8

Points (R,L): 7,6
Widest Spread: 46-4/8
Bases (R, L):8-1/8, 8-0/8

Little is currently known on this great bull met his demise. F.H. Sappingfield was hunting on the Middle Fork of the Salmon River in 1963 when he and this bull had their fateful encounter.

Take a look at that airplane. It looks like the ride in and out of camp could have been even more adventurous than bagging this big bull! It was all likely worth the effort, though, as Mr. Sappingfield looks like he is very happy with his prized set of Idaho elk antlers.

Tim Thomas
360-2/8 P&Y Typical
Clark County, 1996

Idaho Typical Rank: 74
Inside Spread: 46-4/8
Main Beams (R,L): 54-5/8, 55-0/8

Points (R,L): 8,6
Widest Spread: 50-5/8
Bases (R, L): 9-1/8, 8-4/8

On the way back from bowhunting near the divide, Tim Thomas and Ted Laird stopped at a spot in the road and began to glass a hillside. To their surprise, they spotted a bull bedded down on the hillside. They debated its size, with Tim thinking it looked like a raghorn and Ted insisting he was quite a bit bigger. The truth was soon discovered when the bull stood up to stretch. They turned to each other and said, "That ain't no raghorn!"

The bull grabbed his cows and escorted them out of the area and into a big aspen patch. The hunters wasted no time in getting permission from the landowner, and were able to get within about 100 yards of the bull by mid-afternoon. There they waited, for nearly four hours, for the situation to give them what they needed. Just about the time they felt the herd would be getting up to feed, the wind shifted, and like a flash, the elk were gone.

So would go the encounters between Tim and one of the biggest bulls he had ever seen. Over the course of ten days, Tim was equally close to the bull six different times. Something always seemed to go wrong at just the right time, though, and he always got back into the truck and headed home empty.

On the second to last day of the season (Tim's last day), he once again headed up to try for his new nemesis. He was driving along through the sagebrush, when all of the sudden his front end took a dive right into an old cave-like depression, lifting his back end clear off the ground. The rancher had warned him about the gaping hole, but Tim hadn't seen it in time. Thinking this was not the way he wanted to spend the last day of bow season, Tim began the long march back to the rancher's property to get help. Too much time later, they returned and pulled his pickup out.

The rancher left to go check on some stock, and as he made his way down the road, he jumped a herd of elk. Tim just happened to see the entire scene unfold, and watched the elk heading for one of the main canyons in the area. The big bull he was chasing was in the herd!

The canyon was an open and broken one, with quite a bit of sage and large rocks. As such, he was able to watch from a distance as they bedded down. By this time, unfortunately, Tim had to leave and run an errand, so he marked the spot in his mind and decided to come back in a couple of hours.

He returned, only to find a couple of antelope hunters in the area. He chatted briefly with them before leaving, and almost instantly saw elk far off in the distance. The sun was going down, so he would have to act fast. He jumped in his pickup and flew down the hill, parking 400 yards or so away. Even from where he parked, he could see the tops of their heads bedded in the sage.

Rushed stalks are not often effective in bowhunting, but it was either this way or no way, so Tim moved in fast. He practically sprinted for 300 yards before coming to a small draw between them he could use for cover. Before he could get there, though, the elk had him pinned.

In desperation, he cow-called, and they started coming toward him. As soon as they dropped out of sight into the draw, he moved his position as fast as he could behind a large rock.

Now the elk were coming across to him, toward where he had cow-called. They slowly came up the draw. – cow, cow, cow, and so on until nearly 30 head had passed. Finally, the big bull showed and, at 27 yards, Tim was able to finally take the shot he had been trying so desperately to get.

The bull took a few steps, and then Tim could see his legs beginning to buckle. The bull went down and Tim began to get excited. Then, to his amazement, the bull gave a defiant bugle before expiring. It was a sound he would never forget. About that time, Tim heard coyotes off in the distance howling, and he decided it was about time to join them. He cut loose with one of his own in celebration of one of his most glorious days afield.

Tim's giant 1996 bull is nearly more than his little pickup could handle.

Unofficial Trophies*

*Many of the trophies in this section have either been measured for Boone and Crockett Club but were never submitted, or were measured by other records keeping organizations which accept lower minimum scores. As a result, most never made the transition to B&C and were entered only in the Idaho Fish and Game's record books or other books which have a lower minimum standard. It should be noted that while most have been officially scored at one time, many may have to be rescored before being accepted. Until officially verified and accepted by B&C or P&Y, all scores for the purposes of this book are unofficial.

Jerry Neumeyer
393-4/8 Non-typical

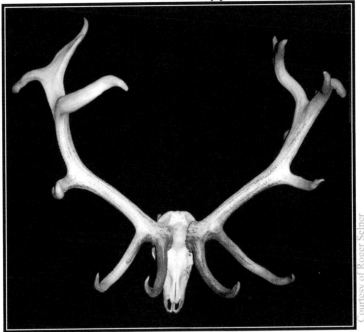

Jerry Neumeyer killed this tremendous bull in northern Idaho. Information seems to be scarce on this bull at the present time. It has been officially measured at 393-4/8 as a non-typical, but no paperwork was ever submitted and no story can currently be found.

This bull is truly one of the most remarkable ever taken in Idaho, or anywhere else for that matter. It's not very often a non-typical elk really gets that non-typical, but this one genuinely fits the bill.

Picked Up by Steve Heitstuman
385-3/8 Non-Typical
Nez Perce County, 1972

Harold Heitstuman's family had been running cattle in the Craig Mountains for many years. As such, he had seen many interesting things in those mountains. During one trip in the fall of 1971, Harold spotted a great bull elk in a pasture near the cattle on Swamp Creek. The bull looked very poorly, and in such bad shape that his head barely hovered above ground as the bull struggled to keep it up. Harold had no tag, so could do nothing to put the bull out of its misery, but he knew the bull was not going to make it long.

After he got home, he told his boys about the big poor-looking bull. Steve and Wayne were very excited about maybe finding the bull, or his shed antlers, the next summer - excited enough that they had no problem remembering it when the time came to go try and find him.

The next June, Harold, 17-year-old Steve, and 14-year-old Wayne headed up the mountain to let the cattle out on the allotment, and more importantly to the boys, to look for that bull. They searched a good long while with no luck. Eventually, Steve went over to investigate a thick scrubby patch of jack pine that had sprung up after a fire. It was thick as doghair as Steve pushed his way through it, but it was all worth the trouble. He found bone, which turned out to be the whole skeleton of the big bull. Harold had been right; the bull had no chance to survive the winter.

Those people driving by the Heitstuman cattle truck in June of 1972 had this view coming at them.

John Abel
384-3/8 Non-typical
Idaho County, 1999

Idaho Non-typical Rank: 21 *Length of Abnormal Points: 24-6/8* *Points (R,L): 8,7*
Inside Spread: 32-2/8 *Widest Spread: 42-2/8*
Main Beams (R,L): 52-1/8, 52-1/8 *Bases (R, L): 10-2/8, 10-1/8*

John Abel and his hunting buddies Bill Schauer, Chris Fulster, and Darrell Ferreira had been hunting the country off of the main Salmon for more than thirty years. They were planning the next year's adventure and eventually decided it was time for a change of scenery. They had a good many memories and fun in the area, but decided it was time to see some new country. They organized a hunt with a guide and headed north for their 1999 season.

Even though the location had changed, the basic scenery had not. It was big, intimidating country, and would be a new challenge. It was typical country for central Idaho – rugged, dry, and full of elk.

The first morning's hunt would be above some of the steep river breaks on more gently rolling terrain. The four men split into groups of two. These tandem groups were each led by one guide. John and Darrell were paired for the day, and they headed out in the darkness full of a brand new anticipation.

As first light began to peak over the mountains to the east, they spotted elk instantly. A quick coin flip determined that Darrell would have first crack at any bulls. They got to within 200 yards and watched as a giant bull and 35 cows made their way through the early morning light.

With the wind perfect and plenty of time to set up, Darrell fired a shot that would break the morning stillness. As the shot echoed through the canyon, it quickly became apparent he had missed. John snapped, "You're shootin' high!"

A second shot followed with the same result as the first. Miraculously, the bull stood frozen, as if his hooves were magically cemented into the ground. Shot number three was as ineffective as its predecessors. The guide was about to pitch a fit in all the excitement.

Finally, on the fourth attempt, Darrell connected – right through the right beam of the big bull, who then shook his head vigorously, likely with the same feeling you have when you hit a baseball wrong and the vibration sent through the bat and into your fingers makes you wish your fingers would just fall off.

Darrell looked up, a hint of sadness and disappointment in his eyes. "I'm out of shells."

John quickly handed Darrell his gun. "Use this!"

"Nope. I'm left-handed. I'm done."

As the hunters seemed to take a timeout to discuss the situation, the bull had yet to attempt an escape! Four loud booms and the slap of a bullet right through the bone on his head, and the bull continued to just stand there.

John sat down and got a good rest on his knees and let a bullet fly from his .338. The first shot hit the bull in a foreleg, but the second shot was right into the boiler room. The bull barely moved before falling.

Darrell's dreadful luck had turned into John's good fortune. Like any good friend, John wishes things could have gone better for his friend that day, but, hey – that's huntin'.

Ben Sonnen
383-2/8 Non-Typical
Nez Perce County, 1977

Other than a few bugs on the windshield, and perhaps a few ants underfoot, Ben Sonnen had never killed anything in his life. At 71 years of age, that would finally change, as Ben would take his first big game animal – a record-class bull elk.

After years of watching his boys futilely put in for a controlled hunt elk permit in the Craig Mountains, Ben decided he would give it a shot. To everyone's astonishment, it was Ben (born in 1906) who would be doing the elk hunting for the family in fall of 1977.

Ben's sons Vern and Ed, along with Vern's friend Jim Beckman, came along to help Ben on the hunt. They left early on the second morning from Greencreek and headed for the area near Soldier's Meadow.

The pieces fell together and soon Ben was face to face with two elk; one was a cow and her companion was a regal bull. Had Ben hunted very long, he might have realized just how special a bull he was looking at, but as it was, he was able to calmly squeeze the trigger of his 7mm Mag. and effectively drop the bull on the spot. He must have been wondering why people thought this elk hunting business was so tough as he walked up on his first elk.

The area proved to be fairly easy to get a pickup to, and they drove right to Ben's trophy. The boys hoisted the bull between two trees, drove the pickup right underneath him, and slickly dropped the bull right into the bed of the pickup. Poor ol' Ben never even got to learn the joys of packing out elk quarters. He probably got over it.

Scott Griggs
368-3/8 P&Y Non-typical
Custer County, 1992

Scott Griggs was bowhunting in Custer County in 1992 when he ran into this monster bull. Scoring 368-3/8 Pope & Young, this great bull is the fourth-largest non-typical ever taken in Idaho with a bow.

Unknown
410 B&C Typical
Idaho, 1960s

LeRoy West (a friend of Neil Hinton's) strains to hold up the massive rack.

The only thing unofficial about this bull seems to be the truth itself. This gigantic typical is in the B&C records book, but the main question seems to be, "Where did it come from?"

It was somewhat coincidentally discovered by the author that this tremendous bull had Idaho ties. A call to Neil Hinton would not only verify that, but lead to an interesting and fairly convoluted story.

In the 1960s, Neil had heard from a friend that there were some gigantic antlers outside on a balcony down the street in his hometown of Walla Walla. Neil wasn't one to turn down a free chance to see something that interesting and went to check them out.

He arrived to find that some college roommates in an apartment were the ones in possession of it. Neil put a tape on it and realized quickly that this bull was something special – maybe even one of the top bulls in the world! He inquired about their willingness to sell the overgrown hat rack but they didn't seem interested. After a pause, one of the boys asked, "How much you offering?"

Neil's offer was a whopping $20. It wasn't a ton of money, but to two young college kids, it was enough to convince them to part with it.

Before he left, Neil made sure he got as much history as he could on it. The bull had a 1943 metal tag on it, and the boys told him it had come out of Orofino off of an old barn.

Neil had them officially measured and then entered them in B&C. They were big enough that they were invited to the 14th Competition Judges' Panel, where the bull received a Certificate of Merit. At the time, it was # 5 in the world.

A couple of years down the line, Neil himself needed some money, and even though he didn't want to sell his prized elk antlers, he did. A northwestern Oregon trophy hunter bought them, to display in a restaurant he was told.

A couple of years later, Neil was at the Spokane Bighorn Show and was stunned when he saw them in the big game competition. The Oregon man that had bought them had them entered into the show as a bull he had shot himself in Washington State. Neil was stunned, at both the coincidence as well as the gall of the man to cheat to such a degree. He reported the charade to show officials and the bull was disqualified.

Yet another few years passed when Neil crossed paths in Walla Walla with a man who was the uncle of the kid he had bought the antlers from. It was only then that Neil got the true story behind the big bull. "Those kids lied to you about that rack," the man said. "That rack came off a barn out of Orofino alright, but not like they said. They just put that old tag on there. That bull wasn't taken in 1943; it was likely taken in the 1960s. Those kids stole that rack off of the side of that barn."

Where the antlers reside now is unknown. Perhaps all that is known is that they aren't where they're supposed to be – hanging on that barn wall out of Orofino.

Picked Up by Bob Harris
392-5/8 Typical
Fremont County, 1971

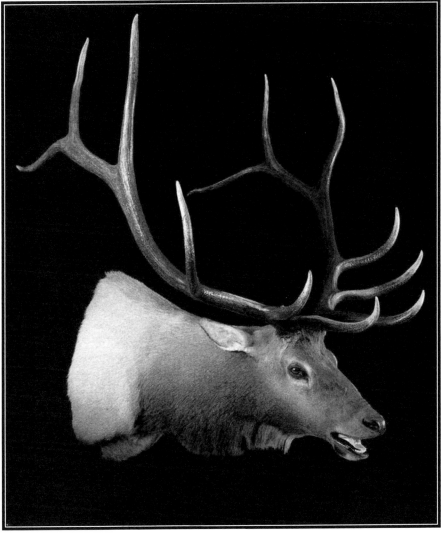

A government trapper named Bob Harris found this giant 6x6 in a gravel pit near Island Park on Ashton Hill. Bob figured it had been wounded by a hunter and died. It had likely been migrating out of Yellowstone when it met its fate.

Blake Jacobsen, of Jake's Midnight Taxidermy, helped with what he knew of the bull that he and his brother Blair now own. If ever officially verified, this bull could be one of the top bulls in the history of the state.

Poached
390-6/8 Typical
Lincoln County, 2000

You might ask why a poached animal is allowed to be placed into the records books. One reason is that these records recognize conservation success, not particularly how the animal died. Another is that it gives credit and adds history to the area from which the bull came. As such, they are allowed in, so long as the poacher will never receive any credit, and that the animal is entered into the records program by a state/public/non-profit-type entity that holds the animal in public trust.

This bull is displayed in the Citizens Against Poaching (CAP) trailer that IDF&G uses to educate the public about how poachers steal from all sportsmen. The following is from the CAP display:

> *This elk was killed a month before the season opened. It was found in a grain field in Unit 52A by an elk hunter that was scouting the area. This area is managed for large bulls. Rifle casings found at the scene indicate there were two shooters. Officers estimated that the animal was killed the previous night. The antlers "green scored" 391-3/8 B&C. Since 1997 there have been enhanced penalties for killing trophy animals. Also, spotlighting is considered a "flagrant" violation. See penalty sections 36-1402, 36-1404.*

Dennis Baird
376-5/8 Typical
Clark County, 1977

Idaho Typical Rank: 21
Inside Spread: 30-2/8
Main Beams (R,L): 55-6/8, 55-0/8

Points (R,L): 7,6
Widest Spread: 47-1/8
Bases (R, L): 8-6/8, 8-4/8

Hunting the Clark County area was an annual event for Dennis Baird, Terry Baird, Larry Rose, and their families. In 1976, they had seen a big bull in their favorite hunting area, but no one had been able to punch their tag with that big set of antlers.

The following fall, they were back at it again. Terry and Dennis were there, as was Larry and his boy Troy, now twelve and just old enough to hunt.

They headed out from camp and had covered a little more than a mile. They then all split up and began to hit some jack pine thickets. Dennis, as usual fell behind a ways. He was a slow, methodical, and patient hunter, and was never in a hurry to get anywhere in the woods. Better to let them come to him. A good strategy most of the time, in Dennis' case it never seemed to work out. Terry and Larry recall that Dennis always seemed to have horrible luck killing an elk.

They hadn't been into the jack pines long when Terry smelled elk. Soon after, he saw them. They were all cows and calves, and were circling around the loosely held hunting group.

About that time, they heard a loud *CRACK-BOOM*. Then another. It was Dennis' 6mm. Dennis had found the bull, split off from the cows, and had given him some air conditioning. The first shot had actually missed, but a second shot to the neck dropped the bull in his tracks.

Shortly after the shot, they heard a yell. "Terry! Come quick!"

They all made good time in getting down to the source of all the commotion and were stunned at the bull lying there on the ground. Dennis was, of course, all smiles.

They were able to drive the Jeep right to the bull after clearing some deadfall out of the way. As they departed, they had the antlers tied to the front of the Jeep and were driving through a quakie patch. There they encountered a hunter, who nearly fainted when he saw that giant rack coming at him.

On the way home, the stopped in Dubois for fuel. A boy stopped by on a bike and yelled, "You guys got that Sheridan elk!"

They asked the boy what he was talking about. He went on to explain that his dad had been chasing that same bull after seeing him from the air while doing aerial counts of elk for the government.

Dennis Baird takes a moment to enjoy one of the prettiest bulls ever taken in Idaho. This photo rates right up there with Idaho's best historic field photos of big bulls.

Ron McCann
369-2/8 Typical
Nez Perce County, 1973

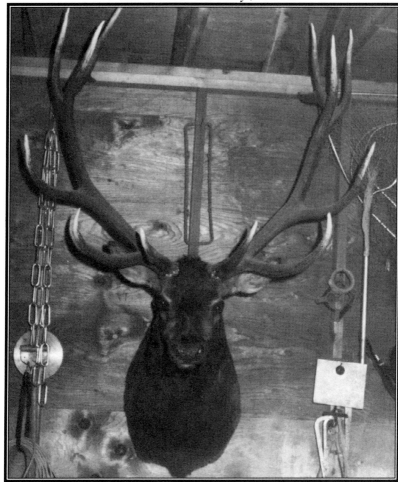

The year 1973 is the first, last, and only time 27-year old Ron McCann was ever able to draw the elk tag for unit 11. He made it count, taking one of the great bulls to come out of the area.

It was close to the end of the season when Ron, his dad Bill McCann, Sr., Ken Bausch, and a couple of others headed out for another day of trying to find a good bull to hang a tag on. They were hunting in timbered country and, as the day wore on, it looked like it was going to be another elkless day.

Late in the afternoon, their luck changed when they jumped a herd. Ron watched as 15 head came around the point of a ridge toward him. In classic style, the big bull was the caboose in the train.

They came through the brush and Ron's shot was going to have to be quick work at short range. He pointed the .30-06 at the bull's lungs at 40 yards and squeezed. It was a perfect hit, and abruptly ended the last day of elk hunting Ron would ever know in that country. It was a good way to end it.

Ron McCann's giant bull fills the bed of Ken Bausch's pickup. That's the way every hunter wishes his pickup looked at the end of their hunting season.

Claude Chaflin
363-7/8 Typical
Shoshone County, 1977

This clipping was all that could be traced down on this great bull. What an awesome old-time photo. The clipping says:

8-Point thrill

Some guys have all the luck. At 7 a.m. opening day on Mercury Creek, north of Prichard, Claude Chaflin, 45, of Squaw Bay nailed this 1,000-pound plus, eight-point elk. The rack measured four feet across at its widest point and the dressed animal yielded 510 pounds for the freezer [likely an exaggeration]. *Chaflin, who has missed only a few years of elk hunting since high school, said this is his biggest bag – yet.*

The Idaho Fish & Game listing has Claude Claflin (different spelling) as the hunter. Regardless of the spelling, it seems very unlikely these are not referencing the same elk.

Joe Yatzun
361-2/8 Typical
Valley County, 1974

Noon is a strange time to see a trophy-class bull walking out in the open, but Joe Yatzun wasn't about to question the gift in front of him. Joe was out on an overlook checking out a drainage when he heard a noise. Expecting it to be his hunting partner, Rudy Mokely, he casually turned and discovered that the source of the noise was a great big bull elk walking his way.

Only one pine tree separated them, so Joe waited for the pine to block the view so he could move into shooting position. At 100 yards, he finally got a shot off, and the bull went out of sight below the bluff.

Joe waited, but couldn't tell where the bull went. Luckily, the bull snapped another twig, in an unexpected location, and Joe was able to get on him again and put him down.

The packout, while less than a mile, proved to be a difficult one. They finally borrowed a horse from the neighboring camp, which led to its own adventure. The horse was as spooky as they come, and the men ended up expending as much energy handling the horse as they likely would have had they just packed it out themselves. Joe notes that the rack only exists today because Rudy was willing to pack it out.

Poached
360-4/8 Typical
Owyhee County, 1996

Unfortunately, not all big bulls are taken by honest, law-abiding sportsmen who realize the integrity of the hunt, and that a clean conscience is what matters at the end of the day. The chance any hunter would have had to harvest either of these two awesome bulls was stolen in what became a high profile poaching case in Idaho in 1996.

The general public doesn't get enough education on the difference between hunters and poachers. By definition, they are mutually exclusive.

The top bull in the photo scores 353-4/8; the bottom bull scores 360-4/8. These bulls are part of the display in the Citizens Against Poaching (CAP) Trailer, which is a public educational display. The signs read as follows:

Juniper Mountain Elk

On November 6, 1996 four bull elk were illegally spotlighted and killed in Owyhee County. Two Jordan Valley residents shot these magnificent animals and then tagged them with Oregon elk tags. The big 6x6 bull would have qualified for the Boone and Crockett record book.

Concerned citizens provided Idaho Fish and Game and Oregon State Police wildlife officers with information that led to the arrest and conviction of four poachers. Penalties and fines were assessed as follows:

- $9326 fines and restitution
- 3 years hunting, fishing, and trapping license revocation
- 180 days jail (60 days served)
- Total of eight years probation
- 100 hours community service
- Written apology to the citizens of the state of Idaho
- Poachers also charged in Oregon for unlawful possession

More Great Bulls

Courtesy of Cabela's

L egendary outdoor writer Elmer Keith is one of Idaho's most well-known names. He spent many years enjoying the wilds of Idaho in the early and middle parts of the 1900s. It was on one such adventure that he encountered this spectacular bull.

Elmer was out in February of 1939, chasing a bear that had "thawed too early," as Elmer put it. During the chase, he happened onto an old bull that was the best Elmer had ever seen on the hoof. "At a glance, I knew it was the finest elk head I had ever seen alive and have killed some good ones and guided others for even better but this head was outstanding in length."

Elmer made several trips back in on snowshoes, checking on the old bull. The elk wasn't in good shape, and Elmer said, "I was sorely tempted to bump the old bull and save his fine head and cape, as he was very thin. However, I waited, thinking I would at least pick up his horns. He died a natural death of starvation, and the horns loosed so I brought them out."

This bull is a great specimen, particularly for his era. Both main beams exceed sixty inches. In 1947, this outstanding elk won the First Award at Boone and Crockett Club's 1st Big Game Competition. This was before the advent of the modern scoring system, and award winners were picked solely on length of the longer main beam. Shortly after, shed antlers became ineligible for competitions.

This bull stands as a giant reminder that not all of them end up in the freezer. Even saddled with a life of packing this monstrous set of headgear, this sly old bull was too smart to fall prey to a hunter.

Courtesy of Roger Selner

Ira Jones took this unique elk in Idaho County during the 2000 hunting season. Ira was spending his birthday looking for an elk, but had no idea that this impressive bull would be his present. After a 45-minute stalk and ten minutes to calm down, Ira ended up with the present of a lifetime.

The bull was radio collared in 1995 by Idaho Department of Fish and Game and tracked for several years. Ira harvested the bull just ten miles from where it was collared and was aged at ten years old.

This fantastic and freakish 8x12 bull has been measured at 400-7/8 non-typical, with a 50-5/8 greatest spread, 47-2/8 and 40-7/8 main beams. Droptines on both G-3s make this bull exceptionally rare.

Photo and portions of story courtesy of Trophy Show Productions.

Courtesy of Boone & Crockett Club

Ray Holes was one of the most sought after saddle makers in the west throughout the last half of the 20th century. He started in 1934 out of Grangeville, and turned his craft into a true functional art.

Ray was crippled, stricken with polio, but didn't let that stop him from enjoying the mountains. He had a well-trained mare, Patty, from whose back he could shoot at anything he desired. Patty was a like a bird dog, and knew when they were coming into elk. She would suddenly stop, and that was often a clue for Ray that they were "in among 'em".

On a 1945 hunt in the Selway, Ray was riding Patty when she suddenly froze. Ray started listening, and could hear a clatter coming. Soon Ray had this big 7x7 bull in the sights of his .300 H&H, performing the shot off of Patty's back with ease.

This bull won 1st Prize in B&C's 1949 Competition. This was before the advent of the modern scoring system, and so the only thing that ranked the bulls were main beam length. With a 59-2/8" beam, it's easy to see how this bull distanced himself from the competition. The bull scores 353 on the modern scale.

Courtesy of the Holes Family

Ray Holes leads a well-built packstring into Idaho elk country.

In 1992, elk hunting was opened in unit 56 on a limited basis. Only five bull permits were issued in that inaugural season, and Larry Anderson was one of the lucky recipients. For decades, the elk population in the area had been allowed to grow and age, undisturbed by hunters. As such, Larry figured there had to be some big old bulls in the area.

Larry was accompanied by Kirk Dahlke on many scouting expeditions. Kirk didn't have a permit, but it was still fun to be a part of unit 56's first elk hunt in many decades.

The area is mountainous but not high in elevation. Moderate to rolling hills, covered in aspen and conifers, give way to sagebrush flats and agricultural fields – prime nighttime grazing for roving bands of elk.

On opening day, October 15th, they saw elk nearly 1000 yards off. They had no luck in closing the distance, however, and ended the day with no tag punched. Several more days of hunting netted similar results. The type of country they were hunting was tough, not so much in terrain, but in the fact that those elk can cover a lot of ground in a night, moving from one food source to another, and catching up to them can be a frustrating experience.

Finally, on October 30th, their luck would change. It started with seeing a nice six-point that Kirk took a shot at but couldn't connect. Fresh off of that defeat, they headed to a new area, and early in the afternoon found themselves looking into a deep draw. Kirk looked down into the hole and said, "There's gotta be elk in there. I'll go swing around a make a push through there. You be ready."

Kirk had no idea how truthful his words would be. The plan worked like a charm. At about three in the afternoon, Larry saw a large, lone bull coming out of the draw. At less than 100 yards, he fired his .270, hitting the bull in the chest. It would be the only round he would need.

Larry and Kirk were stunned at what they had just done. At points during the hunt, they began to doubt if they were going to be able to fill Larry's tag, and now they found themselves looking up close and personal at possibly the biggest bull in the whole unit!

Reality of the work ahead of them was sinking in when they realized they might be able to get a pickup pretty close to his final resting place. Sure enough, with a little effort, they were able to get their rig within about two hundred yards. They dragged him downhill, and eventually loaded the monstrous bull whole.

This Cassia County bull is reported to score over 390 as a non-typical. With lots of long tines, heavy mass, and a few extra points, it's likely this bull might make the all-time records book.

Although Keith Ford had seen a big bull eating way too much of his alfalfa during the summer and fall of 1987, he really gave little thought to the possibility of outsmarting the big bull come hunting season. Elk come and elk go, but it's big country, and focusing on one animal is oftentimes a waste of a season.

On October 7th, 1987, Keith, his wife Helen, his son Ron, and Greg White set out from the Ford family home on horseback. They weren't picky; any antlered elk would do just fine. They had ridden less than an hour before setting up in the rolling sagebrush foothills above their home.

The group had split up in order to watch more real estate, leaving Keith and Helen to enjoy a nice morning up on the mountain. It was a typical early fall day, full of sunshine and dry vegetation.

Suddenly, they saw the dust billowing as a herd of cow elk came directly toward them at a trot. Keith and Helen watched as the herd sallied through the sage in single file. It was fairly evident that, from engine to caboose, no antlers accompanied the train. Nonetheless, they watched intently the forward progress of the disturbed herd.

It was then that something happened that neither of them can explain to this day. One second, the herd was all cows; the next second, they were being escorted by the giant bull that had been stealing all of Keith's alfalfa. There was not nearly enough cover to have hidden the bull, and he didn't come in from any other angle. Like an apparition, he had just suddenly become visible.

Keith wasn't about to look a gift horse in the mouth, though. From 150 yards, he was able to drop the giant Washington County bull with a borrowed .30-06.

A plaque sitting under the now shoulder-mounted bull says that it scores 395-7/8 as a non-typical. This doesn't appear to have ever been verified, but it does appear likely that if the bull is ever officially scored, it would be fairly close to that figure.

It's hard to imagine any elk sweeter than one taken only a mile or so from the family farm. Keith Ford poses with his finest trophy.

At the same time Joe Adams purchased his 393-5/8 typical bull (currently #5 in Idaho), he purchased this bull. This bull reportedly came off of the Middle Fork of the Boise River, probably sometime around the 1950s. Joe has since sold this bull, and its whereabouts are unknown, but believed to be in the San Francisco area.

It has never been officially scored, but looks as though it would be one of Idaho's top-ranking non-typicals, likely in the 400 class. Joe's son, Lee, is the one struggling to hold up the big antlers.

Ron Laird went up on an everyday antler hunting expedition, having no idea it was going to start a long obsession with one particular bull. He had been watching a group of bulls, and when they dropped, he had picked up quite a few sets of shed antlers. A while later, he happened to notice that one of the whiter pair was the previous year's sheds of one of the fresh sets he had just picked up. The bull had a noticeably short G-5 on one side, and so was easy to identify. Over the next year or two, he began to informally track the bull's movements, discovering that the bull summered about eight miles from where he shed his antlers.

Another interesting thing about the bull is that he dropped his antlers like clockwork. March 10th every year (very early compared to the average) this bull would drop his antlers within about a 100-yard radius of the previous year. Ron found them again, although it looked like the bull had had it a bit rough, breaking one tine and regressing a bit.

On the final year, a friend of Ron's told him he had seen the bull, but he didn't look well, lagging behind a bachelor group. When the bull didn't show on March 10th, Ron was worried. He spent about ten days in the next few weeks looking for him, often with friend Dave Leonardson.

On the last day of their search, he and Dave were out one drainage to the east when Ron found him, dead in the snow. It was a sadness Ron really couldn't describe. It was if a good friend had fallen.

It wasn't until much later that they happened to find the cause of his death. A poor shot choice by an archer had sent an arrow straight through the bull's nostril and into his mouth. A large portion of arrow shaft had broken off and lodged inside the nasal cavity, and from there the bull had little chance.

It was a sad end to what was a great bull, but Ron is still happy to have some great souvenirs the bull left behind. Ron's Clark County bull unofficially is estimated to score in the 370-380 class.

Typically, your senior year is not the year to draw a great elk tag. School activities can take a big bite out of more important things, like hunting. Those are the breaks, though, and Conner Jacobs would just have to deal with it.

It was 1996, and he had drawn a "desert" tag for a late hunt in eastern Idaho. The hunt ran the full month of November, so chances were decent of finding a good bull. Conner's brother, Rhett, had also drawn the tag, and had taken a great bull on the second day of the hunt, leaving Conner to go it alone.

After the first few days, he had seen plenty of elk, and quite a few bulls, but he had a good tag and wanted to make the most of it. He continued to hunt after school every day, relentlessly giving all he had to the opportunity.

Then one evening, a friend gave him a tip. This friend had seen what he described as a whole herd of bulls, and they were quite a bit closer to Conner's house than Conner had been. Conner came back, but it was after dark. The hunt for the herd of bulls would have to wait until morning. Needless to say, he got virtually no sleep at all that night.

The next morning, he and Robert Davies headed out before first light. Robert had no tag, but was along just for fun and to help if he could. The area was mostly sagebrush on gently rolling terrain. Most of the cover was either in the sagebrush itself or in a few dry washes that weaved through the nondescript high desert.

It wasn't long until they found the mythical herd of bulls Conner's friend had mentioned. As they surveyed the scene, it was surreal. It seemed impossible, but right there in front of them was a herd of bulls numbering at least thirty!

The herd was 300 yards away, but to complicate things, the big bull was smack dab in the middle. They could get no closer, due to lack of cover, so they had no choice but to wait for him to clear. Finally, he did, and Conner shot.

Conner's bull, as he lay. What a striking and contrasting coat on this fine bull.

The ensuing lack of reaction had everyone equally puzzled. Not only did the bull not appear to be hit, but none of the bulls took off. Instead, they chose to simply mill about and look slightly confused. Eventually, to their astonishment, the bulls went nowhere. To add to the frustration, the big bull was now once again protected by smaller bulls in the herd. For a long and intense half an hour, Conner had to wait yet again for another shot at the bull. All the while, they had to lay motionless and get pounded by an icy cold north wind that had them all wishing they were inside.

Finally, the bull cleared, and Conner made good on a rare second opportunity, dropping the bull with a perfect neck shot from his Sako .300 Win.-mag. One nice thing about hunting in sagebrush – they were able to drive right to him.

Conner Jacobs, Robert Davies, and Ken Cherry with a giant of a bull.

Going into the morning of November 22nd, 1968, Gene Fuqua had yet to take a bull elk. He had filled the freezer with a few cows but, thus far, antlers seemed to be avoiding him at all costs.

He was camped with his wife Lola and his brother-in-law Frank Mullins. Splitting up that morning, Gene had hopped into the old blue '54 Chevy pickup and wound his way up the road to a spot upriver from camp.

The area he was hunting was mid-elevation mixed conifer ground, with open Ponderosa pine/Doug-fir southern slopes and north slopes of white fir. The tops of the ridges flattened out up above, but the pitch he had to fight up from the creek bottom was a real doozy.

Gene had been down in the back something terrible, and so was painfully slow getting up the steep incline. The now completely melted snow and ensuing muddy footing wasn't helping matters any. After covering just a few hundred yards, he stopped to rest.

He had just sat down and was starting to look around when he saw the darndest thing. There in the brush, about 300 yards away, was a great big bull elk bedded down! The bull was watching him, and looked like he had been for a while now.

Gene pulled up his .264 Win.-mag. and intentionally watched through his scope as he pulled the trigger with the safety on. He wanted to see if he was steady enough to take a good shot. He was, and flicked the safety off. This time, he put his crosshairs on the bull and squeezed carefully.

At the shot, the bull rocketed up out of the brush and began contouring around the hillside, mortally wounded with a pierced jugular vein. A second shot followed but never made contact. It was all formality, however, as the bull still tumbled down.

Gene really had no idea of the size of the bull he had taken. It wasn't until after he had gotten his brother-in-law and wife to help him that he realized he had taken a great bull. Frank had repeated a few times what a monster bull it was and that Gene would likely never take one bigger, and Gene suddenly began to get very excited. In his own words, he said, "After I realized what I'd done, I couldn't do nothin' for half an hour! I was useless."

Gene's 7x7 bull was taken in Adams County in 1968. It scores 358-3/8 net B&C, just missing the records book. He is 52-4/8" wide, with beams of 54-3/8" and 55-1/8".

All the ingredients for a winning combination and a successful hunt – the lucky hunter, his .264 Win.-mag., and a big set of antlers.

Brook Stancil has good reason for that big smile. That's one big bull.

It was the 12th day of elk hunting season here in north Idaho and still no sightings. Actually, it was the 12th day of my 12th elk hunting season. Some days I'd even been out both in the morning and again in the afternoon. Since I'm the youngest in an avid hunting family, everyone was trying to help me locate an elk. I didn't even care if it was a cow. Antlers don't seem so important considering all the time we've invested in finding my first elk. But cow season was only five days long and now it was back to bulls only, and boy can those big guys hide!

I was hunting with my husband of seven months and my dad, who not only taught me to hunt but instilled in me a love of the outdoors. We beat the brush and came back to the pickup. Dad had some work to do and we had a birthday party to attend that afternoon.

Dad said he'd like to drive out this road and see what the area looked like. We were sitting in the pickup on a ridge looking across the valley to a clearing. Nothing to see, but since we were up high I decided to call Mom on the cell phone and tell her we'd be heading home soon.

And then it happened. The elk started walking out of the woods on the other side, one by one. They were so far away that they looked like ants walking on a log. Dad was looking through his binoculars and counting, "Four, five, six – no horns but a bull's got to be around somewhere. What do you want to do Brooker?"

I wanted to go for it. About that time a bull came out. Horns!! We jumped out of dad's pickup and grabbed our guns. Down the hill we went, running, slipping, and trying not to make too much noise.

Across the creek, we then headed up the other side. Finally, we were about 250 yards away and Dad signaled that this is where I should take my shot from. My heart was beating hard and I was shaking. I couldn't steady my gun. *How long will he stay in the open*, I thought. Then he turned and headed back for the timber. I dropped to the ground, propped my .280 Winchester Model 70 on my knee, and took a deep breath. My shot rang out and the elk dropped! I couldn't believe it! Then, just as quick, he was up and going.

We took off with Dad in the lead. Dad got to him first. He was pinned under a log. He apparently tried to jump it and wound up under it. He looked up at Dad and bugled, and then he bugled again. But this was my kill and he was waiting for me to get there to make the shot. When I got there I took a deep breath and ended it. My husband looked at the bull and said. "If I'd known he was this big, I'd never have waited for Brook to take the shot!"

Greg and I started dressing him out while Dad headed to the pickup to try and find a closer packout. Three hours later he was back, but it was too late for us to get out with the elk. We quartered and bagged him and hung him in a nearby tree before heading out for the night. The next day we went back in with mules and packed the meat out.

When we stopped at the check station, I was the only female listed on the tally board. Then, back in town at Blue Goose Sporting Goods, my antlers in the back of our red Chevy pickup caused quite a stir. Heads turned as vehicles drove past. The local paper across the street sent two reporters over to get a picture. Were they ever surprised to learn that I was the successful hunter! So surprised in fact that they took my picture and interviewed me for an article that appeared on the front page of *The Gazette Record* (our local weekly paper). As you can see, I don't look like your typical hunter. And that just seems to surprise a lot of people.

The horns scored 355. Lars at Eidnes Furs said they are the second-largest he's seen in all the years he's been in business here.

Perseverance is an important quality of all hunters. After 12 years, a successful hunt. Next year will be harder though. Dad says, "Next time we won't be waiting for Brook to get the perfect shot."

Ron Hamilton was working in Adams County on a timber sale in 1967, and had seen a good number of elk in the area, despite low numbers of elk at the time. For Ron, it was an easy decision on where to be on opening day.

He and Dave Hale, a co-worker, were hiking up to their chosen hunting spot on opening morning when they heard an elk bugle before they could even get there. Shooting light was just coming so they waited. Ron could only make out the ivory tips of the antlers and a black spot toting them around, as he strained in the tricky early morning light to make out his target.

After a five-minute wait, the bull finally came out into a clearing. When Ron shot, elk exploded all around them. They had been in the middle of about fifteen head the entire time.

While only four feet from Ron, Dave had never seen the bull, as a white fir separated them and blocked his view. He had been wondering what Ron was looking at but hadn't asked, and was clueless as to what Ron had been shooting at.

They brought the bull out to their hunting rig (Ron's brand new Camaro) and hauled it out in the trunk! Needless to say, they got plenty of interesting looks as they headed into town.

Ron Hamilton takes a moment to enjoy his great bull from western Idaho in 1967. Ron has hunted hard and taken some great animals over the years. He also killed a 43" mule deer that ranks among Idaho's best. Look for it in the 2nd Edition of *"Idaho's Greatest Mule Deer."* The bull pictured scores 350-2/8.

A very happy Ron Hamilton, posing with his big 1967 Idaho bull. Ron thought his bull would be tops for the area that year, until Jack Sheppard killed the World's Record archery bull in the same county in the same year. You've gotta love Ron's hunting rig!

When Robert Davies left on that 2003 Sunday morning for an elk hunt, it wasn't a new thing; this was old hat. Having put in over 30 days the last time he had this tag, and over 20 this year, he was on a mission to find a great bull or go home empty.

After reaching the upper end of the unit, he found himself surrounded with thick fog. He mulled it over and was thinking of going back to work when he decided to wander through some lower ground first on the way back. He was weaving through the sage and lava when he thought he caught a glimpse of an antler way off in the distance. Further inspection revealed that a giant bull lay there in between a jagged lava flow, with his body well-hidden, but with antlers exposed over the top.

Robert grabbed his .300 Weatherby Mag. and began the stalk. He soon busted a cow elk, but luckily she spooked in a good direction. Continuing on, he got within 300 yards before running out of anymore options.

For the next 2-1/2 hours, Robert lay there in the cold with inadequate clothing to keep him warm. His perseverance was being severely tested as he sat there shivering. All he kept telling himself was, "Don't miss. Whatever you do, don't miss. This is your chance of a lifetime."

The giant bull finally stood up and shook himself off. Robert, with a rest already created, aimed and fired. The bull quickly wheeled and took off, but only managed 40 yards before collapsing in a clump of brush.

Robert got on the cell phone and called J.C. Siddoway to come and help him take care of his massive trophy. When J.C. asked how to get there, Robert replied, "Just go get my mom, and she'll know where to take you."

Robert's fine 2003 Clark County bull gross scores right around 374 but has never been officially measured. After 50 days of hard hunting, Robert had been rewarded with a bull that was easily worth that much effort and more.

In the spring of 1991, this great bull was nothing more than a yearling spike. That was when he was captured by IDF&G and collared as part of a monitoring program. For the next eight years this bull was as sharp as a tack, avoiding hunters at every opportunity and knowing eastern Idaho like he had his own map. Each summer of this bull's life was spent in Harriman State Park, and every winter he would mosey on down to the desert area near Dubois.

Kay Garner is a rancher in the Dubois area, and has always enjoyed the elk. He hasn't ever killed one – in fact, he hasn't ever really even hunted them – but he has always done a lot for them anyway. He has nearly always left a south slope or two on his ranch free from grazing, so that when the elk come in every winter they have something to eat, and they *always* come in. Rather than hunt them, Kay has always been content to simply watch them do what they do. He has even had fun watching them follow him out of curiosity while he was on horseback.

Around the first of December 1999, Kay was out on his place, near the creek bottom, when he made a discovery. Lying there in the willows was a bull elk, and he wasn't napping. The bull had lain down there, and never woken up. It was a radio-collared bull, and no sign of any injury whatsoever could be found. He had apparently just gotten sick and couldn't shake it. Kay later found out the story of his bull, and where he had spent his time. The bull died as a nine-year old, never falling prey to an arrow or well-placed bullet.

This giant 6x6 bull, from Adams County, was found by a rancher that was riding for cattle in the Little Weiser drainage in the mid-1970s. He saw the birds swarming and went to investigate. There in the brush lay a fantastic elk – the kind that makes a person take notice. It was dead, likely the result of a bad shot, as hunting season had been going on. He left it there, but marked it in his mind to return and get it when it didn't stink so badly. He later traded it for some appliances. The bull has changed hands a few times, and is currently owned by John Hammond. This bull is estimated to score in the 380s.

The name of the hunter is uncertain, but Darrell Riste helped with what he remembered of the story. This bull was reportedly taken in unit 15 in the early 1980s. The hunter was on horseback in the fog. It was either sex at time, and he saw a few elk in the fog. He shot the biggest one, not knowing it was even a bull. This bull is reported to gross score around the 373 mark.

Joe and Ron Gastelecutto, with a bull taken by Ron in 1999 in Washington County. This bull is a 7x9 that nets right at the 353-mark as a non-typical. It's hard to believe that this is only Ron's second-biggest bull. His biggest, a 376-3/8 B&C typical, is featured on page 218.

Dave Simons and Gary Finney found this 350-class winterkill in 2001. They also had the four previous years' shed antlers to this bull before he met a slow death of old age and starvation. The bull was aged at 11-1/2 years old. The last set of sheds were found about 100 yards from where he died.

Sheryl Woody took this great long-tined bull in Idaho County. This bull, with its thin but long tines, just misses making B&C with a final score of right at 358. A mismatched beam tip is one of the only imperfections in this otherwise handsome rack.

After the Willys broke down, Brian "Longwalker" Farley hoofed it five miles to his destination in Bonner County in the 1982 bow season. He promptly called in a bull with a voice bugle and cardboard paper towel tube, and arrowed him at 40 yards. This bull grosses 366, and is one of the larger archery non-typicals in Idaho. It's also one of the larger bulls to come from the northern panhandle.

Curtis "Bumper" Yanzick and friend Ed Knowles were struggling to plow through better than two feet of snow in 2003 when they encountered this fantastic bull. They had split up toward the middle of the day and, coincidentally, saw this bull at the same time. Both also fired their .54-caliber muzzleloaders at the same time, but only one connected. Who it was is not known, so they claim it together. This awesome Shoshone County bull is 58-1/2 inches wide. Conditions were difficult in getting the bull out. Ed and Bumper were two tired hunters when they finished the job two long days later.

Gary Finney, who was in Idaho's Greatest Mule Deer with a 247-6/8 mule deer, holds a set of sheds he found from an unbelievable bull that used to roam the area east of Coeur d'Alene. This bull has some eye-catching palmation and flattened points. This bull died the next year when he attempted to swim Lake Coeur D'Alene. Ironically enough, the bull washed up on the beach right next to Gary's brother Jack's home. Below are the antlers he was packing when he drowned. The bull scores in the 350 range.

Kevin Calaway provides reference for this giant bull his dad Blair killed in 1980 in Fremont County. Blair had arthritis and so was riding a horse when he ran onto about 75 head of elk, 15 of which were bulls. This big bull stood out like a beacon over the rest. Blair's first shot rang the bull's bell, slapping him in the antler. The second shot put him down. This exceptional bull would have scored an estimated 380-390 if not for a mile of broken points. He is completely snapped off past G-4 on his left side, and has a busted off abnormal point on the right. This bull also has several noticeable "canker-type" growths throughout similar points on the rack. Several bulls in the eastern Idaho area seem to have this. Whether it's toxicity in feed at a particular time of year (likely June or July) or a disease is uncertain to the author, but very interesting nonetheless. Below are Blair and Kevin, with their fall bounty from 1980.

Kevin Calaway holds a massive set of 5-point elk antlers taken by his dad, Blair Calaway, in the late 1950s in Fremont County. Blair had to cut them in half to get them in their 1949 automobile. They bleached out on the barn wall, and the browtine disappeared after being broken by some rambunctious kids. A rough score puts this great bull at about 340 (counting the broken browtine as being full). Not many 5-points will compete with this incredible bull.

John Opresik came west from Wisconsin by train during the depression, falling in love with Idaho and moving west shortly thereafter. He spent many years in the Selway, guiding, hiking, and photographing. In the early spring of 1975, John and his friend Dennis were on a hike three miles off of the Selway River when he found this interesting bull, which had been dead about a week. The men had no more than a pocketknife, but were in time able to beaver their way through and loosen the head. They took turns lugging the oddly distributed load back to their rig. They later found out that IDF&G had seen the bull just a few weeks earlier from a helicopter, and remarked that it was the biggest bull they had seen during their survey. This 7x9 non-typical, scoring 361-6/8, is truly one of the more unique bulls to come out of the Clearwater country.

Norm Johnson was discharged from the U.S. Navy shortly after World War II. He and his family moved to Boise from San Diego shortly thereafter. In 1947, Norm took this incredible bull, likely somewhere within a couple of hours from Boise. The family has long since lost track of this giant rack, which is a shame. It looks as though it would rate right up there in Idaho's list of non-typical elk. It appears at a minimum to have a 7x7 typical frame and at least one abnormal point on each antler.

Freak Antlers & Rare Occurrences

For sheer shock value, Kevin Calaway's 1997 bull might be the best in Idaho. Not only is this bull a sheer monster, but his antlers are also indescribably awesome.

Kevin had seen the bull for the two previous years, but couldn't draw the tag. The first year it was a 6x3; the second year it was a 7x4, with the left antler growing down and around his ribs. On the third year, he was magnificent, and Kevin finally lucked out and drew the tag. If he couldn't get him now, it wouldn't be because he didn't have the chance.

Kevin was out scouting about three weeks before the season and saw his dream bull. He had grown up even more, and Kevin had many sleepless nights between then and the opener.

When the season finally opened, Kevin found his bull. Unfortunately, it was on ground off limits to hunting. He was with three other good bulls, and they seemed to know exactly where they were and weren't safe. The bull frequented the boundary, however, and Kevin had to hope that he would find him on the right side of the fence – before someone else did.

He and his friend, Ron Laird, talked on the phone that night. Ron was blindly optimistic. "I'm gonna videotape you shooting that bull tomorrow."

They met early the next morning a couple of miles from where they were going to hunt. They parked one rig and took off together toward what Kevin hoped would be the scene of a kill, not just a good viewing.

As they neared their familiar location, they got out and could hear intense bugling in the "no hunting" area. They drove on a bit further and listened again and could hear antlers clashing. Kevin knew the boundary as well as anyone, and knew that those fighting bulls were on the "good side" of the fence.

He and Ron charged up the sagebrush hill as fast as their legs would take them. There they were! Three hundred yards away, they could see two big bulls going at it, and they were both big! Kevin was about to shoot when Ron said, "Wait! Let me get the video."

Ron ran and got the video camera, and they proceeded to then videotape the action for a good 5-7 minutes. Kevin then decided it was time to quit dilly-dallying around and put his tag on one before his luck changed. They had been fighting the entire time, so he hadn't had a chance to really see how they compared. He focused on the one that seemed to have the most mass. The big warriors were still fighting when he pulled the trigger. The first shot pierced his neck, but the big bull didn't go down. It took some heavy insurance to finally anchor the giant.

Kevin's three-year dream had ended with the taking of one of the most unique and impressive trophies ever taken in Idaho. The character and wildness in this bull's antlers have to be as awesome as any ever grown in the state.

Kevin reports that the bull's right antler, if doubled and given an estimated spread, would have been just over the 400-class as a typical. As it is, the antlers are 54" wide by 54" long. The longest point on the bull's left antler is reported to be a staggering 33-1/2 inches, rivaling the longest tine ever recorded in any state.

An elated Kevin Calaway holds the massive antlers of his one-of-a-kind trophy. Look at the size of the body on that bull!

One more look at one of Idaho's all-time best trophy bull elk. Beauty and the beast, all in one elk rack.

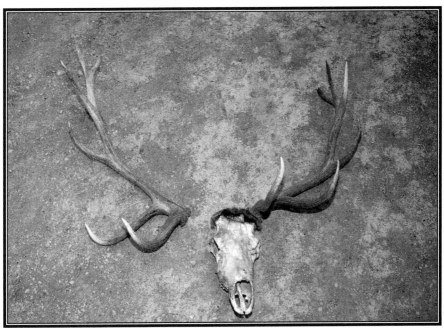

Freak elk? No. Freak occurrence? Yes! Kevin Calaway was searching for shed antlers in spring of 2001 in Clark County when he came across this. This bull had managed to shed his right antler, then died in the narrow window of time before he could shed the other. The odds of finding something like this are likely astronomical. Kevin found the shed antler first and was searching for the other side when he found more than he bargained for 25 yards away.

Courtesy of Lynn Seibold

> D rawing the Idaho Supertag for elk is getting to be "old hat" for Lynn Seibold, who also drew the tag in 2004. On his first attempt, Lynn killed a nice 310 bull after passing up 22 others. He would have liked to let that one walk, too, but at some point, a guy has to go back to work.

Lynn bought one ticket in the 2006 drawing, and it would be all he'd need. The news was welcome, but it didn't leave him much time to prepare. Decisions needed to be made on where to go, when, and how. Lynn decided to focus his efforts on Owyhee County and the extremely limited early rifle hunt during the rut.

He was there on August 30th for the opener, and passed up six 5-point and 6-point bulls. It would be nearly two weeks before he could come back.

He returned on the weekend of September 15th for a four-day hunt. He and Tracy Allred unloaded the horses and rode for higher ground and a quick afternoon hunt. After a while of negotiating their stock into some rolling hills of sage, juniper, and pine, the stopped and gave some cow calls. As they sat and watched, a bull came into view about 400 yards across the opposite hillside.

Lynn and Tracy looked him over and knew that he was a good one. Lynn walked back over to the horses and retrieved his 7mm-mag. One carefully placed shot put this wild-looking bull to bed.

A rough gross score puts this bull at approximately 380, with mass that is shocking. This bull is, without question, one of the most interesting and outstanding bulls taken in Idaho in the last several years.

(Above) Lynn shows off the wild-looking left antler on this one-of-a-kind bull.
(Below) All Tracy Allred got out of the hunt was this photo and to help pack.

The equal and bifurcated branching of this bull's strange main beams is reminiscent of a mule deer. This bull, taken by Randy Hollibaugh, is truly an amazing trophy.

Randy Hollibaugh was hunting with Chris Berry in Nez Perce County in 1989 when he came across one of the more interesting bulls to ever be taken by a hunter in Idaho. With split beams on both sides, this "four-beamed" elk is quite the trophy. It officially scored 361-3/8 P&Y.

Randy and Chris were in unit 11A on an early season bowhunt. They headed into a canyon hoping for some elk action when they heard a bull above them bugling. They moved in slowly, working as a team. Concentrating on the herd of elk in question, they had no idea that another bull was coming in on them from the back unannounced. By the time they knew, it was too late to get the upper hand. Suddenly, this interesting critter came in behind them. Randy was squatted behind a bush, but the bull had him pegged. Chris gave a few cow calls, which managed to bring the bull within ten yards of Randy's position.

Luckily for them, the other herd unknowingly picked that moment in the tense standoff to begin to filter into close proximity. This not only distracted the bull's attention, but also seemed to help set him at ease. He was relaxed enough that he decided to bugle, and when he got to his third chuckle, Randy released the fatal arrow. The bull went 30 yards and piled up.

Randy was ecstatic to see such a big bull go down. He sat motionless, waiting to make sure the bull wouldn't regain his feet or be spooked somehow.

One cow was curious of the events, and went up to investigate. As she stood over her fallen comrade, she caught a whiff of his blood and tore out of the area at world record pace, taking the rest of the herd with her.

Randy went forward to claim his bull, and was stunned at the rack when he got there. He had no idea until that very moment he had shot such a freakish and unique trophy. The bull is an 8x8, with 45-inch main beams.

Randy Hollibaugh's exceptionally non-typical elk is the fourth-largest non-typical ever taken with a bow in Idaho and officially entered in Pope and Young.

Ralph Trethewey's 1992 Elmore County find is one of the more bizarre and intriguing finds in Idaho.

I was in the Sawtooths on a Saturday in 1992. I was driving around with a friend in Elmore County and looking for game. We saw a few deer, and at dusk we rounded a bend and stopped so I could glass a park opening on a distant hillside.

Immediately, I keyed in on a large white elk shed about half a mile away. I wanted to go get it but it was getting dark. My friend said, "Don't worry about getting back on time; go get it!"

I obliged by diving down a steep hillside to the canyon bottom. I crossed the creek and went up into the park and retrieved a great 360-plus 7-point shed antler, bleached but complete. Not a bad find!

The next day I was at an art show in Sun Valley. I was showing my art and had the antler with me. Several people admired it and a couple of them wanted to buy it from me, but I knew if I had time, maybe I could find the other side.

I figured I had four hours to go back and scour the hillside. I drove to the area, slept on the ground, and at daylight I went into the canyon. I seemed to have an antler magnet that day. I jumped a six-point bull, and found a six-point shed antler as I covered the area. I had no luck finding the other side of the big seven-point.

I decided to go back down to the bottom of the canyon. I started "zigging" and found an elk femur bone. I started circling and, in a minute, found the spine and shoulder blades. Then, in the brush and hidden from view, was the head of a bull that would end up scoring 368-3/8. It astounded me! I pulled it out of the tangle and noticed the wire. It was truly an amazing find.

With limited time, I hiked up the half-mile hill to the car. I was driving a Honda Civic loaded with art and an art display booth, so I had to use strapping tape to apply the rack and wire to the roof of vehicle.

The whole contraption weighed 43 pounds. There were several of the twisted vertical spacers between fence posts in addition to who knows how many feet of barbed wire. To my knowledge, the nearest fence was miles away, meaning he had been forced to carry his burden for some time – a sad fate for such a majestic animal.

Paul Snider was hunting the Otter Creek area of the Selway in the late 1950s when he encountered this strange contraption. What he thought was a cow, and then a bull, turned out to be something in between. It's a cow with antlers – sort of. The right antler was about eight inches long and completely covered in hair. The other was only an inch long and not really visible above the hide.

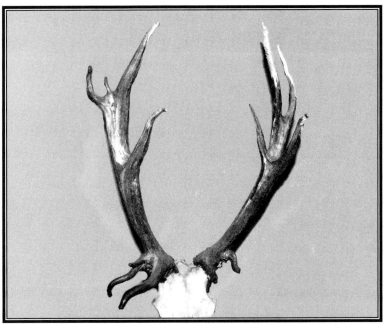

In 1987, the author, along with friend Mike Breske and the author's dad Rusty Hatfield, went on an after-school evening hunt. Mike and Ryan split off and had little luck, but Rusty managed to take this strange 7x6. This bull has five eyeguards that look as though they had a case of antler meltdown, with two bulbous and misshapen bases that are better than 12" each in circumference.

Take a quick glance at this bull and nothing seems abnormal. Take a closer look and see where the pedicle starts on his right antler. A permanent injury to the head likely moved the position of the pedicle to nearly straight out of the forehead. This bull was taken by Robert Linger in Butte County in 1997. The bull reportedly gross scored in the 350s.

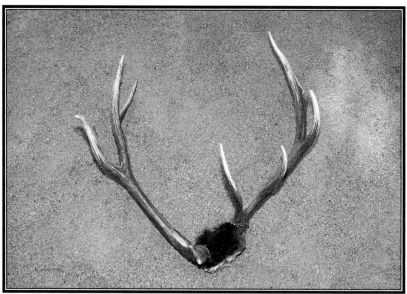

This bull, taken by Gene Fuqua in the Mud Creek area near New Meadows in 1975, is another interesting example of a physically displaced pedicle, now growing from the forehead.

Perl DeFord took this crazy-antlered bull in October of 1952. This unlikely "6x6" has split beams on both sides, with a club-like bottom set coming from the inside and bottom of the top set. Perl (center) and two friends pose with the unique trophy.

Ray Cross had this photo of a very unique bull that was supposedly taken in Idaho, probably in the 1970s or '80s. Unfortunately, nothing is known of the circumstances at the time of printing. It is the bull of a lifetime for sure. The bulbous droptine on the bull's left antler is one of the most massive ever grown.

This bull found a more formidable opponent than he bargained for in taking on a barbed wire fence. How would you like to have been a fly on a tree watching that wild battle? Undoubtedly, it would have been quite a rodeo.

A bullet likely did this unfortunate bull a favor. While not a trophy bull, it is perhaps even more rare a find.

When Dana Dumond took his first bull, in the fall of 2004, he had no idea it would be a mercy killing. Dana was hunting in unit 24 in Valley County with his brother-in-law Shane Anneker. He was packing an old .30-06 Japanese rifle from WWII that his dad, Richard "Pops" Dumond had converted into a big game rifle. On opening day, he caught this bull moving swiftly but silently through the timber. Two shots netted Dana his first elk. As he approached, he could see the bull was in a sad state. The left eye had been gored out, and obvious extreme antler damage existed as well. Dana remarked that the bull's left antler was still partially filled with blood, and was intensely putrid.

Robert "Bobby" Zielinski was hunting near Indian Valley with his brother Harry in 1970 when he took this outstanding bull. He and Harry approached, knowing he had just taken one heck of a big six-point. He got an added bonus when he got closer. This bull has a third antler, with an entirely separate pedicle just below his normal antler on his left side.

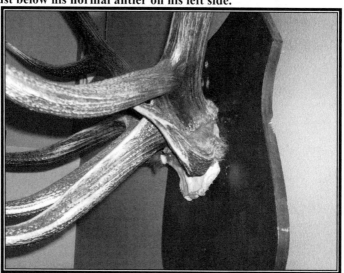

A close-up view shows the small but unique extra antler. If you were to walk up on this little shed antler, it would sure leave you puzzled.

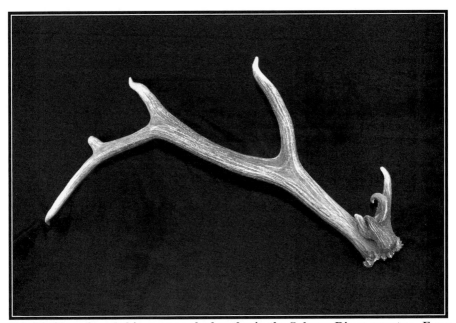

Bob McClure found this strange shed antler in the Salmon River country. Four different points arise from the base/burr area, three of which sputtered and died. This is a really unique-looking growth.

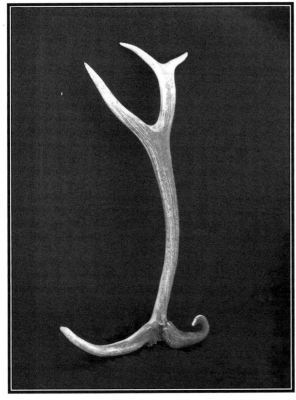

Bob McClure also found this elk antler. The G-2 looks like it was deformed right from first growth, then fused and kept growing in a totally different orientation.

Conner Jacobs took this bull in eastern Idaho in 1995. A beautiful 7-point on one side, this bull couldn't quite make it match on the other. A freak split in the G-2/G-3 area on the bull's left antler makes him a much more unique trophy.

Lloyd Moe, along with a student, Mikey Cutler, and dad Mike Cutler, headed out for a 1994 bowhunt in Kootenai County. Lloyd found more than he bargained for, sneaking up on these two great bulls locked up and struggling. He was in awe as he watched one bull kill the other by snapping its neck. It was a strange situation as the other bull lay there helpless, but Lloyd eventually was able to put him out of his misery with a three-yard shot from his bow. He yelled, hoping that the Cutlers might hear him and come help, but he was answered instead by yet another bull! It was as big as the others, and charged in looking for a fight! Lloyd was allowed to keep both sets of antlers off of the semi-locked bulls. They weren't actually stuck, and had either relaxed from pulling back against each other, they likely could have freed themselves.

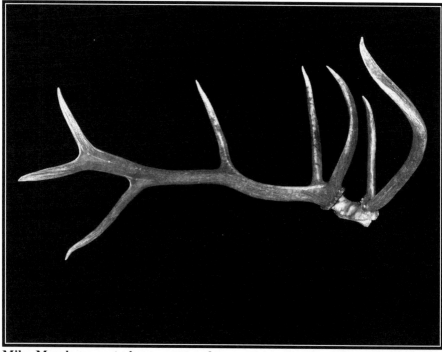

Mike Marek seems to have a natural magnet to strange antler. He harvested the bull above with a bow in Shoshone County in 1996. He had messed up on two bulls earlier in the morning, but quickly redeemed himself. This bull was still bugling and raking a tree. He and his dad, John Hamburg, split up and slipped in undetected. They walked up on him while he was raking.

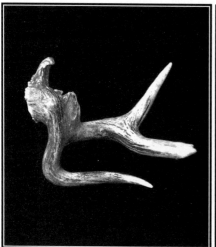 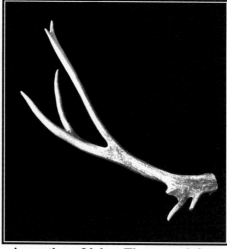

Mike found these two freak shed antlers in northern Idaho. The one at left was found in Kootenai County in 2003. It really becomes much more strange when you imagine how it would actually have looked on the animal. The one on the right is from Shoshone County, found in 2000.

Gary Finney and his nephew Luke found these three sets of sheds, all off of the same bull, in one day of shed hunting. Remarkably, all six pieces to this amazing discovery were located within 100 yards of each other in a secret spot in northern Idaho. What a find!

Luke Finney holds up a shed antler he found in northern Idaho. This is a very unique and unusual find. The bull's left side has two completely separate pedicles, which coincidentally happened to fuse together during growth. They now exist as one solid piece of bone.

It would be interesting to know if anyone ever ended up harvesting this three-antlered bull.

Luke is truly an antler hunting fool. See Luke's magnificent 198-1/8 non-typical whitetail in the upcoming book, *"Idaho's Greatest Whitetails."*

Great Days in Elk Country

Scott McGann was on the trail of this great Gem County bull for four days in 2005. The first three days, the bull simply picked up his cows and split. On September 30th, Scott and his hunting partner called and stalked the bull for over four hours. Finally, they ever so carefully slipped into the middle of the herd. Scott looked away, gave a cow call, and waited. The bull stood up fifty yards away and came right to him. Scott used his Matthews bow to make a perfect shot on an exceptional archery bull. His official score is 343-1/8 P&Y. Lack of symmetry hurt this bull, as his gross score is 361-5/8.

An ecstatic Matt Capka poses for the camera after taking this whopper of a 6x7 bull that carries tremendous mass all the way through the rack. This bull was taken a few years back in the Shoshone County area of northern Idaho.

Paul Snider and son Jack were hunting the Breaks country of Idaho County when they came upon this wide bull. Paul wanted Jack to get it, so held off even though he was within 40 feet. The bull was lying down in heavy brush, and Paul couldn't tell which end was which. He finally had to give up on Jack and try for the bull himself. He made out the bases of the antlers, and finally had the proper orientation for the shot. Paul had the bull down in short order. They were rejoicing when they heard movement coming their way, and soon Jack had another elk down only a stone's throw from Paul's bull. Paul is one of life's true gentlemen and storytellers, and is much deserving of such a fine trophy.

Brian Farley took this bull in Lemhi County in 2004. With 54-inch main beams and some of the biggest backs around, this bull looks to be a record book contender for sure. Unfortunately, upon closer inspection, he seems to have forgotten to grow a couple of G-2s. Brian didn't notice either, until he walked up on him. Still, this bull is a giant, and one of the biggest "5-points" in Idaho.

In Memory of Travis Shane Farley (1981-1998)

Travis Shane Farley, age 14, is all smiles after taking his first bull elk in Lemhi County, October 2, 1996. His Dad, Brian, was there to help. Sadly, this was to be Travis' only bull, having lost his life in an auto accident two years later. Their hunting trips hadn't numbered nearly enough when Travis was unexpectedly taken to better hunting grounds in 1998.

December of 2005 will long be remembered for its early cold snap. No one felt it any more than Lou Griffin. He had drawn a late tag near Island Park and was out in temperatures dropping lower than -20 degrees. After hunting in the a.m., he glassed and found this bull bedded in a bowl, hiding out from a wicked north wind. A cow and calf moose had the bull's attention, so Lou crept forward. He eventually shot the bull with a .300 where he was bedded – the bull never even got up. This awesome bull is 52" wide by 55" long. Unfortunately, the right G-5 is busted off right at the beam. The bull also had an antler tip imbedded between his burrs inside the scalp from fighting. Lou amazingly also bagged a bull that grossed over 400" in Utah the same year.

Judy Griffin decided she wanted to take up bowhunting in 1998, so she went to an archery shop, got outfitted with equipment, and then practiced. She also attended the archery certification class that summer with her two children.

Their chosen spot was in Fremont County. Judy was up the canyon from her husband Lou when a cow and calf came toward them followed by a big 6x7 bull. The cow and calf watered while the bull thrashed in a wallow and bugled for some time.

The cow and calf walked up the trail, passing close to where Judy was standing hidden behind a tree. Soon after, the bull followed. Just before the bull got to Judy, he flinched. Her husband was watching the drama unfold 200 yards away. He thought the bull winded her, but she said it looked like a fly landed on his nose.

The bull straightened out and started trotting up the trail while Judy drew back the 44-lb. bow. At 18 yards, she released the arrow into the bull's ribs. The bull ran up the trail about 50 yards, stopped, wobbled a bit, and fell over dead.

Lou had the great fortune of watching the event unfold, including watching the arrow fly and hitting the bull. He also saw the bull tip over just up the trail.

Judy wanted to wait the standard half-hour, but Lou knew better. He had been able to see the bull tip over and knew he was already expired.

After savoring the moment and taking some photos, they started the work. It was a memorable night with a big full moon and bulls bugling all around them. The animal was nearly all skinned and quartered and hung up in a tree when Lou slipped with his knife and cut his thigh. It bled profusely, but fortunately no artery was cut. They cut the pant leg off below the knee to bandage the wound. He then finished taking care of the animal and hung the last quarter. Late into the night, when they arrived at the emergency room, Lou drenched with blood, the medical personnel thought no person could survive with that much blood loss. They were relieved to learn that it was 95% elk blood.

The Finney family is among the most successful of any group of hunters in Idaho. They are much deserving, however, as they spend as much time as possible in the field. Gary Finney took this nice "whale tail" bull in Shoshone County on September 1st, 2001, with a great shot that passed clear through the bull. Russ Grant and Gary's nephew Luke were on the hunt as well.

Gary Finney took this awesome 6x9 with a muzzleloader on the St. Joe River in 2003. It was so cold that Gary couldn't scrape the snow off of this bull's great rack. It was one giant "elkcicle." It took getting the rack out of the mountains and time to thaw before he could really see any of the detail in the antler.

Jack Finney took this massive bull in Shoshone County in 2003. It was opening day, and the bull practically walked right to him. Jack could hear the bull coming, and by the time they met, the distance was 30 yards. The bull scores approximately 343. He was hunting with his son Luke, brother Gary, and friends Dan Ratza and Eric Kacalik.

Two years later, in 2005, Jack was able to follow up with this 337 bull, again in Shoshone County while hunting with Eric Kacalik. They were on a vantage point when they heard bull bugle. They kept sitting and eventually saw some cows. They staked them out and, 20 minutes later, out came the bull. Jack downed him with a 500-yard shot. Jack was having leg trouble at the time, which they later determined was cancer. He's still recovering.

Mike McClure was hunting with his son Michael in 1998 when Michael took a nice big bull. The family went in the next morning to help him pack it out. Mike, accompanied by his sister Cindy Moffis, decided to hunt their way down to the site of the previous day's kill. This big bull was the result.

Gary McClure shows a couple of big bulls he has taken over the years in that vast, all-encompassing beast called Salmon River country.

DanMcClure's best bull is his 386-2/8 non-typical (p. 122), but this 6x7 isn't too shabby, either. At 357-6/8 P&Y, it is one of the largest bulls taken with a bow in Idaho. Dan was on a 2002 Idaho County bowhunt with his brother Mike when he cow called this giant in to 30 yards. Beam lengths on this big boy are 54-1/8" and 53-1/8". Dan also has the shed antlers to this bull from two years previous.

Dan McClure, with another big bull from around 1997. Dan seems to be a veritable elk magnet.

Michael Marek had bugled this bull in for four nights in a row prior to opening day of the rifle season in Kootenai County, and felt he had him pegged. Unfortunately, Michael was greeted on opening morning to rain and howling winds. Through persistence, he was able to find the herd eight hours later in an odd spot for northern Idaho – a Ponderosa Pine/Doug-fir mix with very little brush. A shot from Michael's .338 Ultra-mag. at 30 yards did the trick on this great bull. He grosses near 343, with some great 53" beams.

Richard Hansen takes an extra moment to take in the results of an emotional elk hunt and remember his son. Richard lost his son Douglas in 1998. In the fall of 1999, he went up to their favorite hunting spot in Washington County, in his mind already dedicating the hunt to his son.

Instead of taking his normal route, he decided to hunt Douglas' canyon. It turned out to be a good decision. He was able to get to 49 yards on this bull when he released an arrow and put it right through the bull's heart.

Idaho's Greatest Elk

Courtesy of Bill Scouten

When Bart Miller found out he had accidentally applied for the wrong unit in 2004, he was understandably upset. To add insult to injury, he soon found out he had drawn the hunt! He didn't know the area and had no idea what to expect, and not much more of an idea where to go. Luckily, his long-time friend Bill Scouten (right) was a bona fide hunting fool and knew the area very well. Well enough that he had been trying to draw the same area for over 20 years, with no luck.

Bill had scouted the area through the summer and knew where some nice bulls were hiding. On their first attempt, they had no luck, but came back for another run at it four days later. Nate Harker was along for the hunt this day.

On this hunt, they found the mother lode. They had been hiking since long before daylight, and were in position early to see a great sight. Dozens of elk, including a few bulls, were hanging out down in the river bottom.

It was bitterly cold and the hills were steeper than Bart could believe, but it was worth it as they watched the big bull for over two hours. Unfortunately, they had no way to move in on him.

As they sat there and debated their next move, their decision was suddenly made for them. Someone else had come in from the bottom and spooked them off. Bill had a hunch where they were headed, so he and Bart headed over to cut them off. Luckily, they had an easy route to get in front of the elk.

They set up in a barren draw and waited for the elk to funnel through. The big bull did just as they hoped, and Bart made good on a 138-yard shot with his 7mm.

After all those years of applying, Bill still had not drawn his favorite area. He had, however, taken a great amount of enjoyment watching a good friend do something special. As he says, "I can't think of a better way to spend quality time at peace with nature and in the company of good friends."

Zeke Haubrich had some close calls with some big bulls in the 2005 archery season but nothing had clicked just right yet. This awesome bull and 25 cows actually ran across the road in front of him at 5 a.m. as Zeke and a friend headed to a different spot. They figured they would have no chance, and drove off. A change of heart led Zeke back to give him a run. Zeke started tracking the herd and eventually gave a cow call. The response was a screaming bugle, followed by the bull charging in hard. Zeke loosed an arrow from 40 yards and the bull just stood there. Zeke thought he had missed until the bull suddenly staggered and fell over dead. Final score on this big bull is 348-7/8 P&Y.

Zeke's Grandpa, Benjamin A. Haubrich, took this nice bull on Round Top Mountain, in the Selway country, in 1958. For a Clearwater bull, this one is a whopper. The G-3s on this bull are outstanding.

George Bettas is nothing but smiles after taking this big bull. George was hunting the Snake River breaks in 1991 when he encountered this bull in some rugged country.

Of many bulls taken by George in Idaho over the years, this one is his best, going 342. As usual, this one was quartered and packed out on horses.

George Bettas, with another big bull taken from Clearwater County in 1981. George was hunting with Jere Dick that day. Jere stopped long enough to admire George's bull, then continued hunting. In less than an hour, he had a 320 bull down as well – quite an hour of hunting.

Matt Dyche (left) and his brother Ashley were hunting near Island Park on September 13, 2006 when they had the encounter of a lifetime. Ashley was about 50 yards away and calling when this enormous bull came in quiet and unannounced. Matt saw him coming through the thick trees, so he chose a small, narrow shooting lane. The bull miraculously passed through it at 20 yards, so Matt passed an arrow through his lungs as he went. The bull went 30 yards and fell over dead. This bull is reported to score 350, though he looks bigger in the photo. Regardless, you just have to love how this great 6x7 is built.

The Golden Era and Other Days Gone

A successful hunting party from 1939 takes a moment to pose for the camera following a successful hunt in northern Idaho. The big 6x7 in the foreground looks as though he is at least as long as six men would be wide. Those poor horses didn't know what they were about to be used for. From left to right: Red Mellis, Dooley Cramp, Bill Williams, Bill Robinson, and Jack Shaner. They were hunting above Avery near Pass Creek Saddle. Aaron C. Robinson (his own bull, scoring 370 B&C, is featured on page 243) took the photo.

A gritty looking pioneer, with the results of an early Idaho hunting trip. The bloating in the abdomen suggests he might not have found it right away. The rifle is an 1886 Winchester.

Bob Carroll (right) and son Richard hold up Bob's big elk taken during the 1947 hunting season. Bob and his neighbor got up at 4 a.m. and headed from Boise toward Idaho City with his Pontiac and a trailer. Bob shot this great bull at first light with a .32 lever-action rifle. The bull headed downhill, and died less than forty yards from their car. They were back to Boise by noon with their trophy and supply of winter meat.

Perhaps the most famous and revered outdoor writer of all-time, Jack O'Connor (right) spent a good portion of his life based out of Lewiston. Jack hunted the world, and more than a few were held captive by his adventures in Outdoor Life over the years.

This hunt, with Dave Christensen (left) of Moose Creek Lodge in the Selway, took place in November of 1964. Jack's wife Eleanor was also along on the hunt, as was Ray Speer, of Speer Bullets. The O'Connors were being guided by Christensen; Ray headed out with Vance Baker.

Eleanor had first crack at this bull. She had been on point across the basin from Jack and was sitting with Dave when this nice 6x7 came out. Eleanor had problems with her Mauser (she had loaded the round into the chamber rather than running it through the magazine, not allowing the extractor to jump over the rim) and had to use Dave's .30-30 with open sights in desperation. Four shots yielded no hits, and the escaping bull headed straight to Jack.

In the heavy brush, Jack couldn't tell what was going on below him, but could see Dave across the basin with his arms wide and pointing for Jack to head downhill. Jack obliged, and eventually made a difficult shot on this bull from 125 yards through some brush. Jack was noted for his fondness of the .270 rifle, but this bull was one of few that he took with a 7mm Rem.-mag. Of the meat on this big bull, Jack stated, "That old bull didn't have an ounce of fat on him, but you could stick a fork in the gravy – if you had a sharp fork."

Rex Bassett and Junior Bitton (fifth and sixth from the left, respectively) and the rest of their hunting party eye their bounty, including Rex and Junior's big 368 B&C bull (page 250). This successful hunt took place in the Dry Valley area of Caribou County in 1956. This photo is amazing.

An unidentified woman in the early 1900s inspects her elk with her 1886 Winchester, likely a .45-70. Her Sunday-go-to-meetin' clothes suggest she likely wasn't the hunter, or at least wasn't intentionally elk hunting. Who needs camouflage and hiking boots? Maybe feather hats and a bustle are what it takes to bring those bulls running in? You try it first.

Dean Evans, left, and Henry Daniels, with a nice six-point bull taken near Deadwood Reservoir circa 1953. There weren't a lot of elk in far western Idaho at that point, so they headed to Boise County, where they had a better chance.

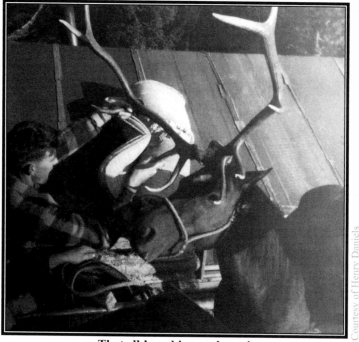

That elk's as big as a horse!

Florence Manwill may pale in comparison to this big bull elk, but she probably felt pretty big the day that she punched her tag with this great eastern Idaho bull. The bull was taken on Thurbin Creek in October of 1953. Florence worked as a cook on the Railroad Ranch out of Ashton; her husband was a wrangler there. She made the most of her free time, and these photos are the lasting legacy. She looks as if she could fit right in between those antlers. Another photo of her with the bull is shown on the next page.

Florence Manwill, with her prized bull, in the back of an old jeep. Does she look proud, or what?

Mary Mikolasek and Rhoda Engel pose with their trophy elk. They were hunting near Holly Mountain, along with Rhoda's husband Bill. They had been on stand while Bill tried to run something out to them. Rhoda wandered around the hill and saw a buck. She downed it promptly, and then the ladies went to work field-dressing it. As they worked on the deer, they heard noises. They went to investigate, and found this bull coming out of the trees. The ladies opened up on him, and got him, too! They then went to work on field-dressing their second animal of the day. By the end of the hunt, even though there were several men on the hunt, the women were the only ones to bring home any meat.

Lewis Daniels and Oren Jacobson, with a few cow elk down on Rainey Creek near Irwin. This photo was taken in the late 1920s. Lew spent nearly four years patrolling the Idaho-Wyoming line on snowshoes and skis tracking down elk poachers for the federal government.

Elmer Thomas, Loren Hatfield, and Ernest Daniels, also on the hunt mentioned in the upper photo, prepare to ride their elk out of the mountains. Oren Jacobson (background) worked on yet another elk as Lew took the photo.

Two elk taken by Lew Daniels' hunting party, circa 1925. Notice the faint lettering at the bottom of the photo – "CAMP MEAT". Dropping an extra elk or two to feed a big hunting party was not at all uncommon in days gone by. In fact, it was more than likely expected. The rifle is a Savage 99 takedown.

This photo of a successful eastern Idaho elk hunt was in Lewis Daniels' collection, but it isn't known who took the photo or for certain who it is. It was likely a friend or family member. This photo, as well as some of the others taken by Lew, are likely some of the older field photos ever taken in Idaho. The young man in the photo is holding an 1895 Winchester, likely a .30-40 Krag.

Lew took this photo of another great elk hunt in eastern Idaho. Two bulls down and just the right horse to pack them out. This stout old horse looks to be a draft horse cross, likely used in that era for pulling the primitive farming and ranching implements of the era. Notice the second bull and hunter in the background at center.

Jess Wages and Cal Binkly stand with two cow elk taken in eastern Idaho in the early 1900s. Bulls were not a focus in that time, as the primary reason to hunt was to provide meat for the table, not as a leisure activity.

Lathen Jacobson looks over a fine six-point bull and another elk taken on Palisades Creek in the 1920s. It would have been unlikely that those antlers were ever even packed out of the hills that day. That would have meant an extra trip, and hardworking people of that era had little time for extra trips. Lew Daniels was the other hunter, and took the photo.

This amazing photo was reportedly taken following a successful hunt into Idaho in 1945. It's hard to beat a great old classic photo like this one. Nice big bucks and bulls all the way around. The photo was resurrected in the Spokane Spokesman Review many years later.

Tom Sanders (above) hunted the Featherville area near Crosscut Trail in 1962 when he downed this nice six-point bull. Younger brother Harry and their dad helped with the packout, which involved getting not only this bull out, but also an awesome double-droptine mule deer that Tom shot on the hunt. Harry (below) poses under the rack and in front of the primary hunting vehicle, a 1942 military jeep.

Larry Rose displays the nice six-point bull he bagged in Clark County in October of 1978. This bull was taken near Sheridan Reservoir. Larry's dad had given these antlers away long ago, and Larry was just recently able to actually track them down and get them back. Great picture!

Ken Wodin took this big, wide bull near Clarkia in 1973. He had quite the stylish hunting rig!

Joe Gisler (story on page 203) took this photo of his hunting partner, Lamont Herbold. Lamont is showing us the other part of elk hunting – the work! This photo followed what looks to be a very successful hunt in the Bear Valley area, likely in the 1960s.

Gordon Larson, who killed a 390-6/8 bull on the Clearwater in 1973 (p. 115), shows us the rewards to be reaped by a little bit of sweat and a lot of fun.

Paul Snider is all smiles after bagging this big bull in 1959. Paul was hunting on Otter Creek in the Selway.

Paul's oftentimes hunting partner Jim Jensen, not to be outdone, killed this great bull two years later in 1961. This hunt was also in the Otter Creek area.

Carly Herbert and Jim Jensen show off their party's luck during the 1960 elk season. The photo was taken in Otter Saddle on the Selway River

Emil Pike (third from right) was a guide back in the 1930s. This trip, in the 1940s, looks as though it gave them all good reasons to be smiling. The photo was taken at Emil's Auto shop in Pullman, Washington, after returning from their elk hunt in the Selway.

A TROPHY TO ADORN HIS DEN was brought home to Euclid, Ohio, by William Dietz after a hunting trip in Idaho. The elk was bagged in Chamberlain Basin on Oct. 15.

This was in the November 3, 1966 edition of the Idaho Statesman. Mr. Dietz must have been one happy hunter. This elk doesn't appear to have ever been officially scored, but looks as though it was a great bull.

The following seven pages are of photos from the Martin Young and Robert Young families. Robert, you might recall, had the huge 42" buck that was the first photo in Idaho's Greatest Mule Deer. That buck looks as though it would push the 400-lb mark with ease. The Young family was ahead of their time in having the foresight to take a second or two to preserve some memories in the field. The photos on the following pages are priceless. It looks as though they spent many a day in the field in Idaho during its best glory days, with many memories I am sure we all wish we could have been a part of. I received these photos before the mule deer book came out, and have been excited for some time to be able to share these photos with you.

Robert Young holds up a great trophy bull he killed on Indian Creek in Blaine County, likely in the 1950s. This bull would likely have scored very well with those great fifth points. This is a great photo.

Bud Mizer stands by Robert Young's big Blaine County bull.

Bruce, Wallace, and Robert Young, along with Bud Mizer, with Robert's bull.

Martin and Robert Young, in the Selway in the early 1940s. They did a lot of hunting together over the years, and had plenty of good times along the way.

Paul Reed (left), along with the Swansons – Red, Chuck, and Joe, on a successful hunt in 1948. This hunt took place in the Selway at a place called Hell's Half-Acre.

Robert Young, holding an 1894 Winchester carbine (likely a .30-30) stands with a nice calf elk taken in the Selway in 1940. This elk was taken in Moose Creek. Sixteen years later, Robert would take the trophy of a lifetime – a monstrous 263-1/8 non-typical mule deer that would stretch the tape to 42" wide, with a body that would be much bigger than this elk.

Hunting was much different back then. The first priority was meat. The second priority was fun. Antlers were not on the list for most people. With the main focus being on table fare rather than antler size, all segments of the herd were harvested, allowing for more mature animals in the herd structure.

Alexis Young stops for a quick breather and photo opportunity while she packs out a huge set of elk antlers taken by Martin Young. The same bull, below, is shown on the right. With those tremendous eyeguards and frame, this bull would have been a whopper. This photo was taken near Bear Valley in 1945. Another nice bull, taken by Robert Young, is shown on the viewer's left.

Robert Young, at Mountain Meadows, Bear Valley, 1945.

Martin and Robert Young, with the results of a good hunt in Bear Valley, 1945

Bruce and Martin Young, on Moose Creek in the Selway, circa 1940.

Dale Abbot, along with Robert, Martin, and Bruce Young, stop for a snapshot after taking this great bull. This photo, along with the bull, was taken in 1950.

Packstrings & Elk Quarters

What good would an Idaho elk book be without a few token packstring pictures? Here are some to make you wish you were out on the trail.

Roland Wilson leads a string down the mountain after a successful hunt in the Selway in the early 1960s.

Clarence "Shorty" Finnell worked in the Selway as long or longer than anybody in the business, putting in over 50 years. He also packed out more elk than just about anyone. There's worse ways to spend your life than getting paid to be in the mountains.

George Bettas and his always well organized setup packing out a big bull in the Clearwater in the 1980s. I was with George on a pack-in hunt once when we met another outfit coming the other way on the trail. The man in front leaned over, looked at George, and said confidently, "You ain't an outfitter."
George replied, "How do you know that?"
"Your stuff's too good."
That's what makes George a great elk hunter. He never does anything halfway.

George, Rebel, and Hawkeye, packing out a bull in prime Idaho elk country.

Martin Young, in 1957, with the fruits of hard labor. This photo is one of the author's personal favorites.

Packhorse Rojo, hard at work, takes a break to enjoy a view of his home country – St. Joe National Forest, 1988.

Brian Farley packs a nice bull out of the Buffalo Hump country in 1992. Buffalo Hump can be seen in the background at center.

Travis Farley leads out on Buck, with Max packing the meat and antlers. Lemhi County high country, 1996.

Ferd Muller, Henry Daniels, Dean Evans, and an unidentified man on their 1953 pack-in elk hunt to Boise County.

The McClure clan, with Gary in the saddle, coming out of the backcountry with another nice bull. If you want a big bull, you have to go where they can live a while, and packing in is still the way to go.

The Rocky Mountain Elk Foundation
Ensuring a future for elk country in Idaho and beyond

This 2,100 acre ranch formerly known as the Quarter Circle O became part of Idaho's Tex Creek Wildlife Management Area in the late '90s. Rather than sell to developers, the owners sought conservation buyers in hopes to preserve open space and maintain public access. The Elk Foundation teamed with Idaho Fish and Game, the Bonneville Power Administration and other partners to purchase this critical piece of elk country, which helps provide habitat for around 1,000 elk and 300 mule deer each winter. And as the sellers had hoped, the land is now permanently open to the public. *Photo by Terry Thomas*

Whether roaming the wilds of Idaho, the hollows of Kentucky, or the high deserts of the Southwest, elk are one of our nation's grandest game animals. As a migratory species, elk require landscape-scale conservation efforts. It was in 1984 that they found a champion in the Rocky Mountain Elk Foundation. Founded by four hunter-conservationists, the Elk Foundation is a leader in elk country conservation with a mission of ensuring a future for elk, other wildlife, and their habitat. The Elk Foundation has protected and enhanced millions of acres of wild landscapes in its short history, benefiting elk, deer, bears, raptors, antelope, lynx, trout and more. In Idaho alone, the Elk Foundation and its partners have spent $16 million toward habitat protection and enhancement, wildlife research, and conservation education.

By conserving the vast expanses of elk country, you help everything that calls it home. And when elk country is protected, so is the future of our outdoor heritage. Like elk, sportsmen need room to roam. The Elk Foundation and its partners have opened access to a half million acres of wild landscapes across North America for public hunting, fishing and other recreation. Thanks to these efforts, Idaho alone has tens of thousands of additional acres open for public enjoyment. And the Foundation will accomplish much more with committed help from hunter-conservationists and outdoor-enthusiasts from all walks of life. People just like you.

Answer the call of elk country today. Visit www.elkfoundation.org to become a member and learn more about what the Elk Foundation is doing in Idaho or wherever elk country is found. Or feel free to call (800) CALL-ELK.

Ridge Boss

Over the Top